Romancing the Home

ROMANCING THE HOME

STYLISH INTERIORS FOR MODERN LIVING

Stewart Manger

WRITTEN WITH JACQUELINE TERREBONE
FOREWORD BY BUNNY WILLIAMS

RIZZOLI

I dedicate this book to my parents,
Lynn and Bill Manger;
my brothers, William and Charles;
my sister, Lilian, and brother-in law,
Porter; as well as my nieces,
Samantha and Catherine, and
my nephew, Jackson.

JOHN CAGE
ARCHITECTURE INSIDE-OUT
EGYPT
A TOUCH of style
SULTAN
VINCENT VAN GOGH
LENNON ON LENNON
THE MECHANICAL SMILE
PETER LINDBERGH
JOHN DERIAN
MESSAGE TO THE FUTURE
oceania
Modern Art in Detail
A FRIENDLY PURSUIT
Morris Lapidus
MOZART
Magna Carta
THE LIVING FOREST
APPEARANCES
ARTISTS
VIENNA
LÉGER
North Carolina
KANDINSKY
A Life with Artists
Fashion

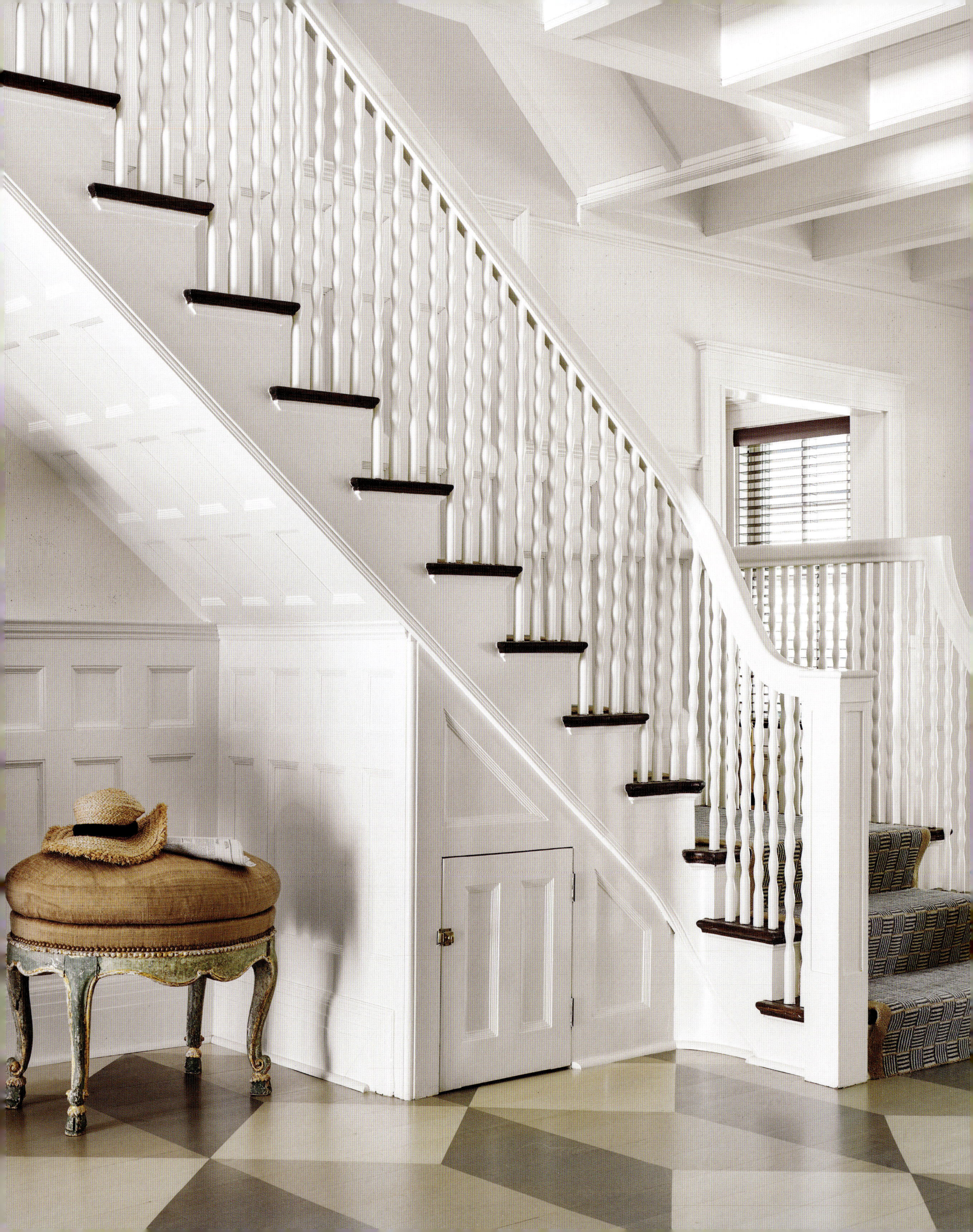

TABLE OF CONTENTS

Foreword *8*

Introduction *10*

A SUNNY SUMMER RETREAT *18*

PARIS PIED-À-TERRE *48*

SEASIDE IN NEW ENGLAND *74*

PENTHOUSE WITH CONTEMPORARY FLAIR *90*

NEW ART COLLECTION SPARKS REDESIGN *106*

A POLISHED LONDON TOWN HOUSE *112*

YOUTHFUL URBAN CHIC *132*

PRESERVING A SCOTTISH CASTLE
ON THE NORTH SEA *144*

RESTORING A SHINGLE-STYLE COTTAGE *164*

MALLORCA MODERN *184*

A POSH SOUTHAMPTON COUNTRY HOUSE *208*

TOP O'DUNE *220*

YOUNG AND BOLD IN THE HAMPTONS *244*

Acknowledgments *254*

FOREWORD

I think it was a Thursday morning when I saw on my schedule that Stewart, who was working for me as a designer at the time, had asked to see me. Usually there was a client name attached to a meeting, but when I saw there was none, my heart skipped a few beats. I knew what this was about, and while I was devastated, I also knew it was time and the right thing for him to do. He was going to start his own firm: Stewart Manger Interior Design.

From a young age, Stewart was no stranger to great interior design. He grew up in a house in New York and a fabulous house on Long Island that he still occupies with his extended family. He was lucky to be instilled with a strong sense of home early on, and this is what brought him to pursue interior design.

Part of what puts Stewart at the top of his profession is his curiosity and breadth of knowledge. He has studied the decorative arts and has an unerring eye for the best furniture and objects. Traveling extensively has only further stimulated his work. Whether he is working on a New York apartment, a London town house, or a Hamptons beach house, he always has a sense of place.

Throughout his early career, Stewart worked with two of my dear friends, David Easton and David Kleinberg, where he learned how to manage projects and the business side of interior design—an essential skill for starting your own firm. Again and again, he was exposed to amazing projects around the country, and I was thrilled when he approached me about coming to my office.

One of the many things that makes Stewart so special is that he listens intently. He wants to hear what the clients' dreams and goals are. His gracious personality coupled with his passion for design and his understanding of the way people live make him a star in the field of interior design. I will always miss having him in my office, but I am still so fortunate to have him as a dear friend.

— *Bunny Williams*

OPPOSITE: The library of a Southampton house comes alive with custom plasterwork inspired by Henri Matisse's cutouts.

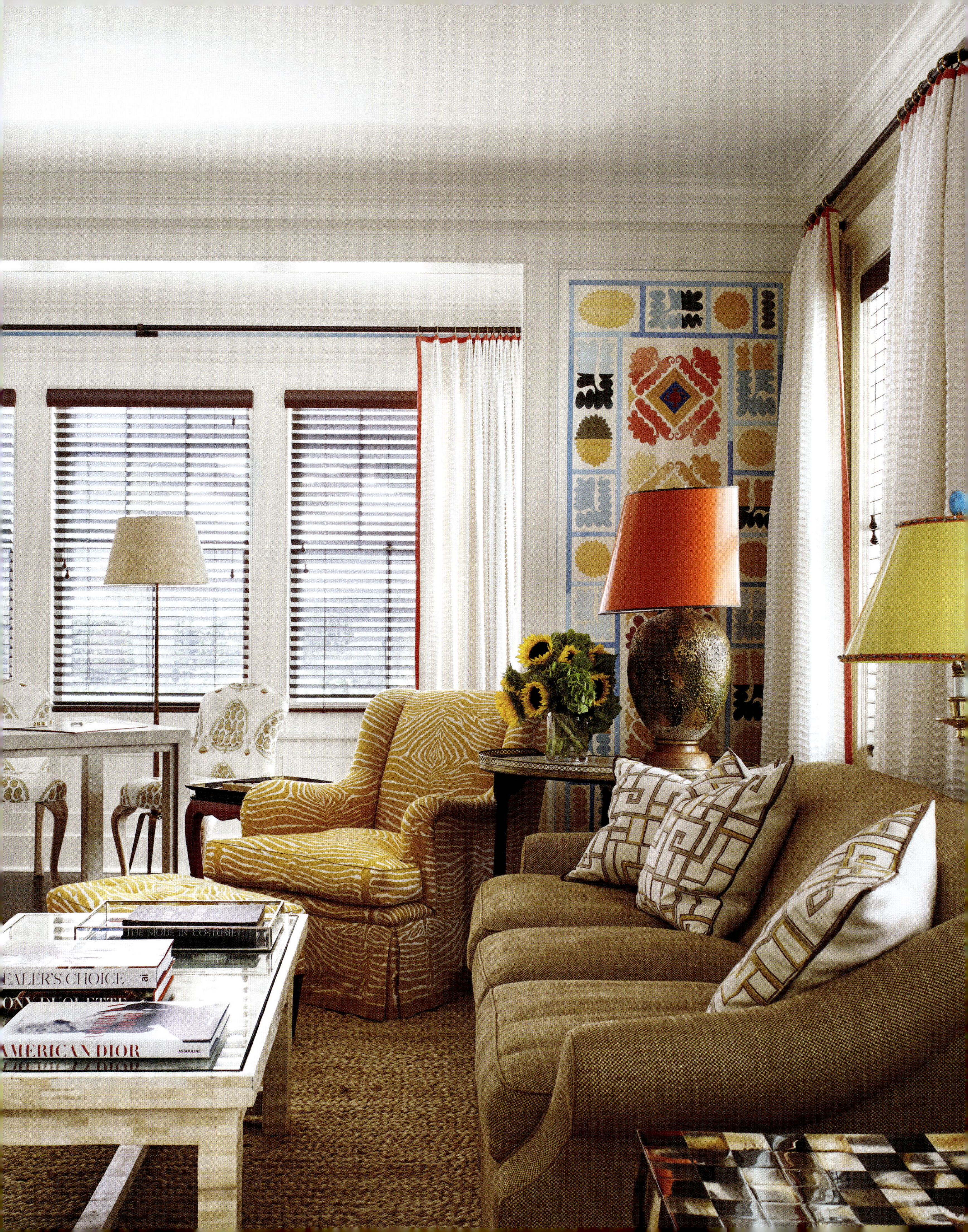
THE MODE IN COSTUME
EALER'S CHOICE
AMERICAN DIOR
ASSOULINE

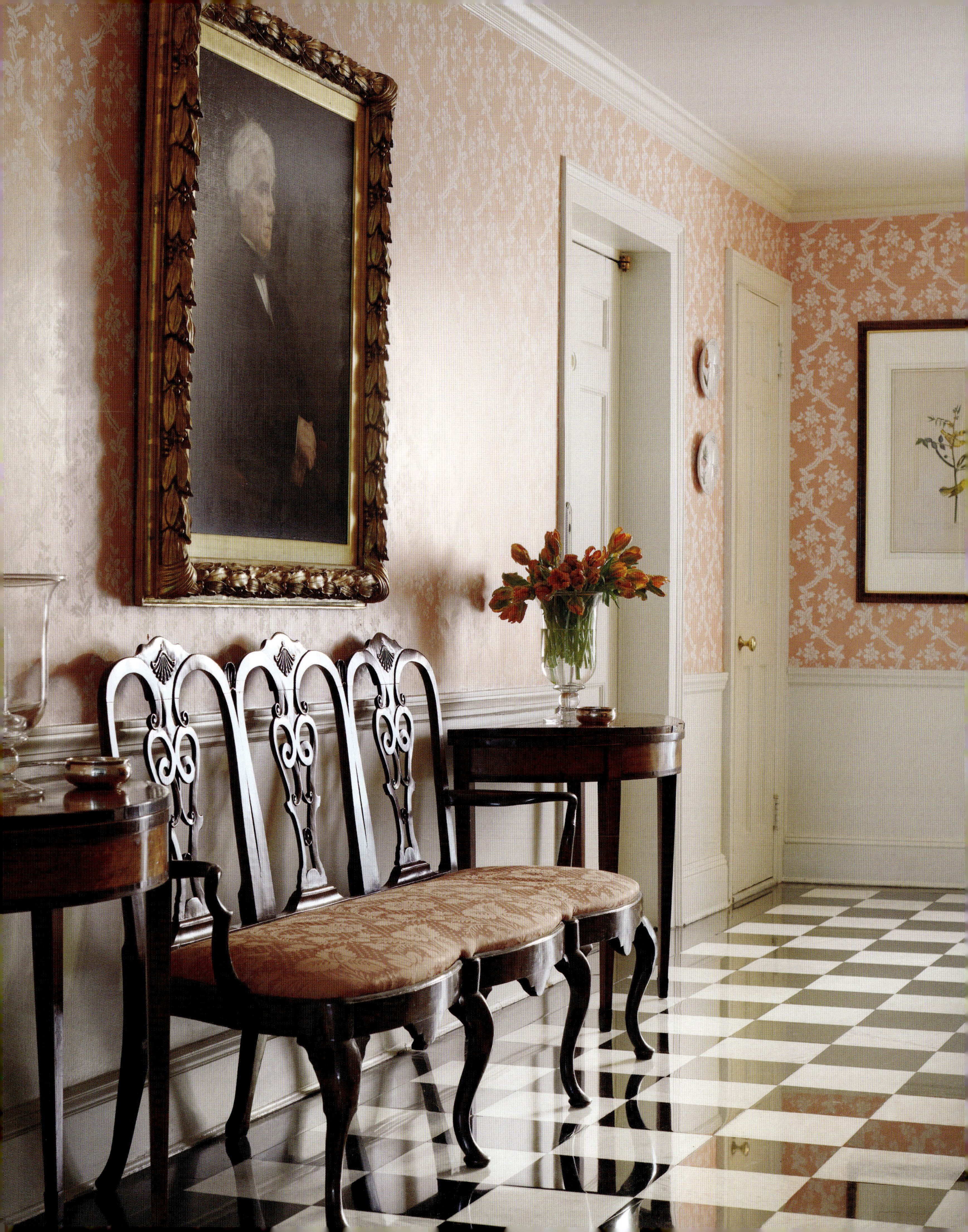

INTRODUCTION

My first big design job came at the age of fifteen. This might sound shockingly young to most, but it felt completely natural to me as I rushed home from school every Wednesday to meet with my mother and her decorator. It was the 1980s, and chintz was decidedly in fashion—especially for those living in an Upper East Side town house in New York. We would visit the D&D Building on Third Avenue and explore all the latest oversize florals. Despite the trends of that period, we made some excellent choices that have stood the test of time, and my parents still live in the same house where these design decisions continue to animate the space.

Although we now think of Gracie wallpapers in dining rooms as a classic, they were quite a new thing then, but mixed well with my parents' traditional tastes. In the dining room, the Georgian two-pedestal table and the French chairs are arrayed atop a rug that was my grandmother's, while in the library strong interior architecture creates the ideal backdrop for comfortably stuffed upholstery in pinks and greens. These types of rooms represent the kind of timeless style that I grew up surrounded by and laid the foundation for my personal approach to creating spaces today.

Through college and graduate school in England, I veered toward a more curatorial approach, studying fine and decorative arts. Back in New York, internships at the Metropolitan Museum of Art and the Brooklyn Museum continued to sharpen my eye, and eventually a stint at the Getty lured me into the world of set design in Hollywood. After trying my hand at that for a few months, a call came from the ever-prescient Marian McEvoy. An icon of fashion and design, she served as the founding editor of *Elle Decor*, and now she had decided I needed to move back to New York and work for her.

OPPOSITE: In the entry hall of the house I grew up in near the Metropolitan Museum of Art, a black-and-white checkerboard floor and mahogany settee welcome you. The walls feature a family portrait and an Audubon print.

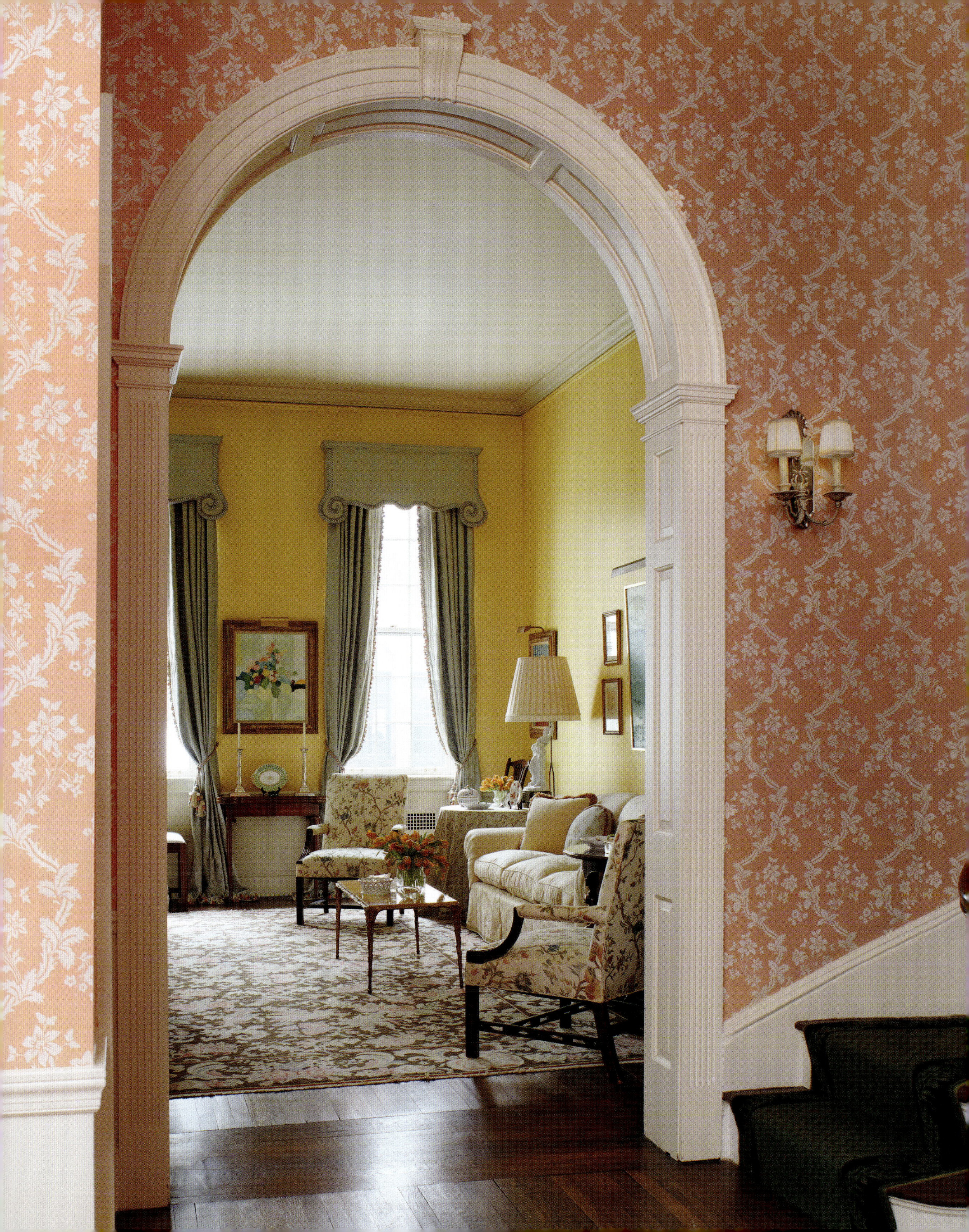

I was ready to return East, and we collaborated on so many wonderful creative projects, such as a Greenwich, Connecticut, landscape garden fair. Through the magazine, she introduced me to another icon—David Easton.

With Marian's encouragement, I took a job with David, although I really knew very little about design. From my stint in the European furniture department at Christie's New York, I did have a knowledge of antique rugs and fine furniture. David turned out to be an amazing teacher—patient, with a great sense of humor. He readily took me under his wing and taught me how to build a room. Color interaction, symmetry and asymmetry, furniture plans—all the basics that so many have now forgotten were exactly what he steeped me in for five years. The importance of draperies and trims was also on the syllabus. As a dutiful apprentice, I soaked up every valuable lesson, and I still call upon this experience to map out rooms today and often think of David fondly when I decide to add a hand-embroidered leading edge to a curtain.

Having that incredible base of knowledge, I went on to assist another pillar of design—David Kleinberg. At his firm, everything was more contemporary, and he encouraged a breaking of the rules. Things no longer had to match perfectly. It reminded me of learning to play bridge—once you know all the rules, you can have fun with the game and start ignoring them. But there was also so much more to learn. David immersed me in the highest level of twentieth-century style while demonstrating how to expertly mix great pieces by legendary furniture makers and artisans—always thinking about the whole. Now I seek out just these types of pieces to create a sense of cohesion and individuality in the rooms I devise. I'm constantly searching for that Milton Avery that will transform a wall or the Émile-Jacques Ruhlmann chairs that create a dialogue with a Eugène Printz desk.

The third in the trio of legends I worked under is the inimitable Bunny Williams. By the time I arrived at her office, I really knew how to devise and execute beautiful spaces, but she doesn't design houses just for the way they look. She wants families to feel comfortable in their homes and guests to feel welcome. In Bunny's interiors, people immediately sit down and feel at ease. There's a place to set a glass and a lamp to read by.

OPPOSITE: From the hall into the drawing room, the classic architecture of the house is complemented by Brunschwig & Fils wallpaper.

There's also a quality whereby rooms don't look too done. Every room is beautiful, but you can tell someone truly lives in them.

When I speak to young designers, I encourage them to work for established decorators for as long as they possibly can. This served me immensely well and allowed me to not just learn but to also internalize what each of these three masters taught me. Eventually, it was time for me to leave the nest. But when I hung up my shingle, I could now infuse every design with the wisdom I had gained from each and bring all the lessons together in a manner decidedly my own. I want my clients to have something special. Every room, every painting, every pillow matters. I wouldn't want to have it any other way.

Now, as a professional decorator, I'm thrilled when people walk into a house that I've just installed and think it doesn't feel decorated. Nothing is too perfect, but everything is part of a whole. There's a unifying voice, theme, and curation of art and furniture but still a level of comfort. In addition to the projects throughout this book that showcase my portfolio of work in Paris and London, Newport and the Hamptons, and throughout New York City, I've taken on several major redecorations of my family's home in Southampton, this time as a professional decorator with many years of experience. In those inviting rooms, I can see the influences of every stage of my career. But in the end, every house is a reflection of the people who live there—and that's exactly what good design needs to be and should be.

RIGHT: English mirrors flank a portrait of my mother with her children by Aaron Shikler, who painted the portrait of Jacqueline Kennedy that hangs in the White House.

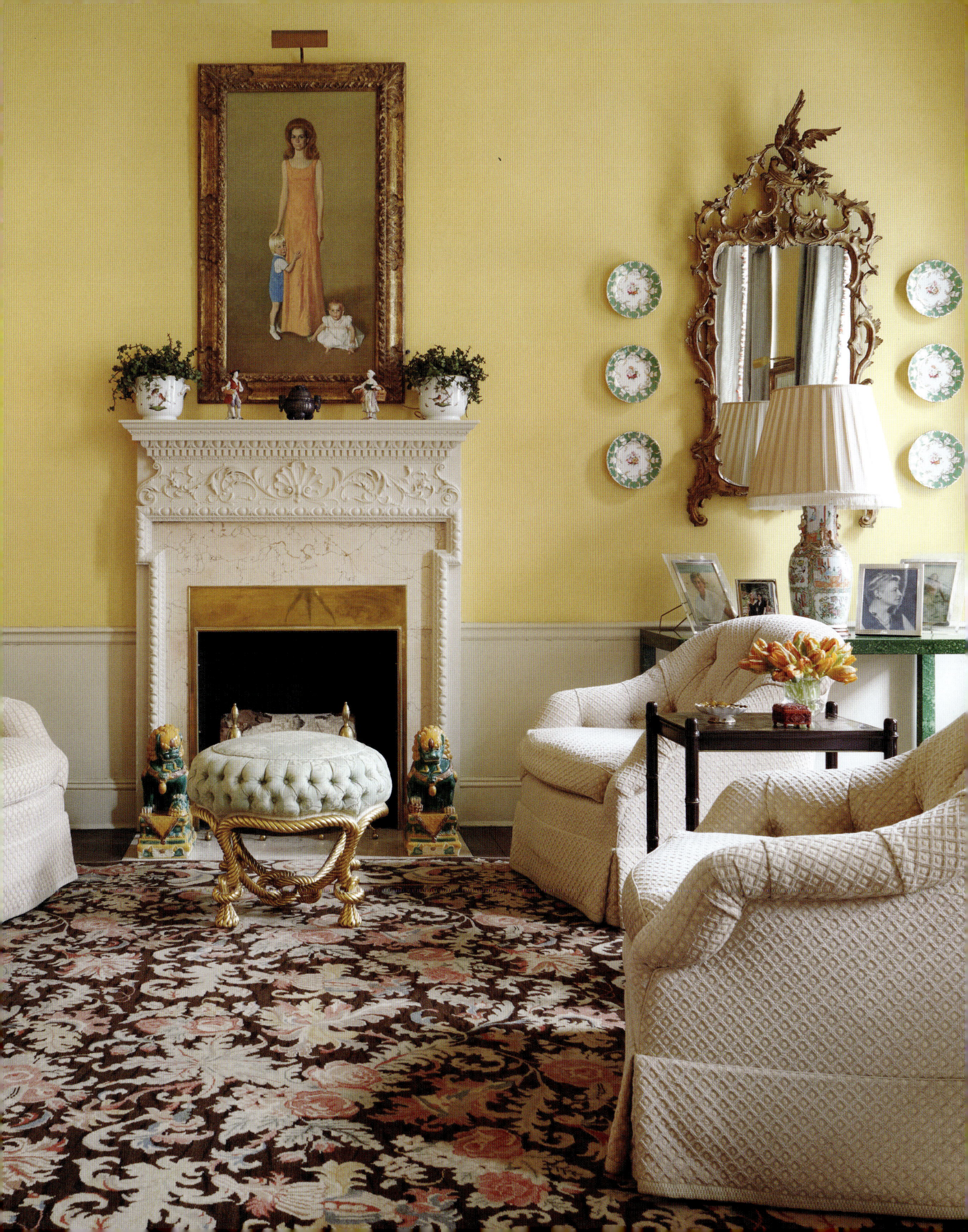

ABOVE: The pine-paneled library with mahogany doors opens onto the stair hall. OPPOSITE: Scenic Gracie wallpaper animates the dining room, which leads into the breakfast room.

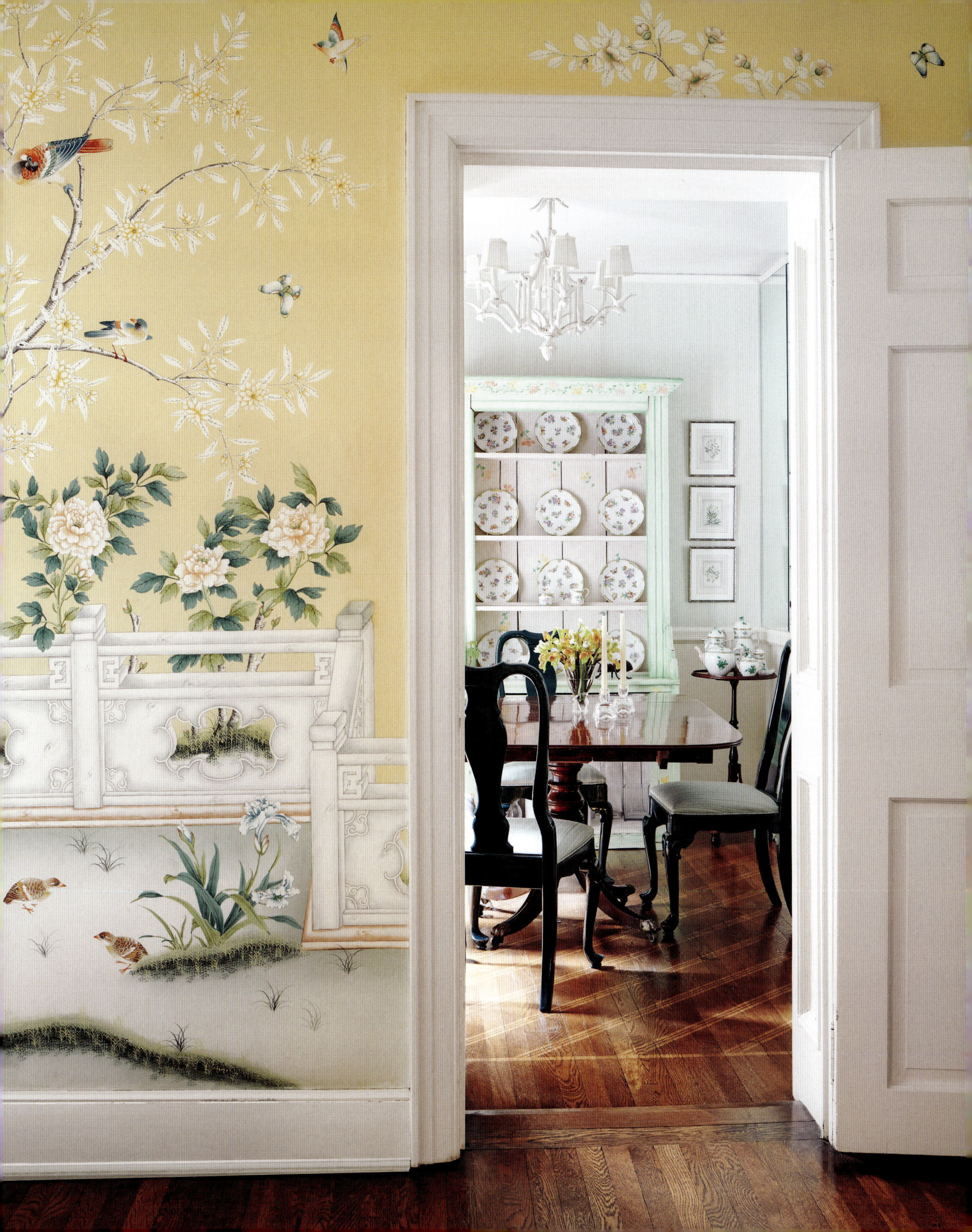

A SUNNY SUMMER RETREAT

Like many design aficionados, I've always loved the staircase at Villa Necchi in Milan. A staggering period house, this architectural gem by architect Piero Portaluppi was designed in 1935 with the goal to stand out from the city's other dazzling palazzos. In many ways, architect Doug Wright and I had that same intent when conceiving this house on the ocean in Southampton. The shingle-style exterior of the new build references the local artist's colony, including homes of the 1880s. His interiors push the envelope in creative and artful ways, including our take on that famed balustrade, which we then used again as a motif in a screen looking from the entry through to the triple-floor stair hall. There, a Damien Hirst butterfly artwork brings a punch of color, while a Stephen Antonson double-disk plaster chandelier punctuates the center.

Throughout, the colors blue and white, practically a Hamptons tradition, anchor the palette, although accents of cerused, bleached oak bring warmth here and there. The library serves as a prime example of this, with handsome shelving imbuing the space with a warm glow. While most of the furniture features white upholstery, the eye doesn't read the room that way—instead moving to the peacock blue of the Ruhlmann-style chair as well as the Penn & Fletcher embroidery on the curtains. Plus, that small wonder of a metal chair by Elizabeth Garouste resembles a three-dimensional drawing with its curving black lines.

Along that same palette, the dining room has a sophisticated tension between the graphic artwork by Enrico Castellani and the blue walls stenciled with mother-of-pearl detailing. The custom oak table and sideboard feel beachy but elegant, especially

OPPOSITE: In the stair hall, the design is influenced by the Villa Necchi. A custom plaster dish light by Stephen Antonson echoes the shape of the round Damien Hirst butterfly painting.

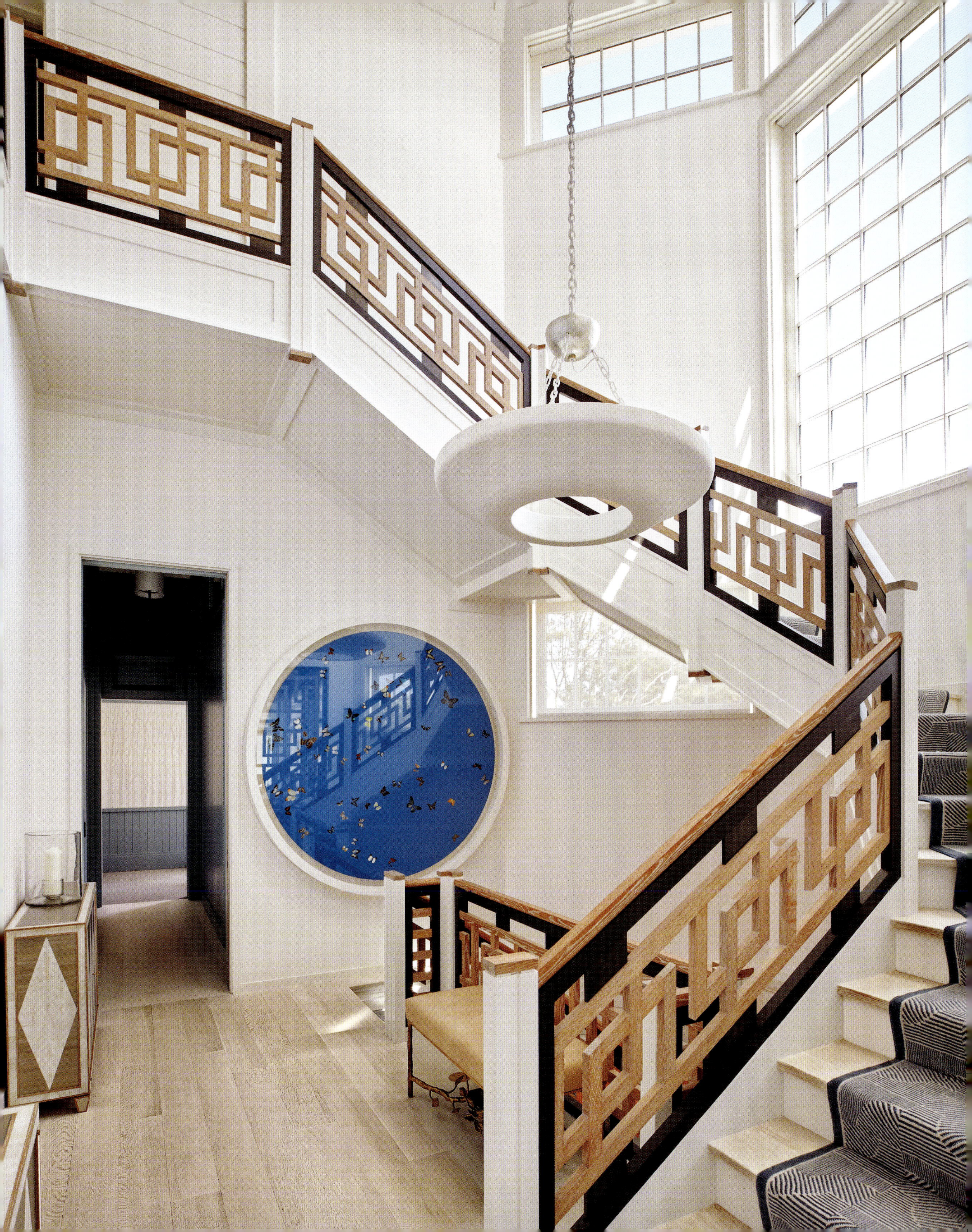

ABOVE: On the second-floor landing, a lamp by Marc Bankowski sits on a plaster console by Patrice Dangel, which is surmounted by a W. P. Sullivan mirror. RIGHT: The entry hall's faux painted ceiling resembles sandy-colored malachite. The color theme continues with a lantern by Stephen Antonson and sheers in a fabric from Holly Hunt.

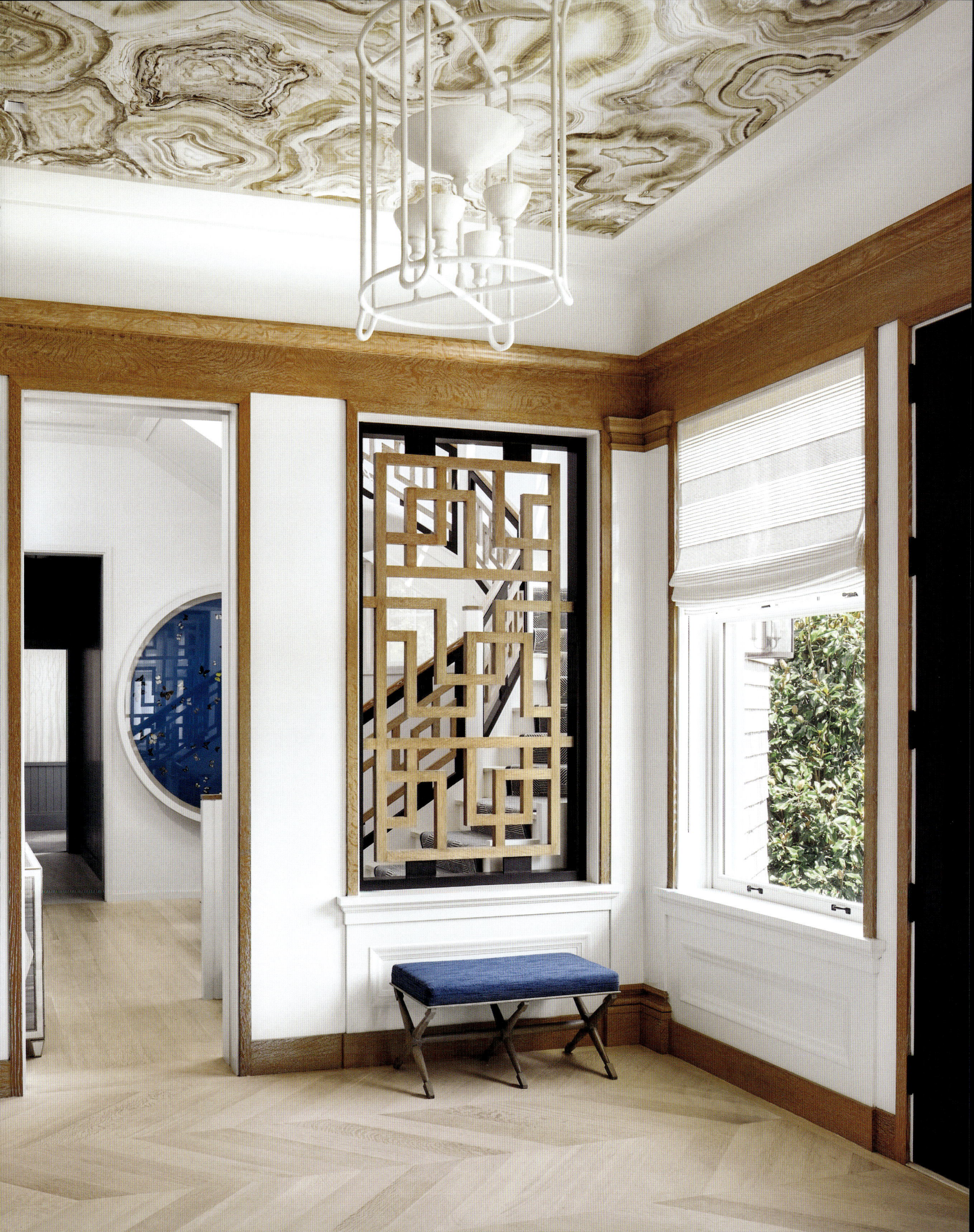

when accompanied by a Claude Lalanne candelabra, a Patrice Dangel light fixture, and bouclé upholstered dining chairs. The primary bedroom is a sea of blues, from the frost-colored upholstered walls to the more saturated blues of the *degradé* curtains. Plus, the denim-hued kitchen, an Iksel wallpaper-covered guest bedroom, and the blissful pool house keep the theme going in uniquely spirited ways.

We did, however, break from the theme in the living room. Pulling from the green in an extraordinary Günther Förg artwork, which was so large the wall had to be built to meet its dimensions, I tapped Tara Chapas to weave an incredible fabric for the lounge chairs, rested a ceramic work by Kate Malone atop the Fredrikson Stallard table, and included an array of pillows in various fabrics reflecting the colors in the canvas. It's fantastic how these natural, cheerful shades of green pick up on the landscape just outside the window. In another guest bedroom, I also called upon the shades of nature to evoke the golden sand dunes and summer grass. And nothing could be more Hamptons than that.

ABOVE: The shingle-style exterior reflects local homes from the 1880s. OPPOSITE: The Ribbon bench by Pierre Renart is framed by the landscape designed by Landscape Details. FOLLOWING SPREAD: A work by Günther Förg presides over the living room, which features an artful mix of furnishings including an acrylic Fredrikson Stallard coffee table, Mattia Bonetti chairs, a ceramic Kate Malone object, and a bronze coffee table and light fixture by Philippe Anthonioz.

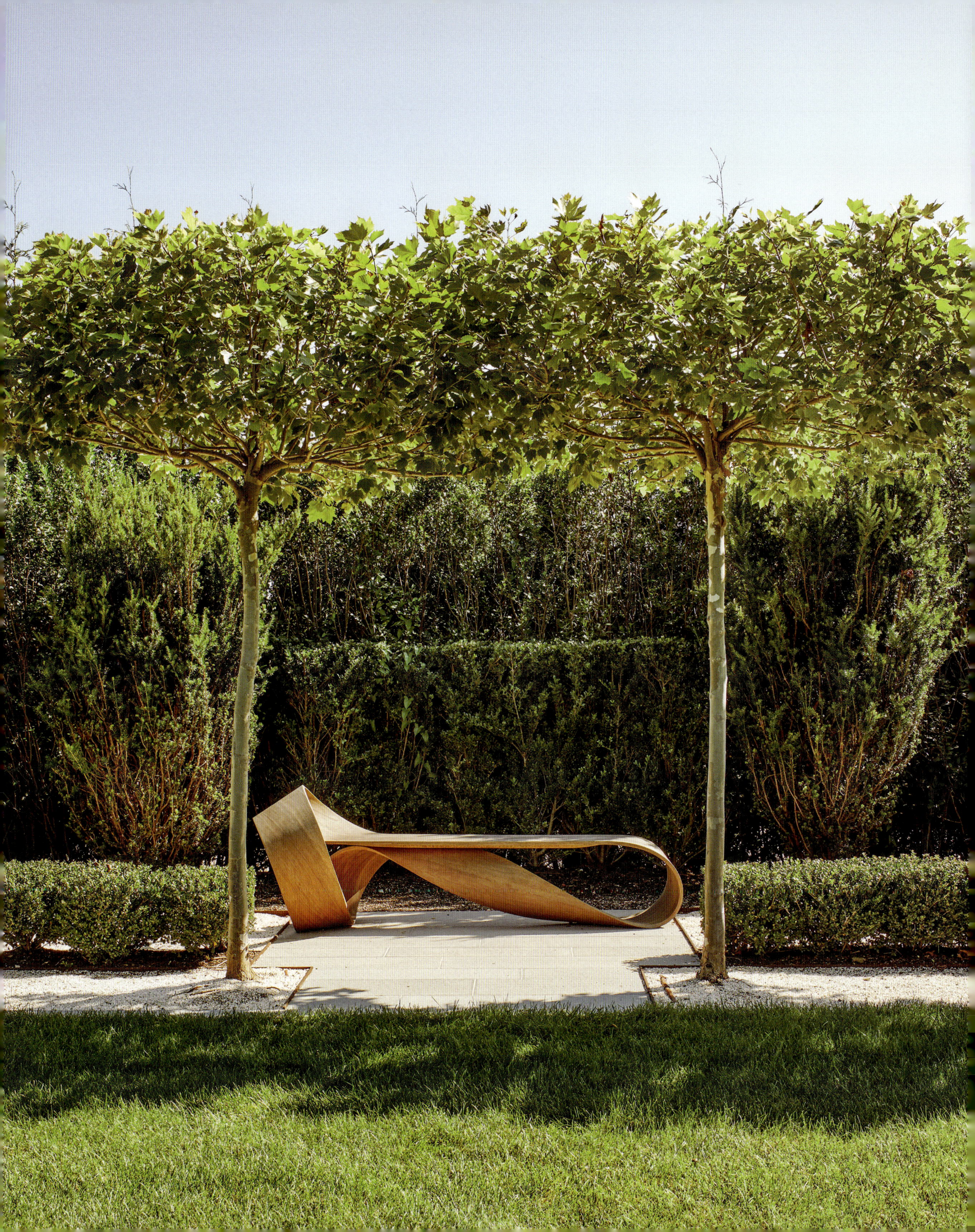

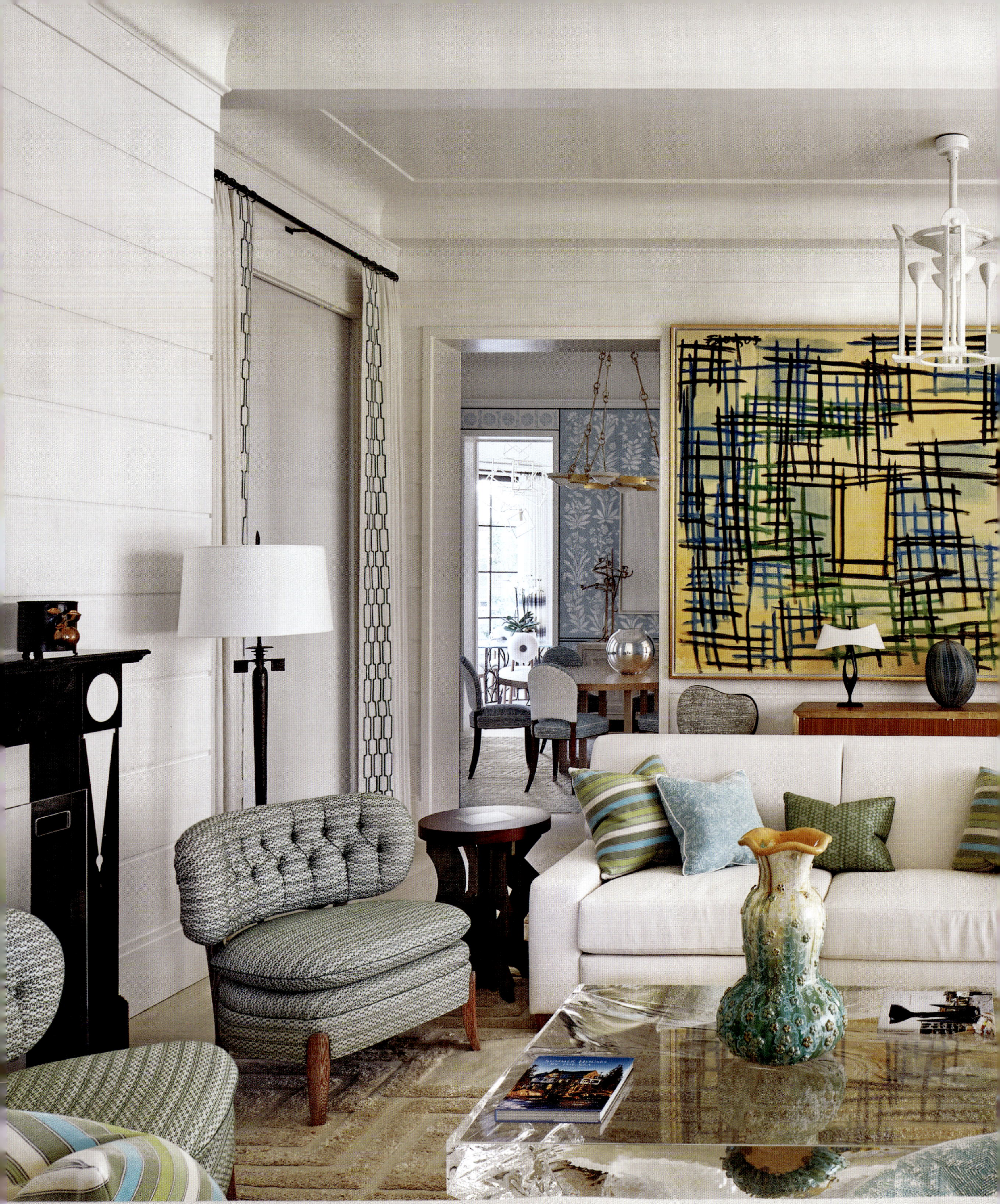

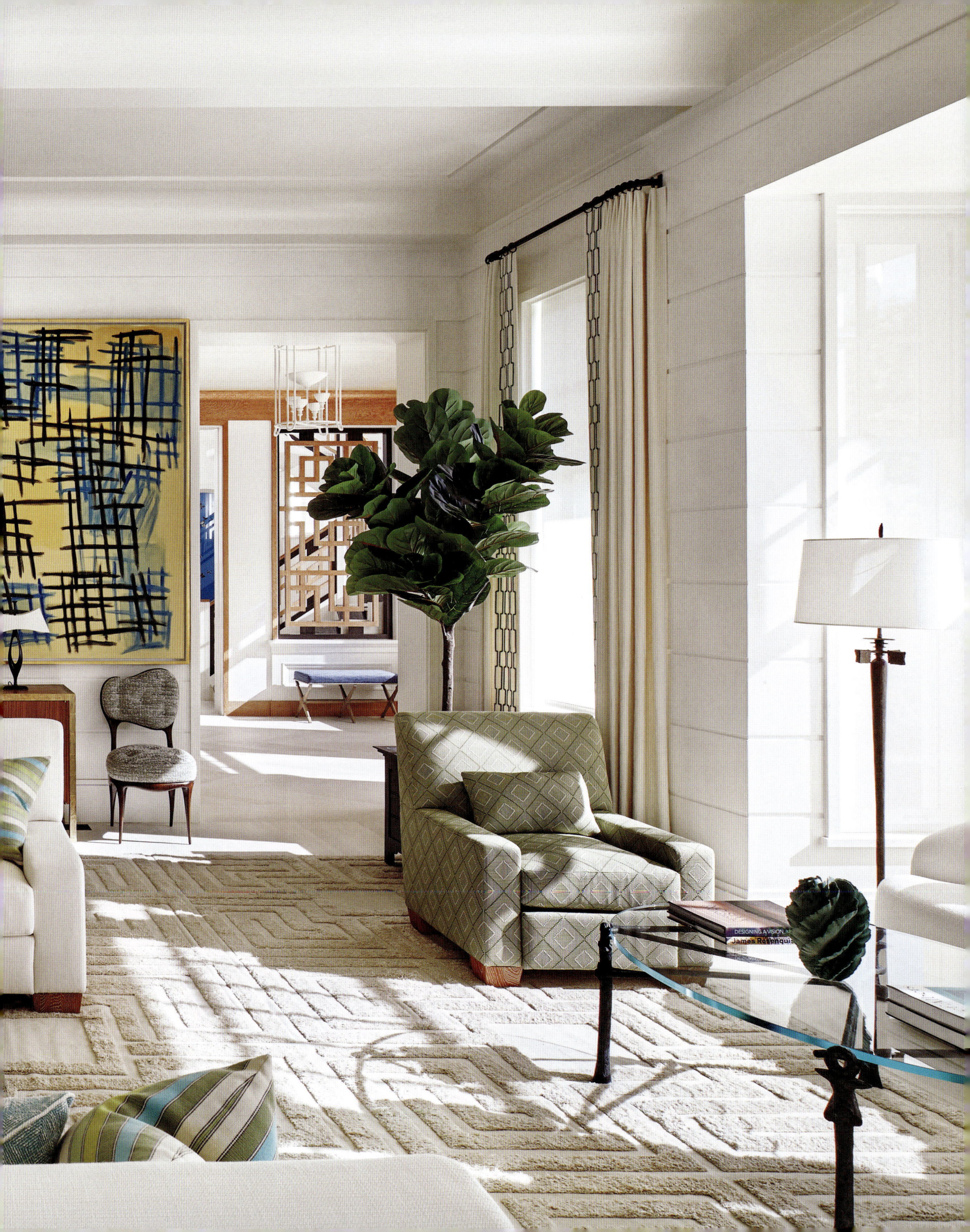
DESIGNING A VISION

RIGHT: In the opposite view of the living room, a dynamic painting by Frank Bowling surmounts one of two Jean-Michel Frank–style shagreen bombé commodes.

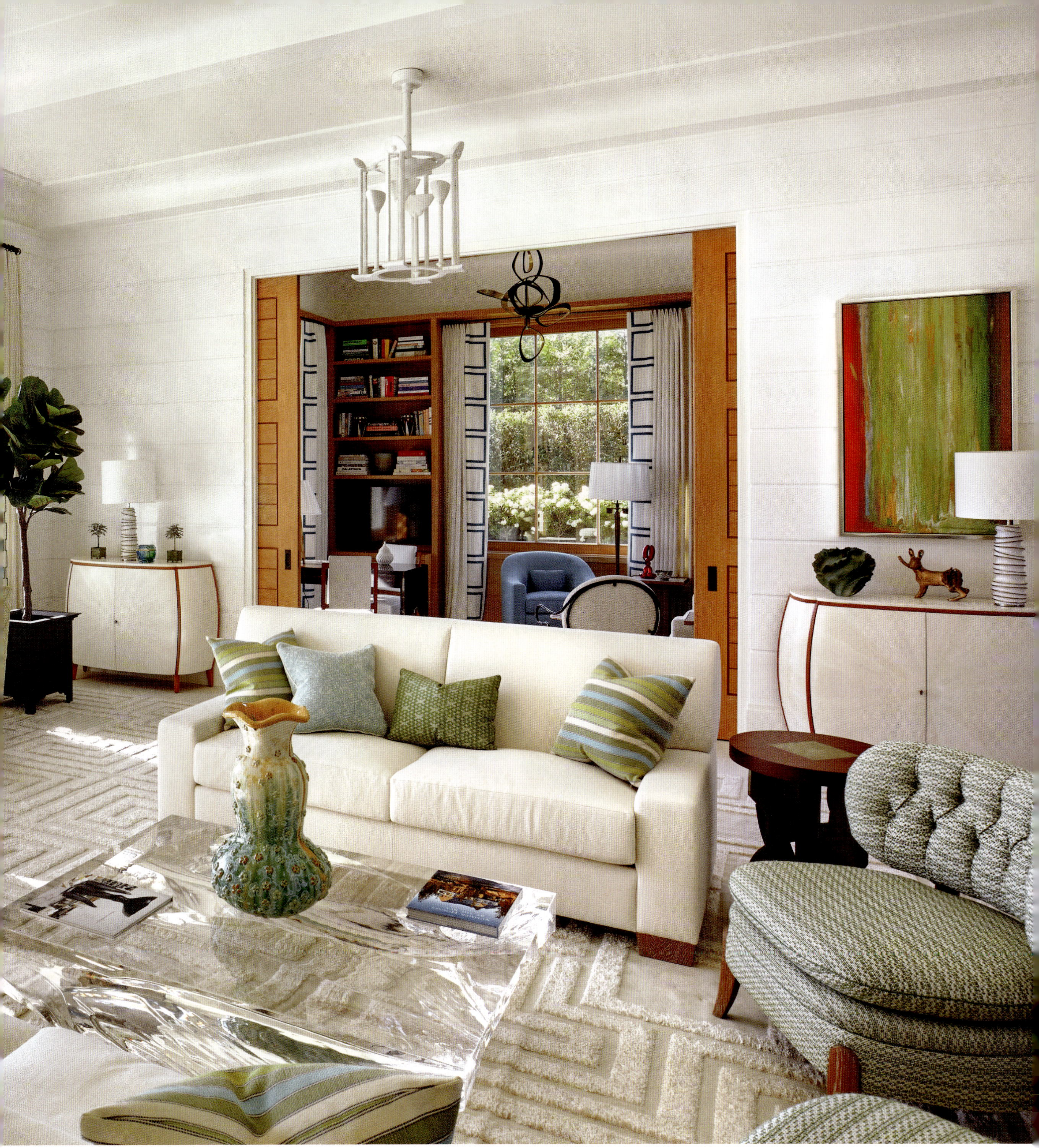

RIGHT: An Elizabeth Garouste metal chair along with a Ginkgo coffee table by Claude Lalanne lend sculptural notes to the library. Penn & Fletcher embroidery on the curtains adds color and pattern in an unexpected way.

HEROIC
Art Nouveau Architecture
PENCIL POINTS
HOUSES
FACADES
RAFAEL VIÑOLY ARCHITECTS
STONE
SMALL
Renoir

ABOVE: The entry hall, featuring a green canvas by Lucio Fontana and a mirror by Frank Evennou, frames the passage into the dining area. OPPOSITE: The dining room is enveloped in custom-stenciled walls with a mother-of-pearl inlay. A Claude Lalanne candelabra rests on a cerused-oak sideboard, above which an Enrico Castellani painting hangs.

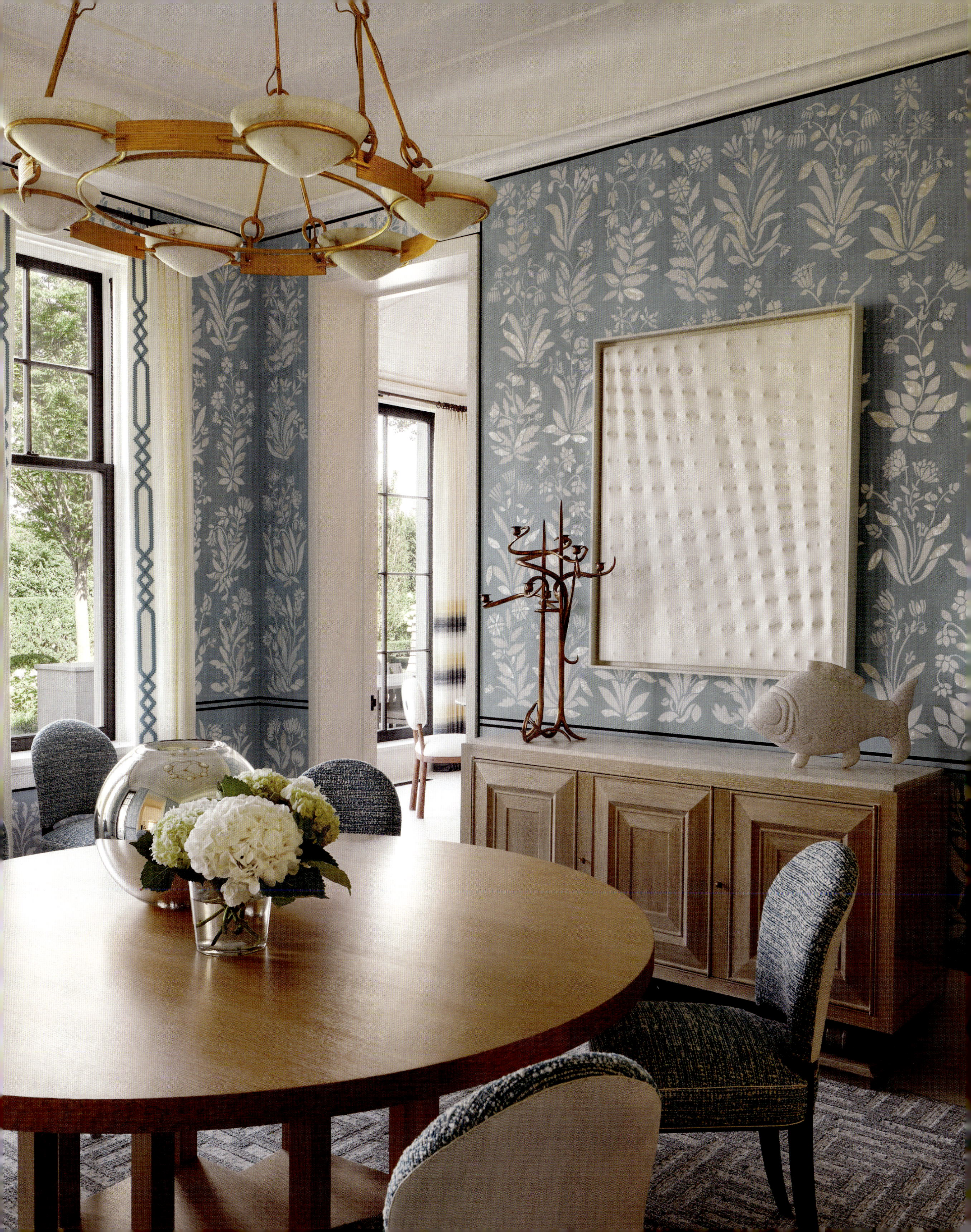

Pattern Play

When I travel, I pick up on patterns that are part of other cultures around the world, whether from a mosaic tile, an unexpected weave on a rug, or even a wood carving. Later, I reinterpret them to fit a variety of different projects, and they may turn up as a wallpaper or upholstery fabric in an altogether different scale or colorway. This project in the Hamptons is loaded with pattern at every turn but never comes across as busy. Often the patterns are set in white and there aren't too many other colors, so they come off a bit more muted and mix well with other prints. Pairing two seemingly different motifs on a headboard and Studio Four wall fabric creates just the type of tension that adds interest. The wonderful Fermoie stripe almost looks hand painted and the kaleidoscopic circles by Studio Four reverberate in a manner that aligns them. In the family room, a Borneo pattern resembles wall carvings or something out of the Arts and Craft movement. In the dining room, the blue and white walls feel beachy but with an Americana twist. In the boldest use, the scenic Iksel wallpaper in the guest room has a completely transportive effect, making visitors never want to leave. If you ever want to get lost in design possibilities, I highly suggest a visit to the Iksel showroom in London's Chelsea Harbour.

OPPOSITE, CLOCKWISE, FROM TOP LEFT: A Fermoie fabric is paired with a Studio Four printed headboard. The design of Borneo prayer mats inspired the pattern for the wall stencil. An Istanbul wallpaper by Iksel dominates a guest bedroom. Custom-stenciled walls are inlayed with mother-of-pearl. PAGES 34–35: A denim-blue kitchen gets extra oomph with an Hervé Van der Straeten chandelier above the breakfast table and custom-woven curtains by Lauren Hwang.

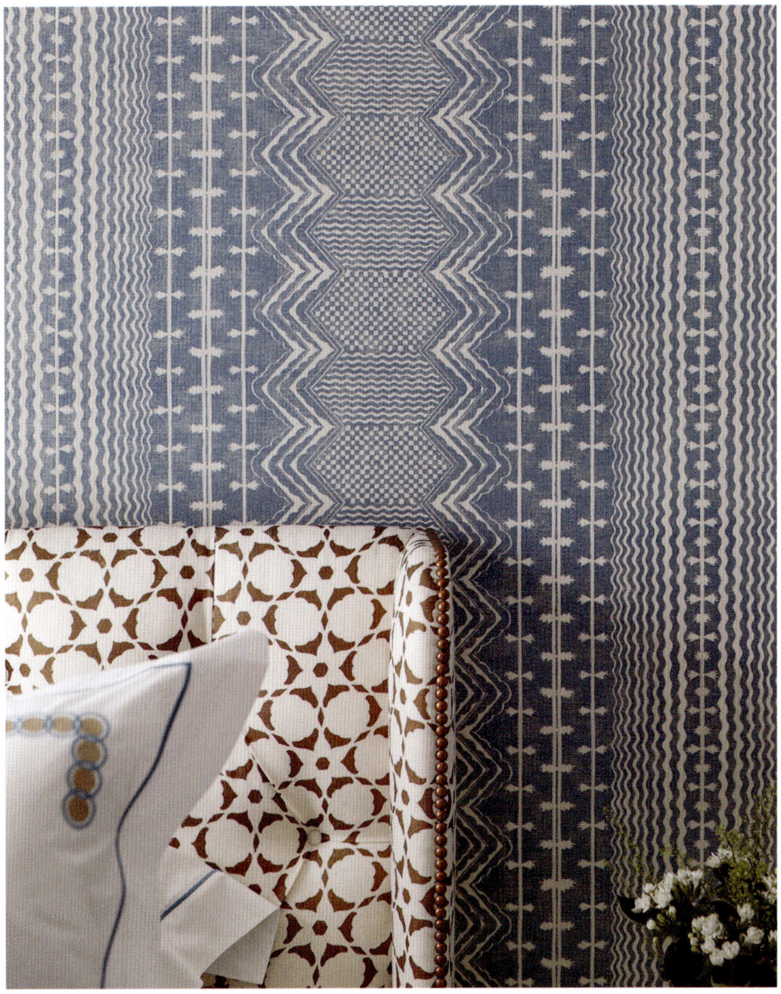
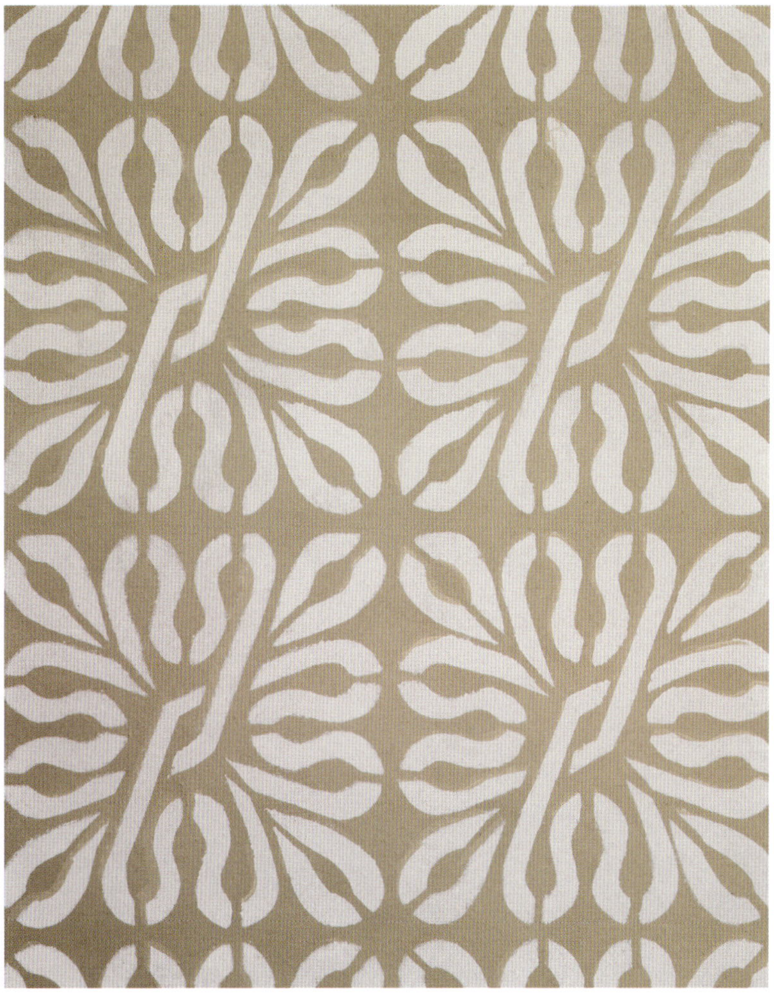
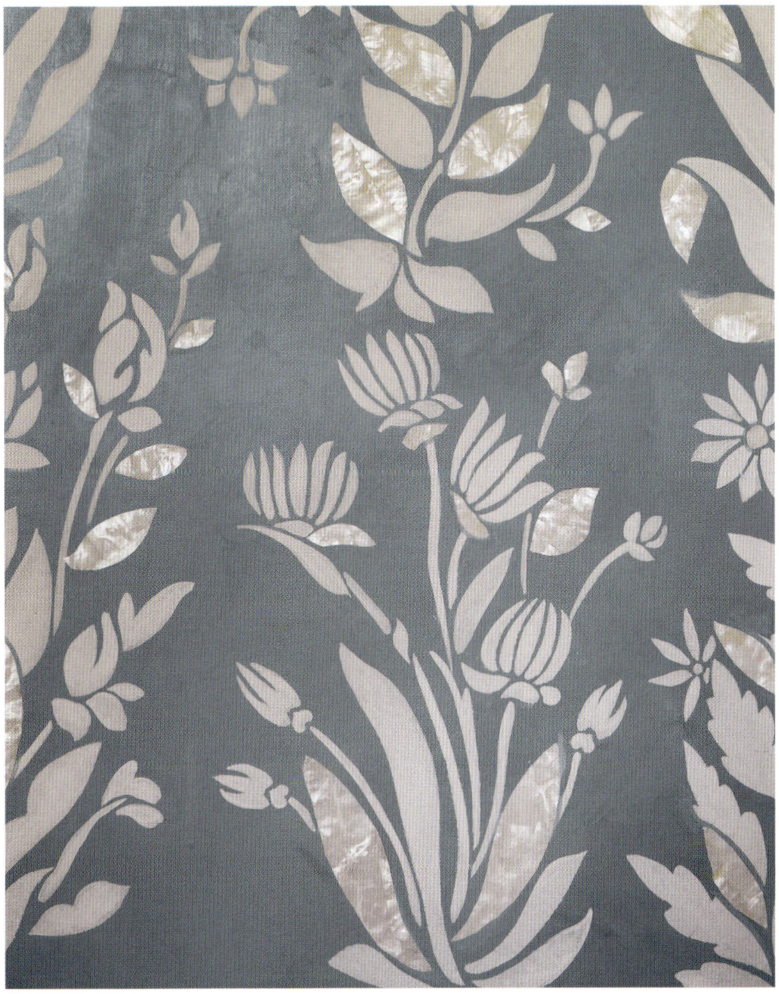
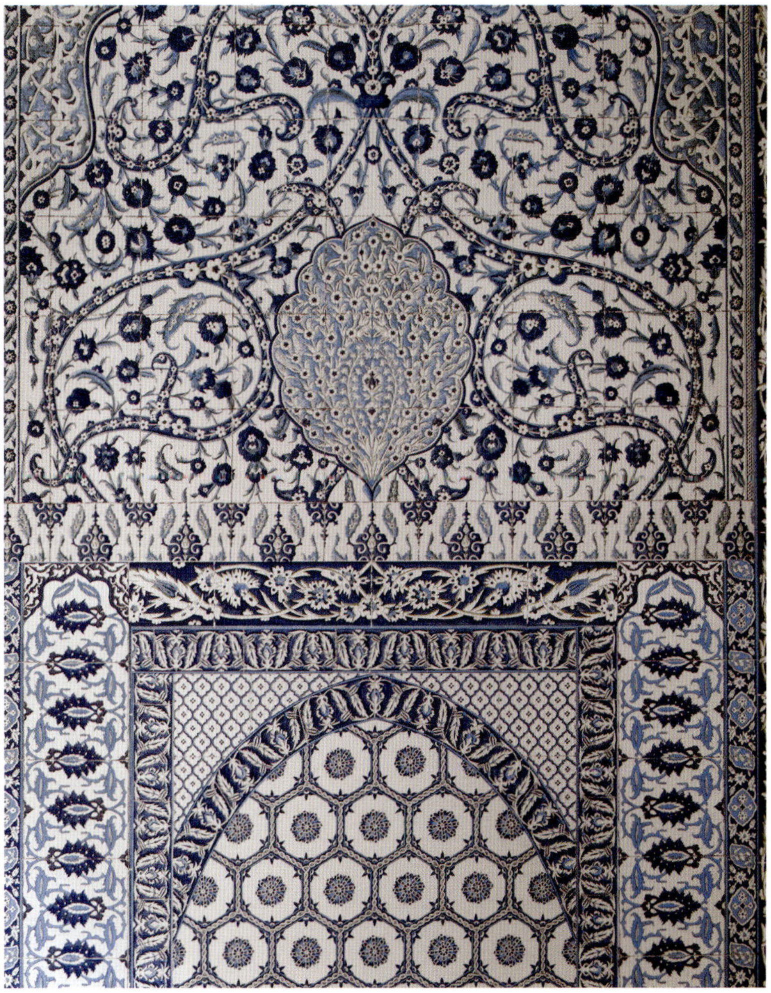

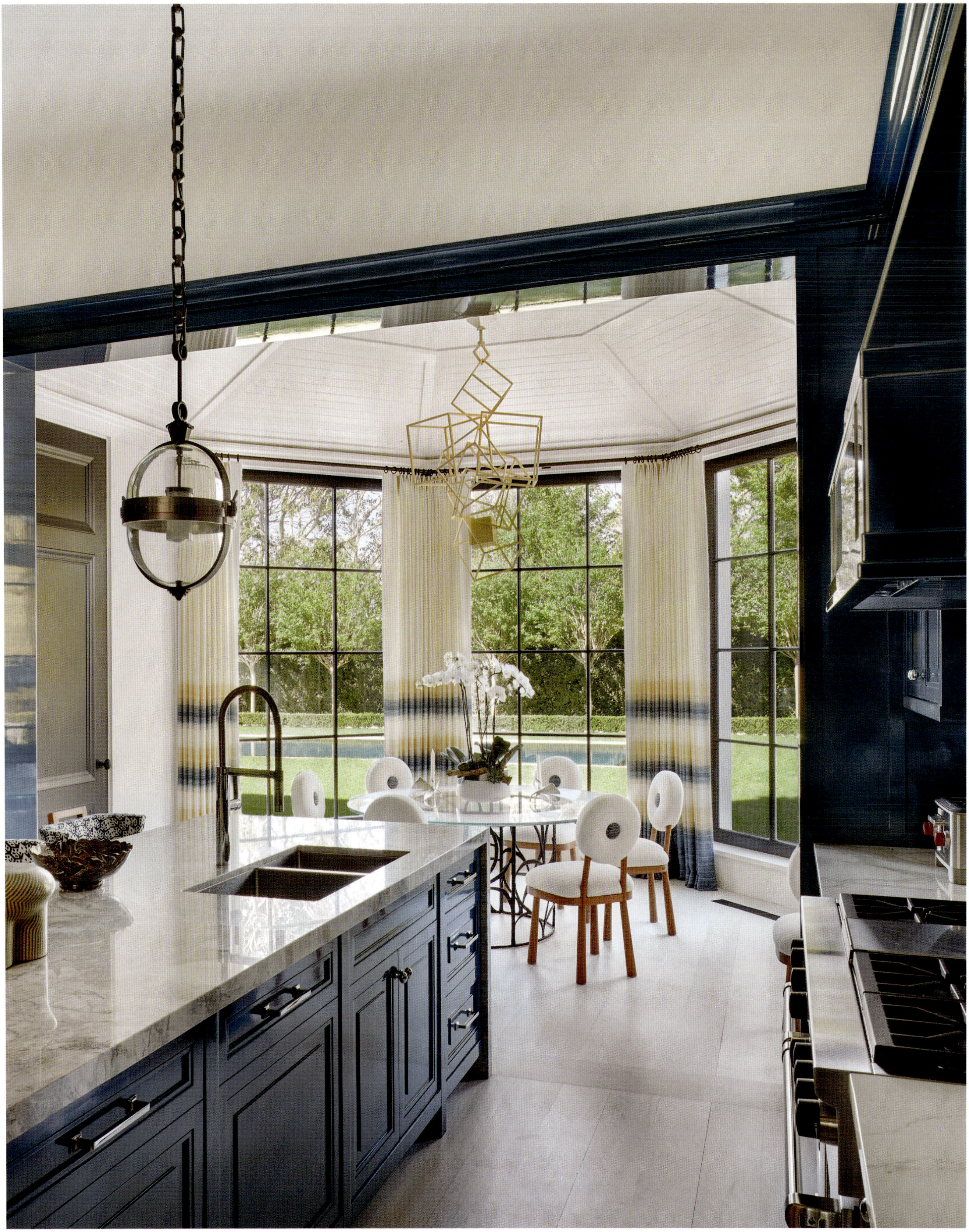

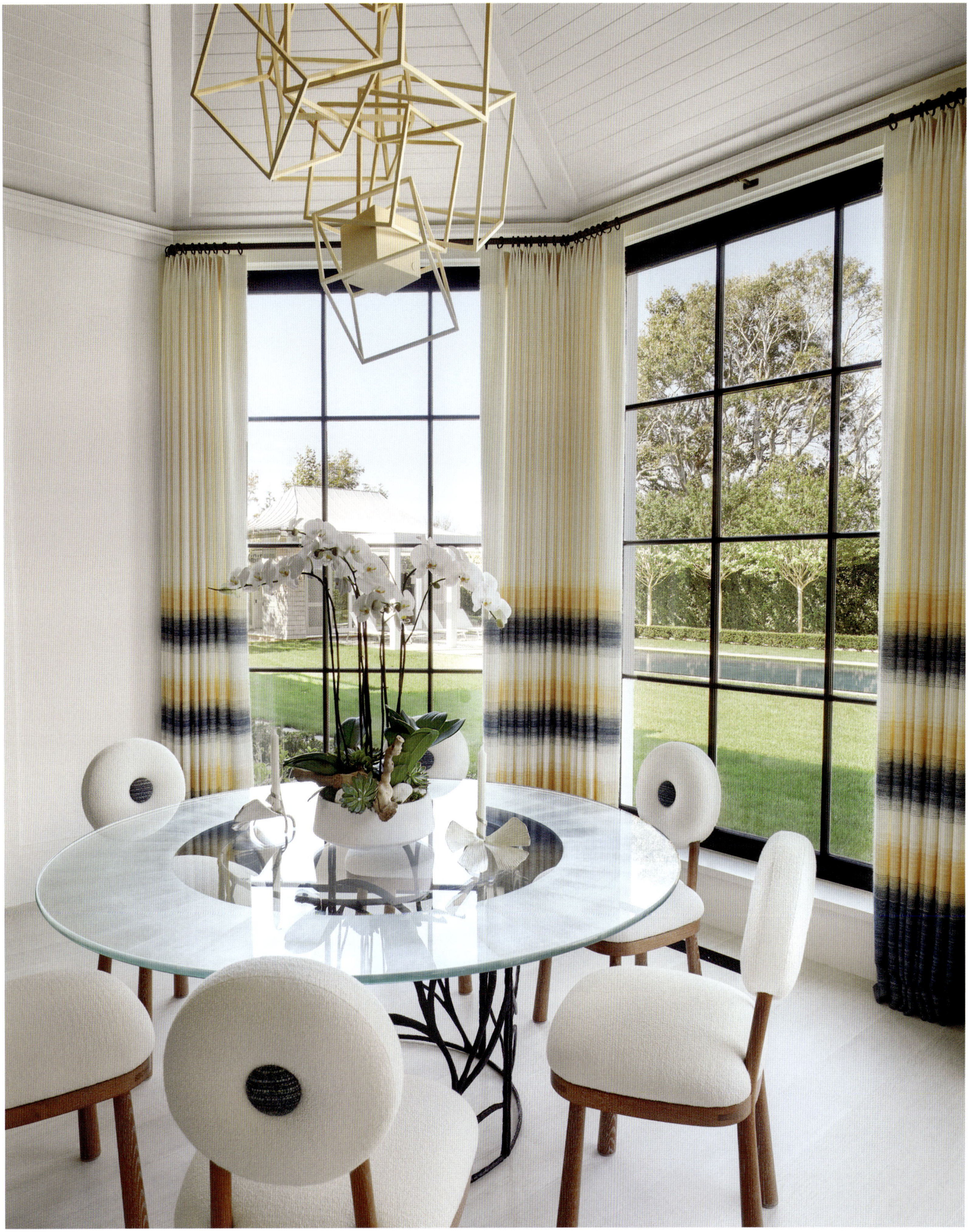

ABOVE AND RIGHT: A Borneo-inspired custom-stenciled paper sets the tone in the family room, which includes a Stephen Antonson mirror, a Chesneys mantel, a Philippe Anthonioz plaster light fixture, Christopher Spitzmiller lamps, and a Günther Förg lead painting.

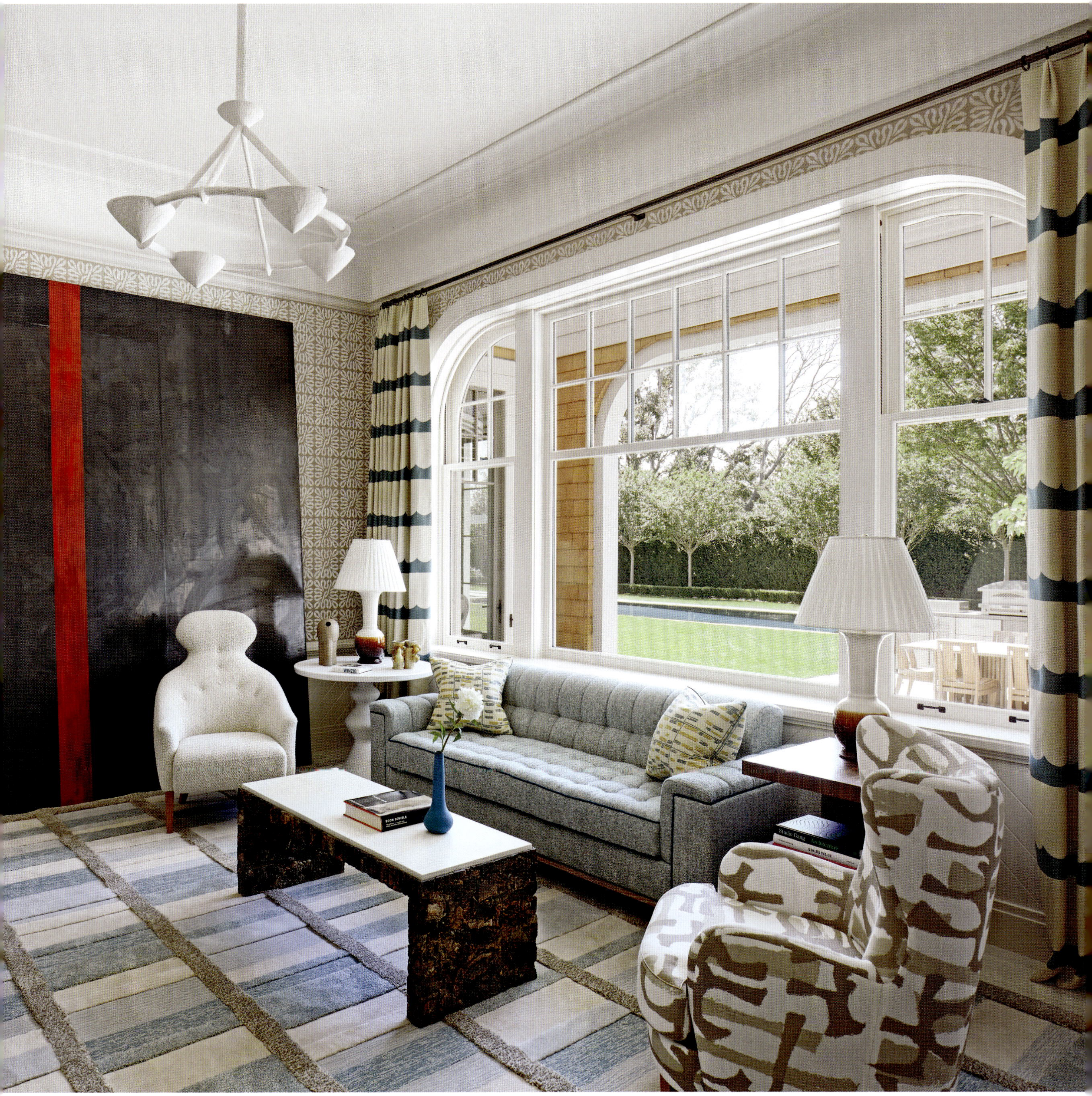

ABOVE: On the second floor, a Liaigre desk overlooks the Stephen Antonson fixture in the stairwell. RIGHT: The airy family room on the second floor is anchored by a Günther Förg painting and is accented by Penn & Fletcher embroidered curtains, which complement the Hubert Le Gall chair, inspired by birds kissing.

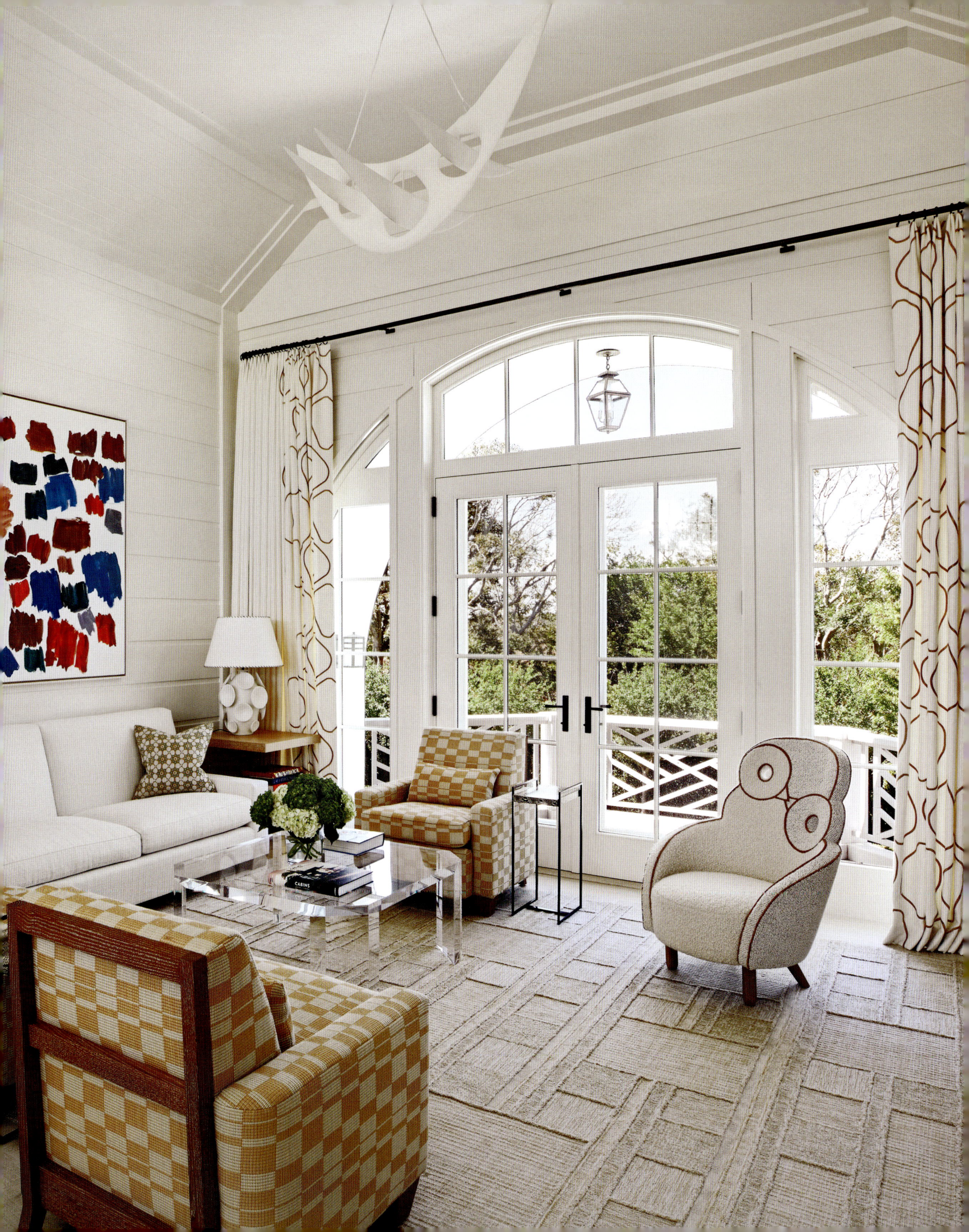

ABOVE: In the primary bedroom, straw marquetry commodes paired with 1940s mirrors flank a hall of closets. RIGHT: Dreamy blues define the space with a patterned Beauvais rug, tufted headboard, and *degradé* Pietro Seminelli curtains.

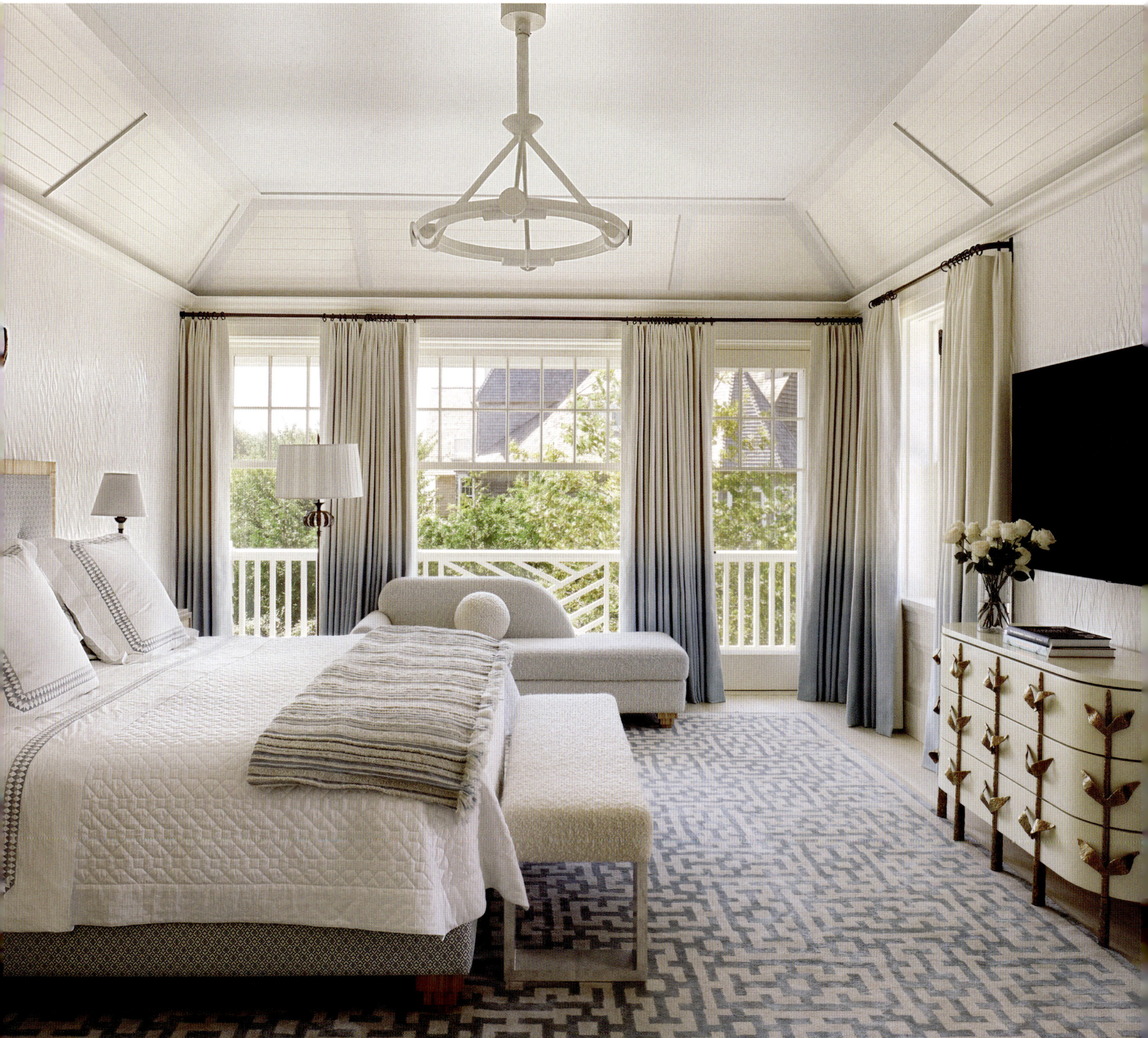

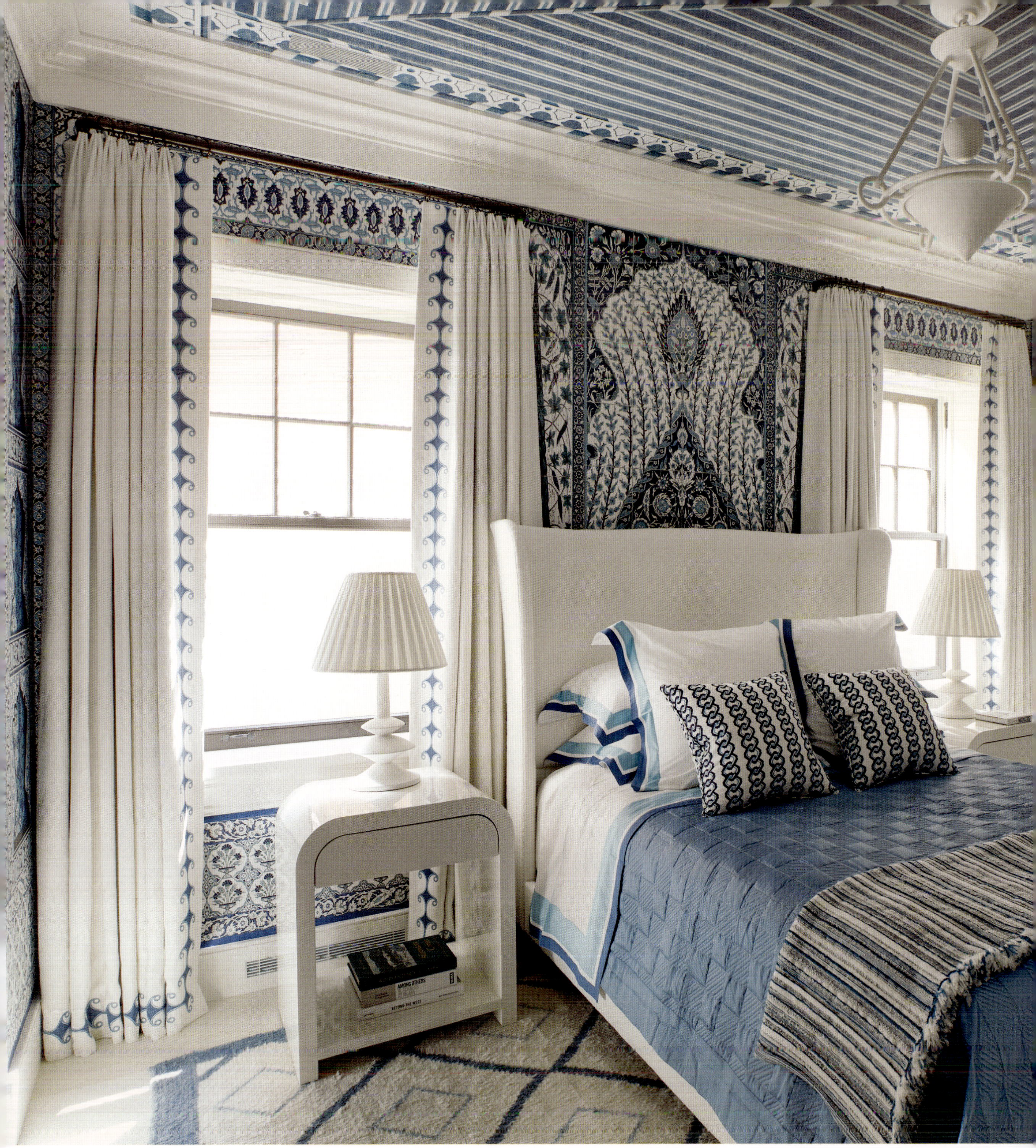

LEFT: Guests never want to leave this bedroom defined by the bold Iksel wallpaper and a striped, tented ceiling. Holland & Sherry curtains and a Beauvais rug complement its bold look.

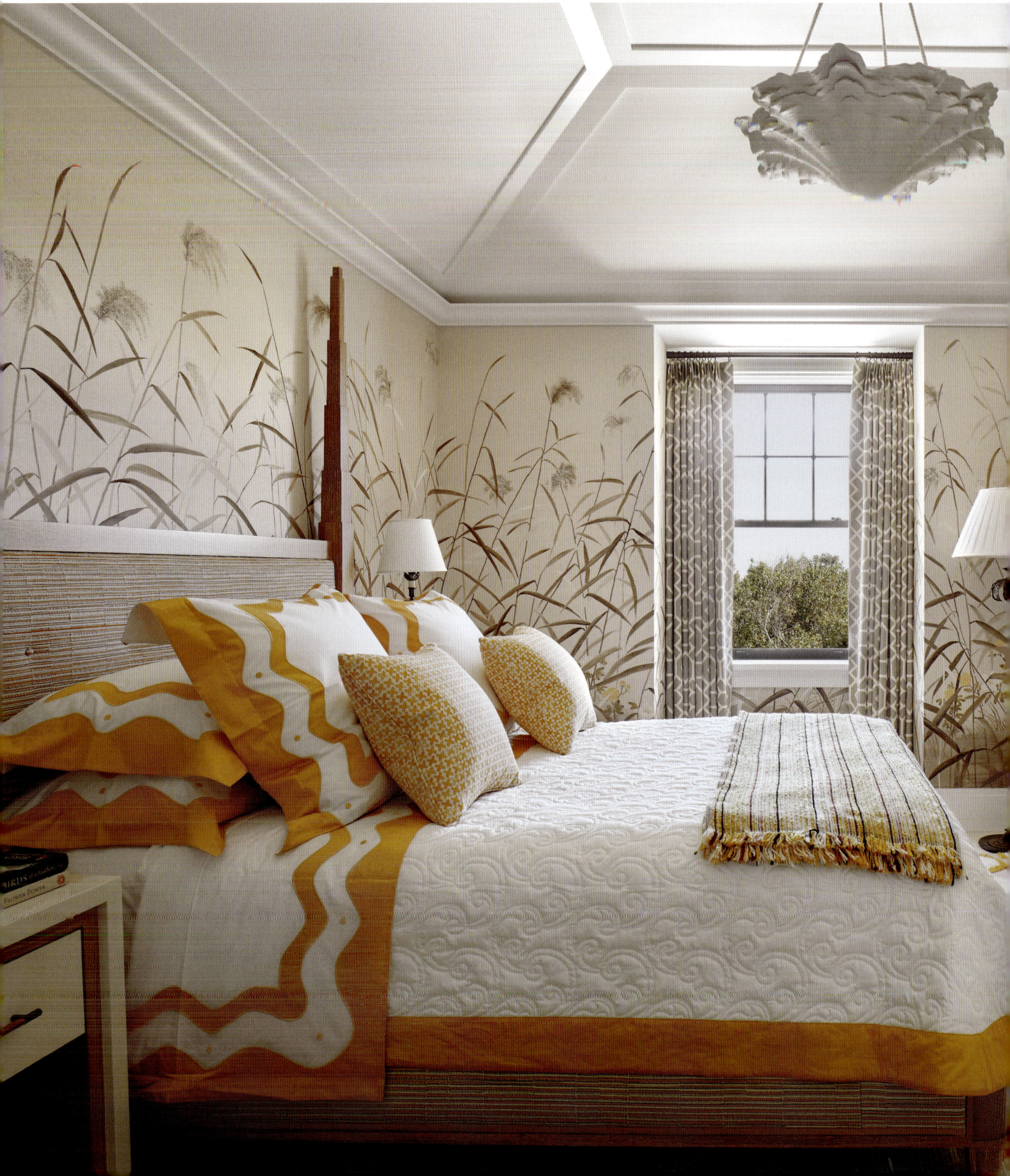

LEFT: De Gournay windblown wheatgrass wallpaper sets the tone in this guest bedroom, where elements, including a Caleb Woodard chest of drawers, Maison Gerard light fixture, and cerused-oak bed, echo the design's movement. ABOVE: A yellow lacquered guest room features Penn & Fletcher embroidery on the roman shade and a Patterson Flynn Martin carpet.

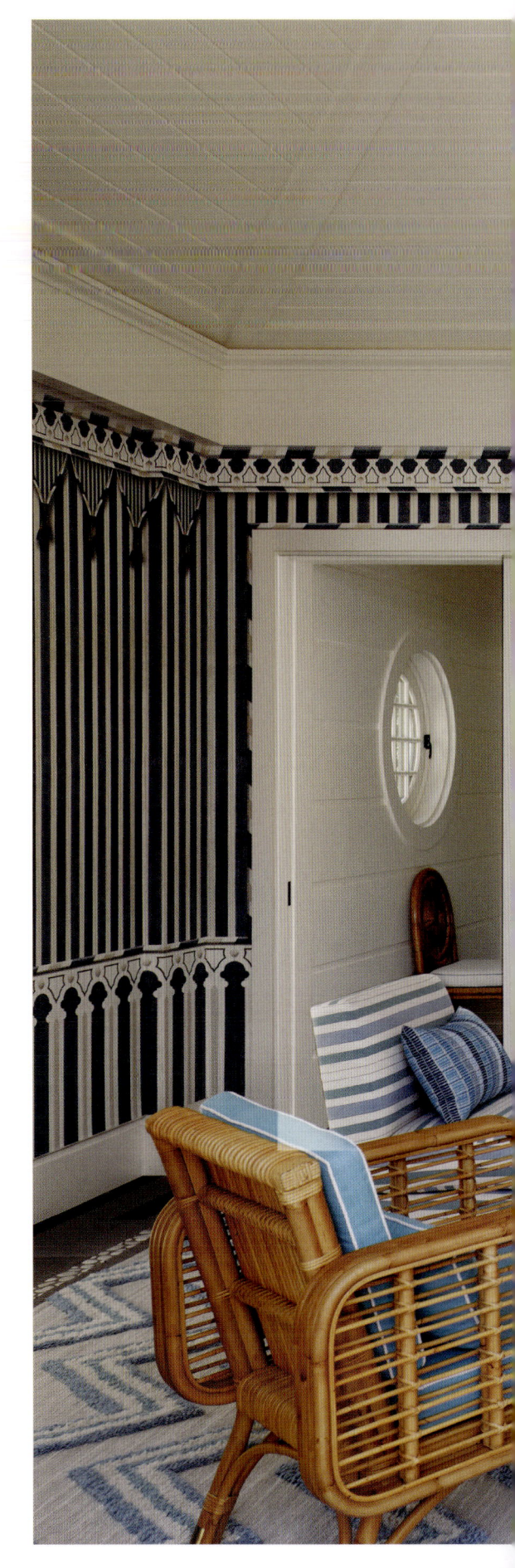

ABOVE: A garden view of the pool house with a sculpture by Wendell Castle. RIGHT: The Iksel-wallpapered pool house is furnished with a snakeskin coffee table by Lobel Modern and India Mahdavi chairs.

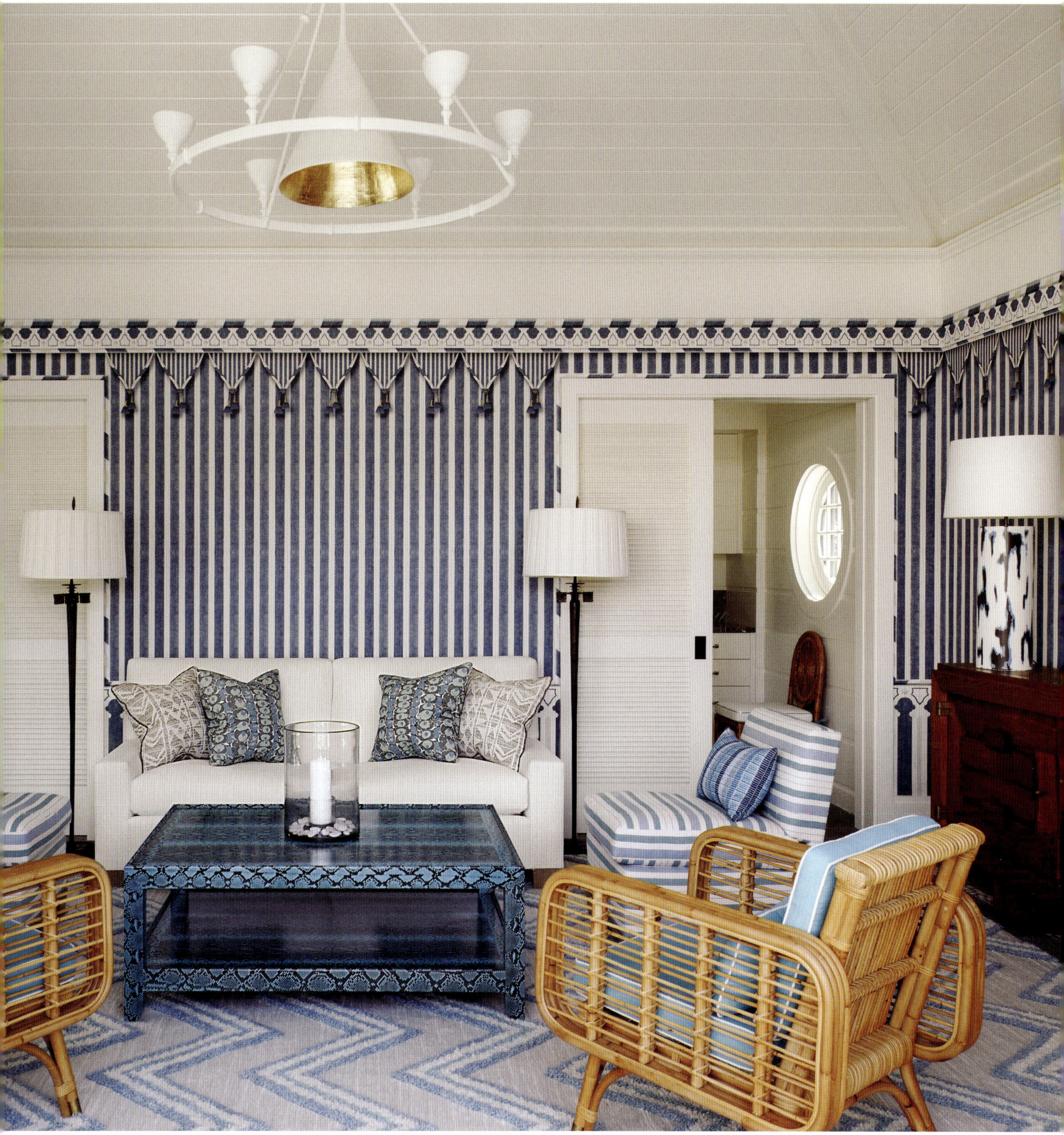

PARIS PIED-À-TERRE

Many of the greatest creatives who have made their names in Paris weren't French at all. Fashion designers, painters, and writers can find new depths of inspiration in the City of Light without being a slave to the Gallic rules and customs. For this pied-à-terre in a Beaux-Arts building for American clients, I sought to tap into that same type of magic—taking the best of local architecture and craftsmanship but shaking things up with a rebellious flair for blending provenance, periods, and styles.

Working with local architecture firm Kasha, we stripped everything down to bring the apartment back to its original beauty. As part of that process, we gracefully updated floor plans and made tweaks for modern comforts. To integrate the space's innate grandeur with the client's vocabulary of pared-down luxury, we needed an overhaul that blended the best of the past with an appreciation for some of the greatest craftsmen working today. In order to strike that balance, we embraced all the benefits of the soaring ceilings and generously proportioned rooms while adding interesting architectural details to breathe new life into the space. A marble floor goes beyond traditional black and white with the addition of a border of mushroom-colored stone, a trick I picked up from classic Rosario Candela buildings in New York. The library's mood is lightened with cerused-oak paneling. For a decidedly modern touch, all the doors are painted black.

Throughout the four-bedroom residence, the mix of major contemporary art and design represent an absolute wish list of artists, artisans, and sources. Nowhere

OPPOSITE: The entrance hall establishes the pied-à-terre's collected sensibility with a pair of sconces by Hervé Van der Straeten flanking a mirror by Serge Roche along with a Louis Cane commode and a pair of Mattia Bonetti chairs.

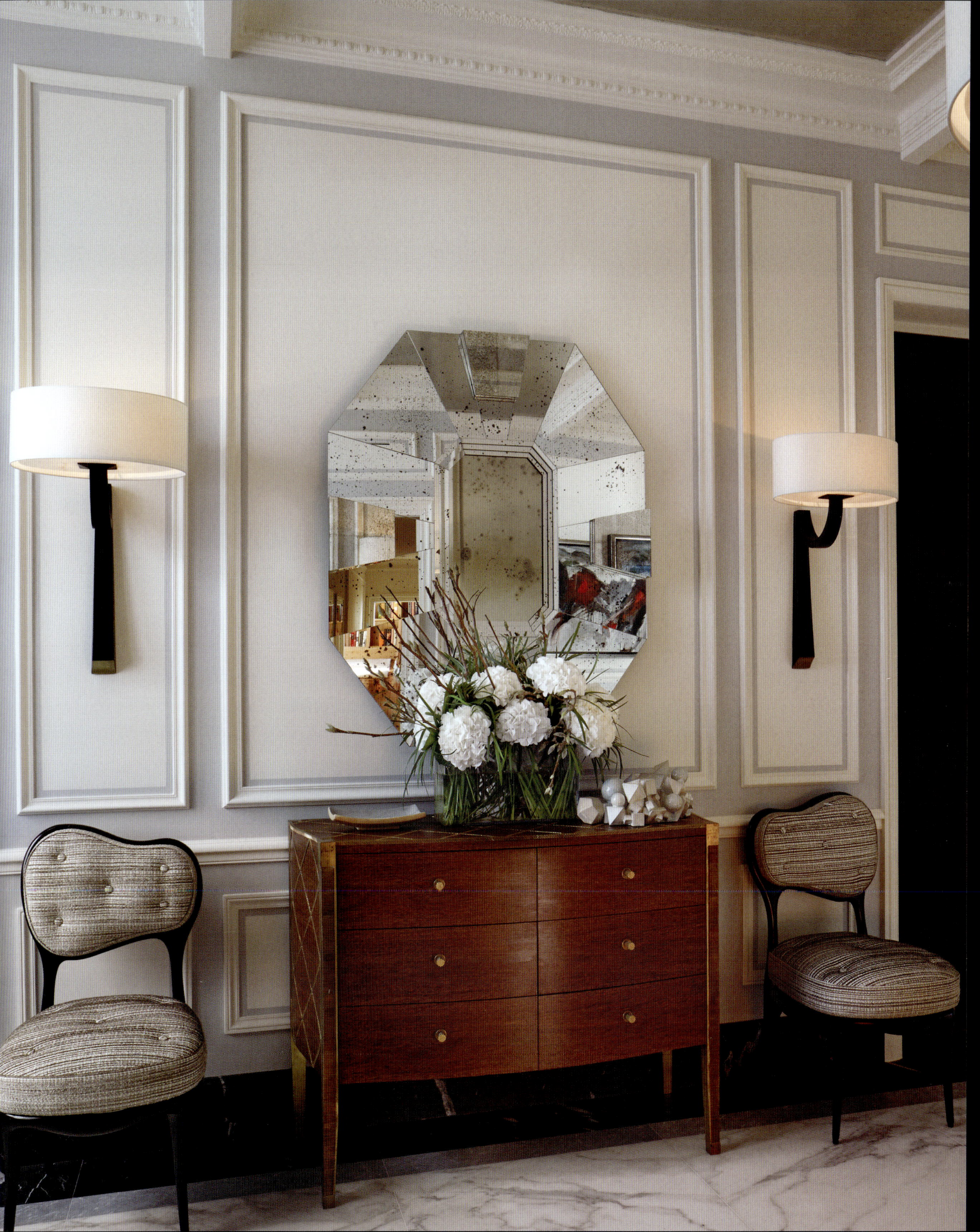

is this combination more richly on display than in the salon, which also serves as the dining room. Everything revolves around a palette of ivory and honey tones from the custom Beauvais rug to the degradé curtains that frame views of Boulevard Saint Germain. I had the entire layout in my head the first time I saw the space. Starting with the rug, I juxtaposed edgy and energetic pieces, including a Fredrikson Stallard acrylic table, an Hervé Van der Straeten cabinet, and a side table by the Campana Brothers, with more refined ones such as Ruhlmann chairs, a pyrite mirror from a dealer on the Left Bank, and a Philippe Anthonioz chandelier.

Having all that and being in Paris is just the dream. To reflect its location, there's a dressiness that highlights the spirit of the glamorous city—with Rateau-inspired de Gournay paper enveloping the primary bedroom and Line Vautrin mirrors lining the walls of the bath. Everything had to be just that special, yet we made the decision to keep the exposed radiators. After all, it's a nineteenth-century space, and we wanted it to feel inviting and warm.

RIGHT: The entryway greets visitors with a marble floor banded in gray and black as well as a dynamic painting by Per Kirkeby. FOLLOWING SPREAD: The living room shines in shades of beige, honey, and caramel, all captured in the *degradé* curtains. A screen featuring polar bears by Anne Midavaine at Atelier Midavaine mirrors the deep black doors for a symmetrical appearance without architectural intervention.

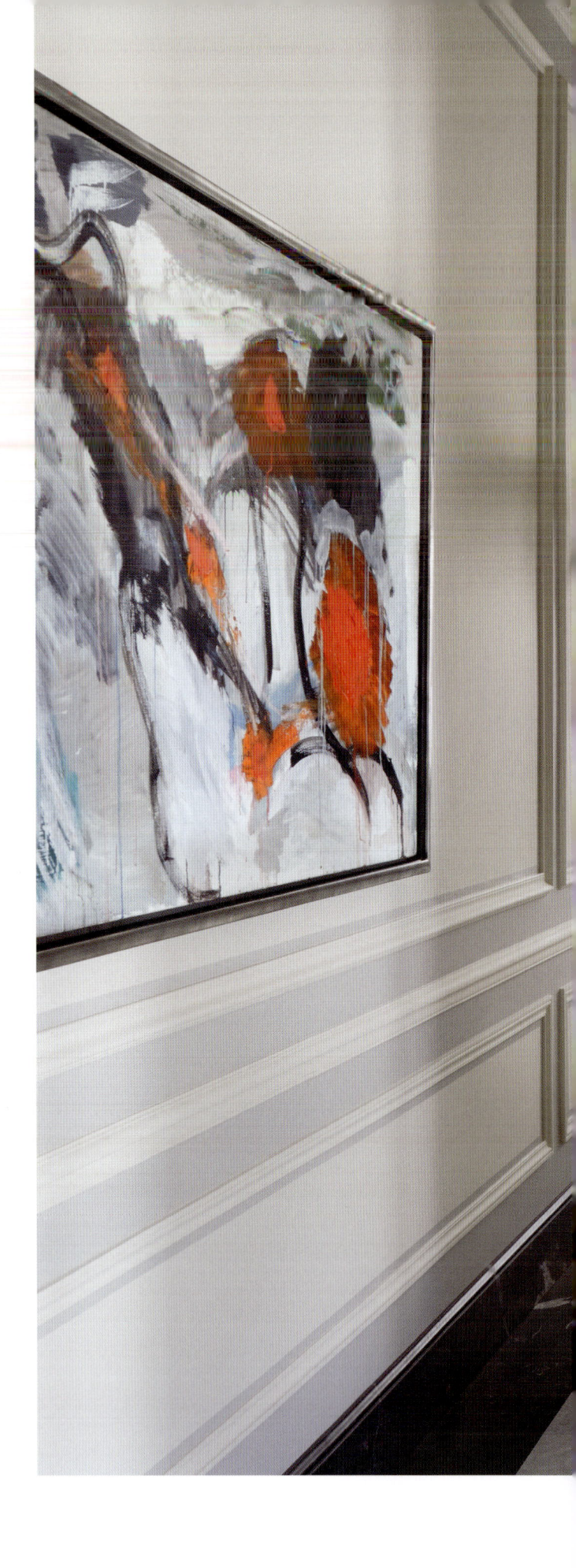

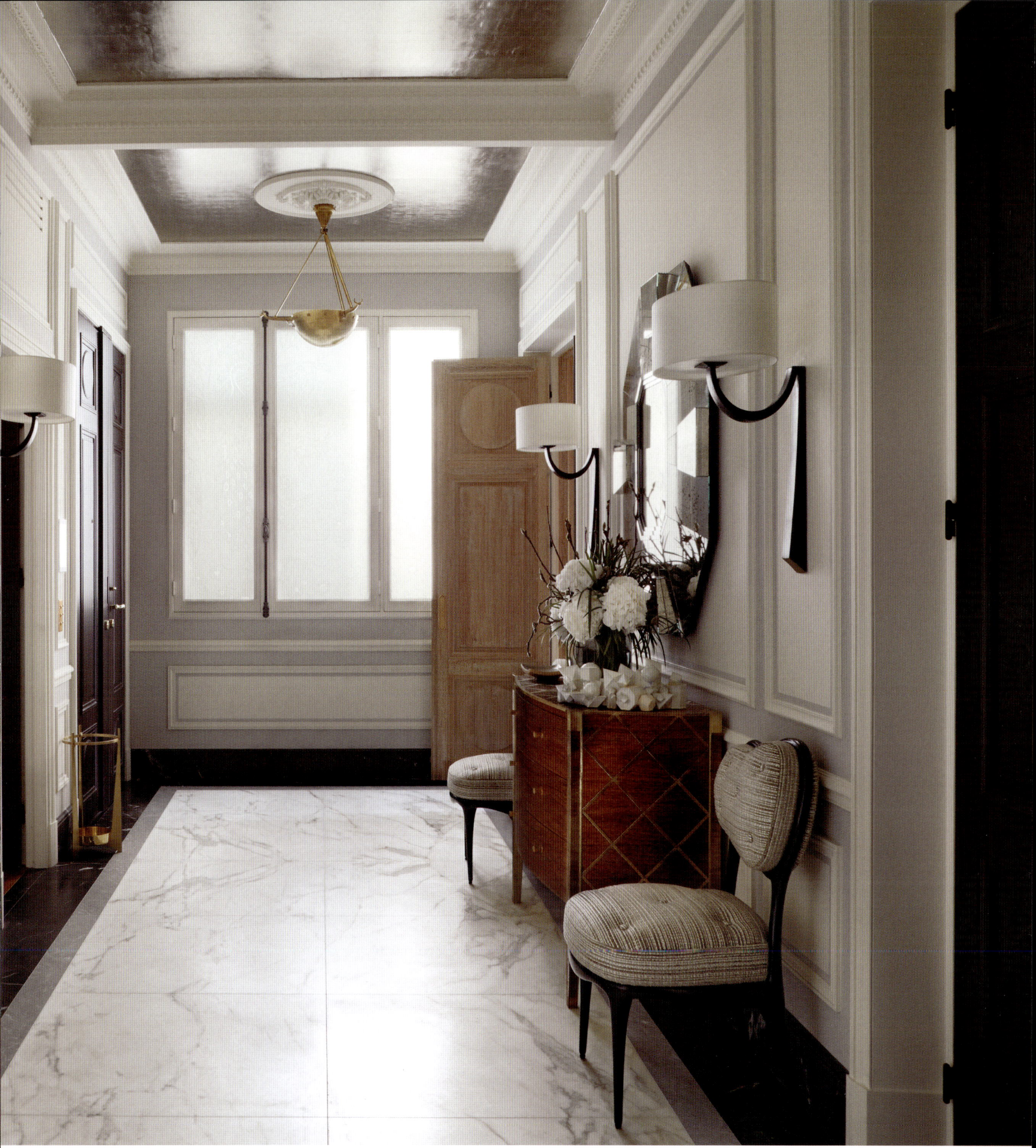

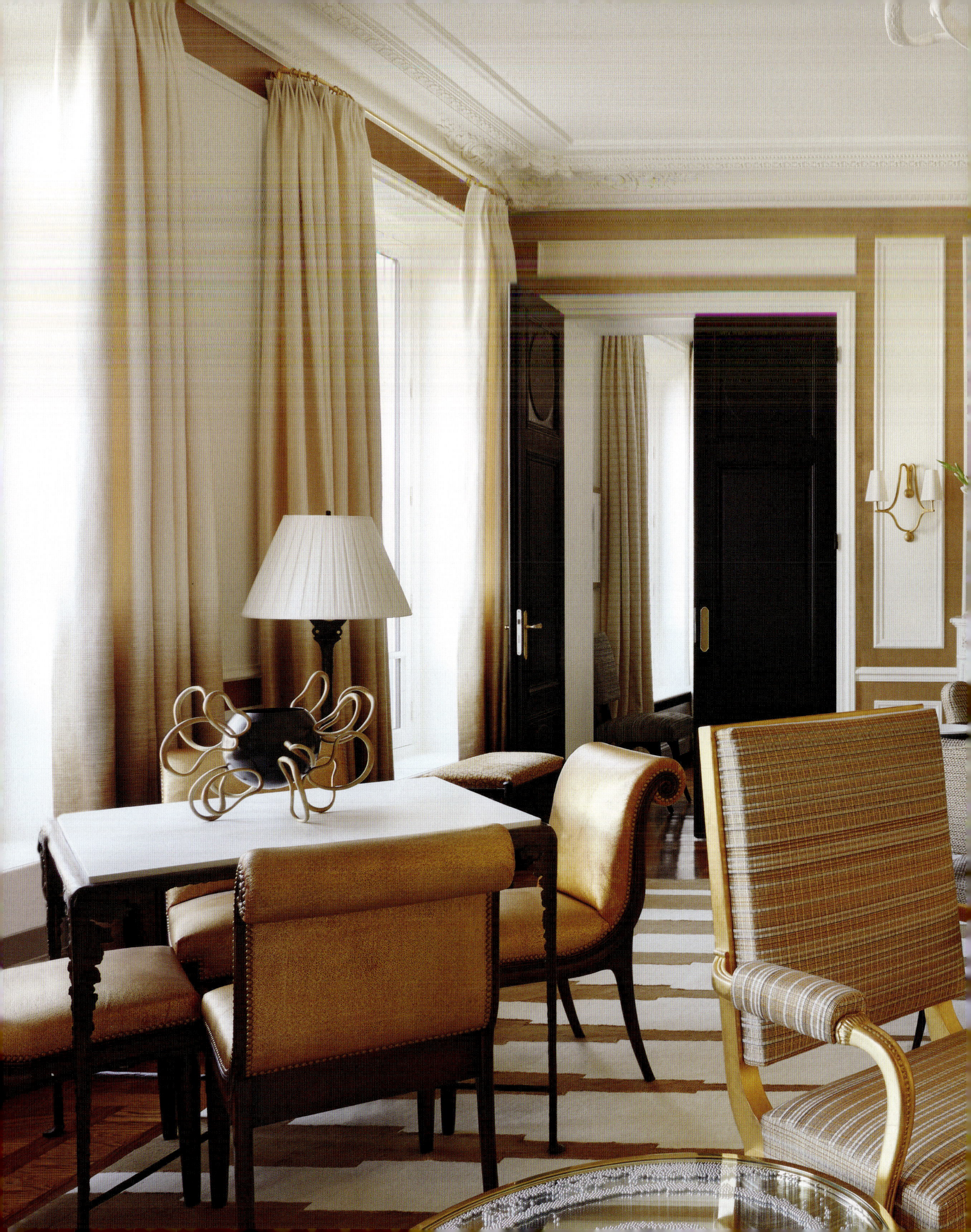

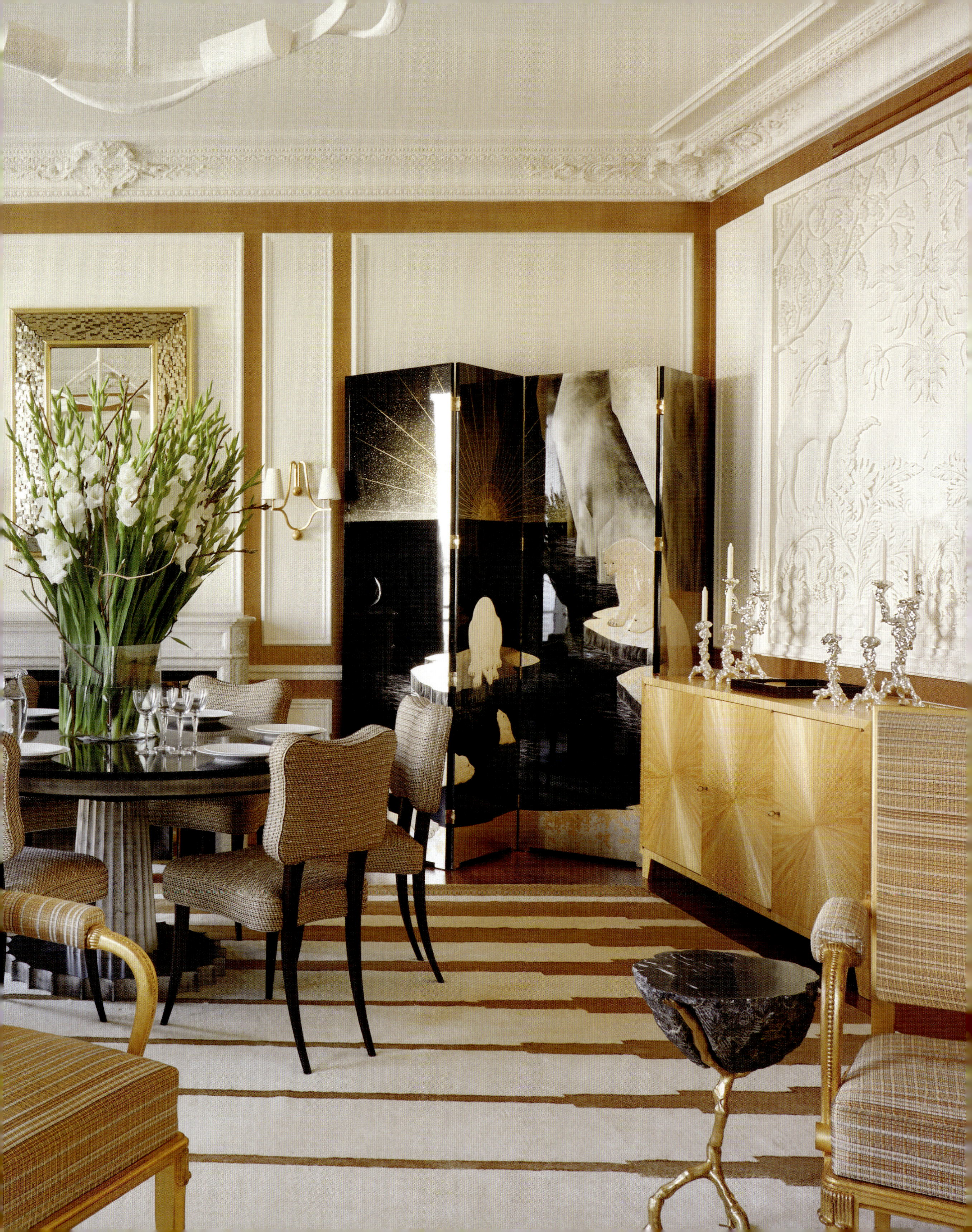

RIGHT: With views of Boulevard Saint-Germain, the room acts as both a sitting room and dining room with the addition of a W. P. Sullivan card table and Armand-Albert Rateau chairs covered in a gilded leather from Meriquet.

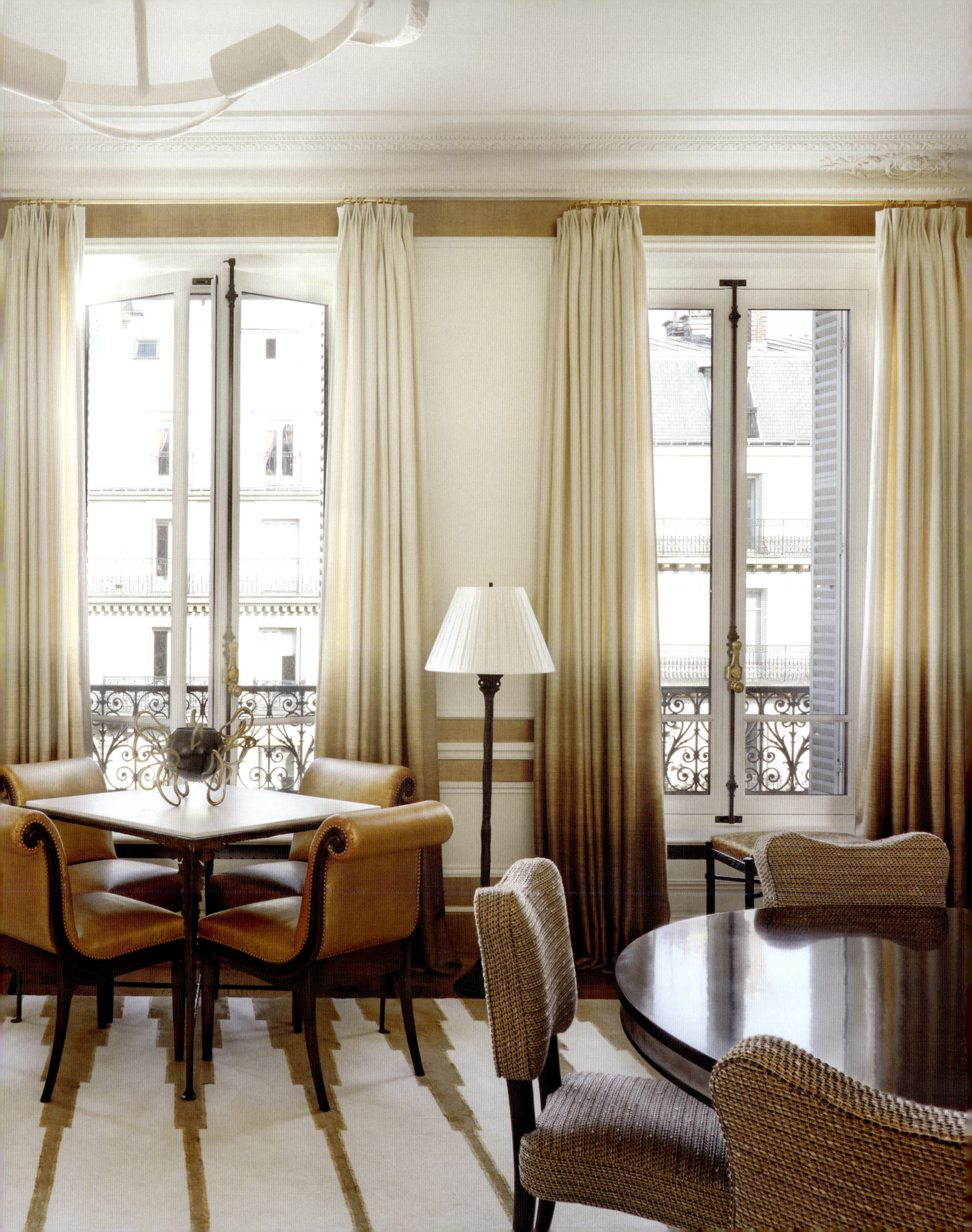

RIGHT: Although the Beauvais rug sets the tone of the room, the Gerhard Richter painting casts a powerful presence. Also assembled in the seating area are a Jouffre sofa, a Fredrikson Stallard acrylic table, and a marble-topped Campana Brothers side table.

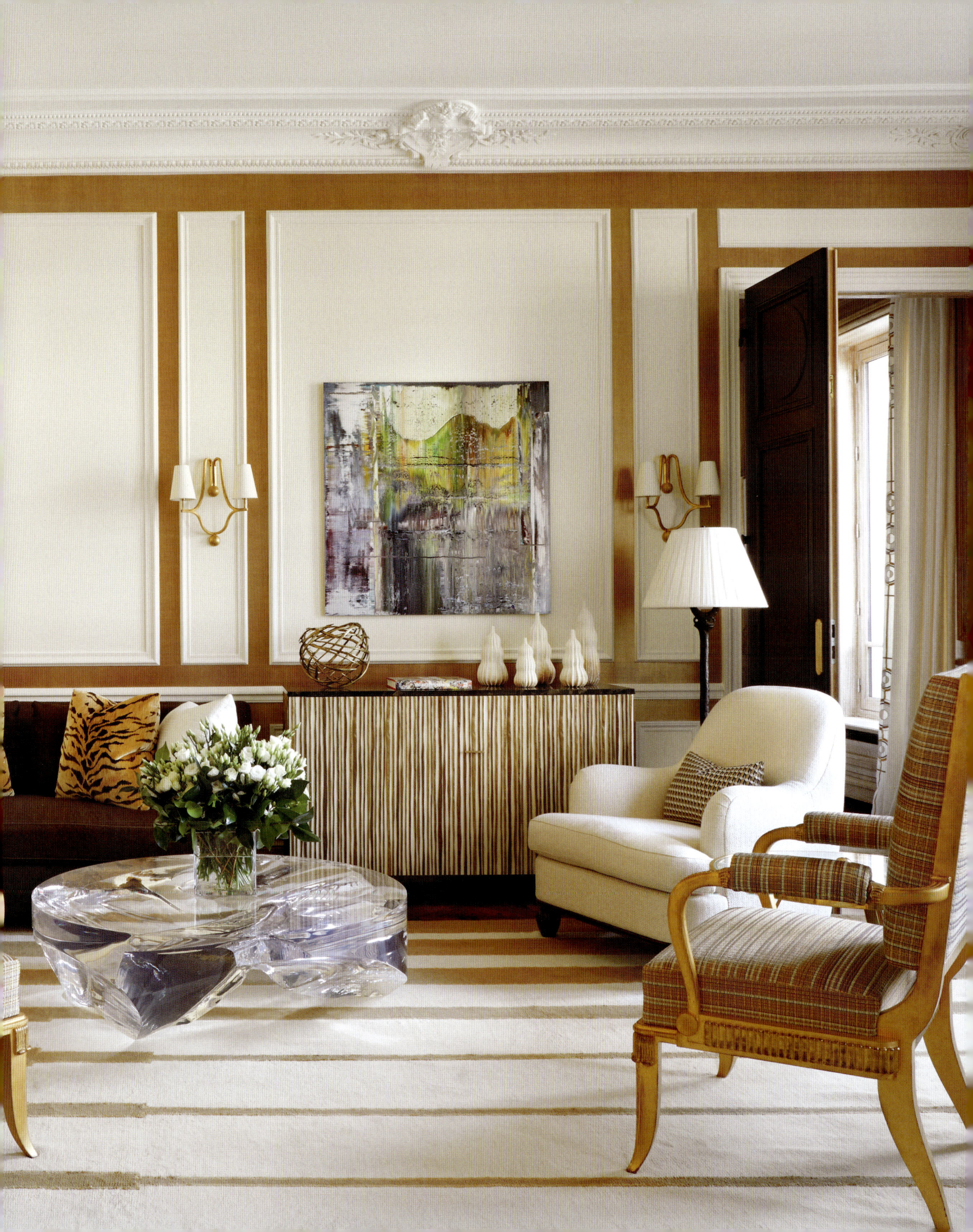

Committing to Local Artisans and Makers

One of the greatest joys of developing a project is connecting with artisans and makers who can handcraft one-of-a-kind pieces. Not only do they elevate the beauty of the space, but they also lend an aspect of customization that allows the residents to be surrounded by collected furnishings and objects. Of course, this direction comes with added expenses and elongated timelines, but clients who are on board are always appreciative and thrilled with the results.

For such endeavors, I often turn to local makers, so working on a project in France means there's a wealth of regional talent and artistry. For example, for this Left Bank pied-à-terre, I collaborated with workrooms that I consider the Giacomettis of tomorrow and whose creations will only appreciate with time. I visited Lyon twice to customize furniture with Jouffre, known for its exceptional upholstery such as the primary suite's Hollywood-style bed. For a bedroom lighting fixture, Alexandre Vossion created a chandelier of rock crystal that really lives up to being jewelry for the room. When it came to marquetry work, Lison de Caunes created a cabinet of such detailed beauty. And I cannot recommend more highly the intricate embroidery of Ligne au Coeur for everything from curtain embellishments to custom bedding.

Across the decades—even centuries—few *maisons* and makers of this caliber remain, so it's a pleasure to support them in their craft. Beyond that, the results are always magnificent—and there's real value in investing in these types of pieces, which are rarer now than ever.

OPPOSITE: The plaster panel in the living room was inspired by Armand-Albert Rateau.

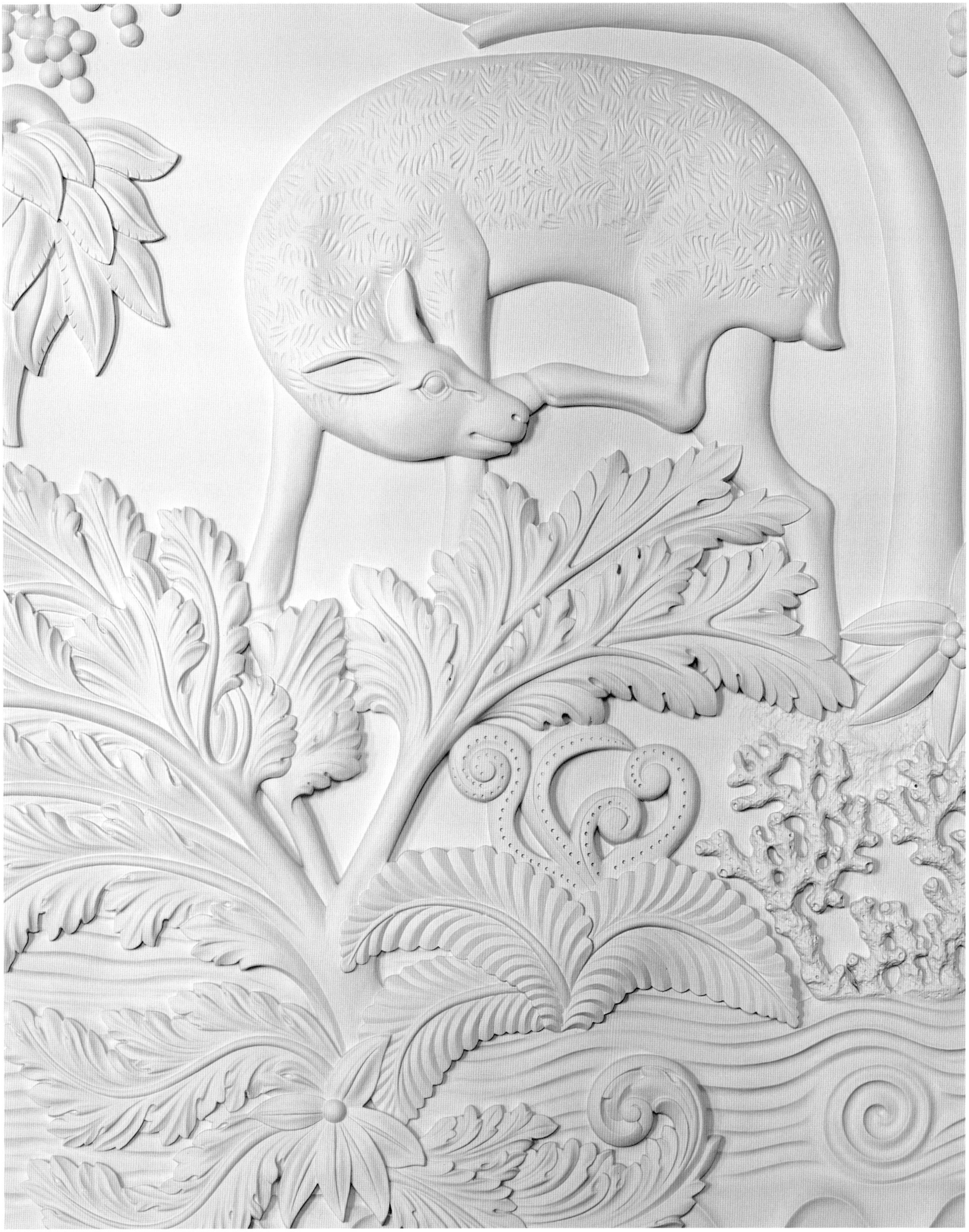

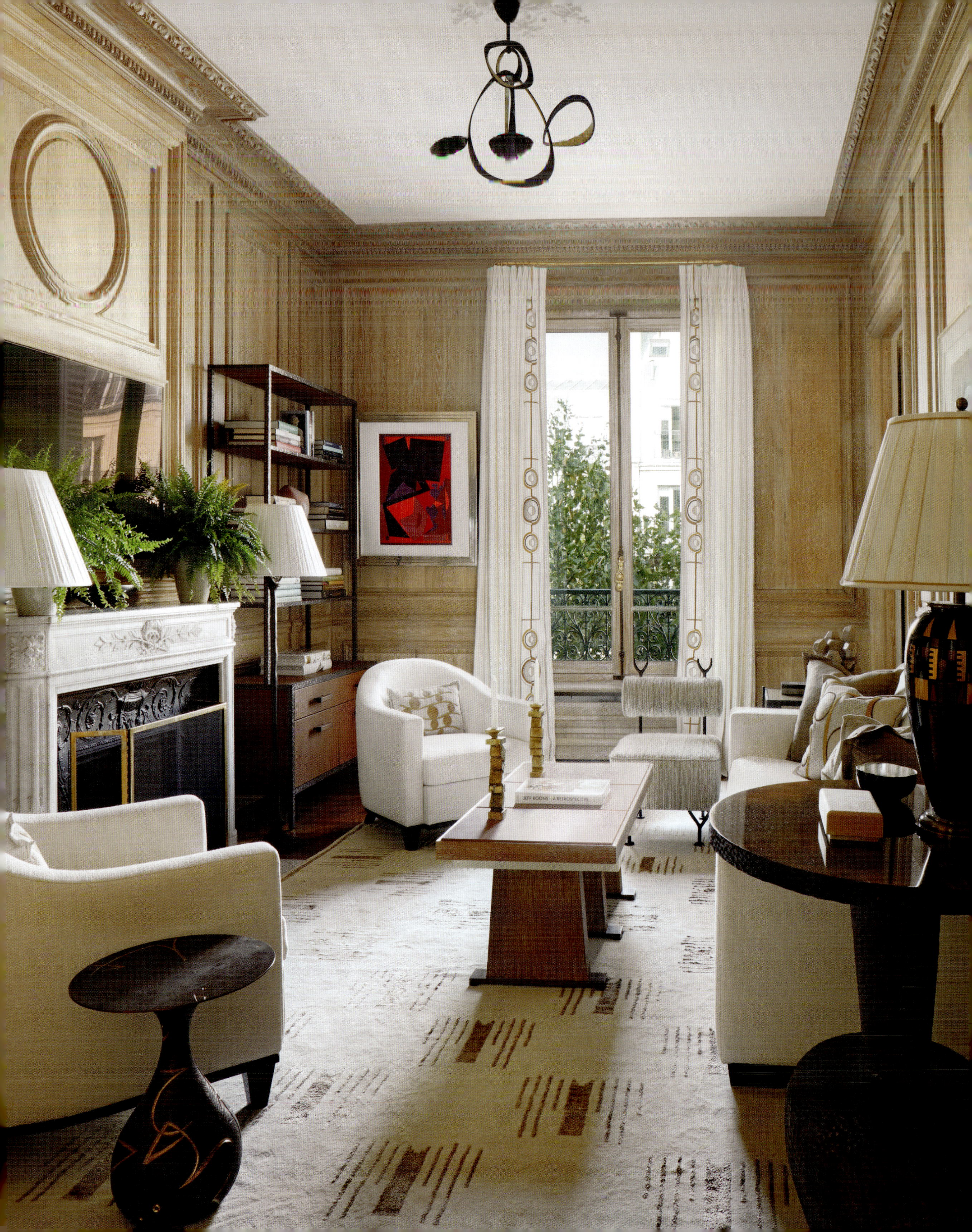
JEFF KOONS A RETROSPECTIVE

OPPOSITE: The library, clad in cerused-oak paneling, presents a spirited mix, including an Hervé Van der Straeten light fixture, a leather-clad table by Marc du Plantier, lounge chairs in the style of Ruhlmann by Jouffre, and a striking artwork by Victor Vasarely. ABOVE: The curtains were custom-embroidered by Ligne au Coeur.

RIGHT: Works by Pablo Picasso and Marc Chagall add to the library's collected character. A Kate Malone ceramic sculpture rests atop a side table by Patrice Dangel.

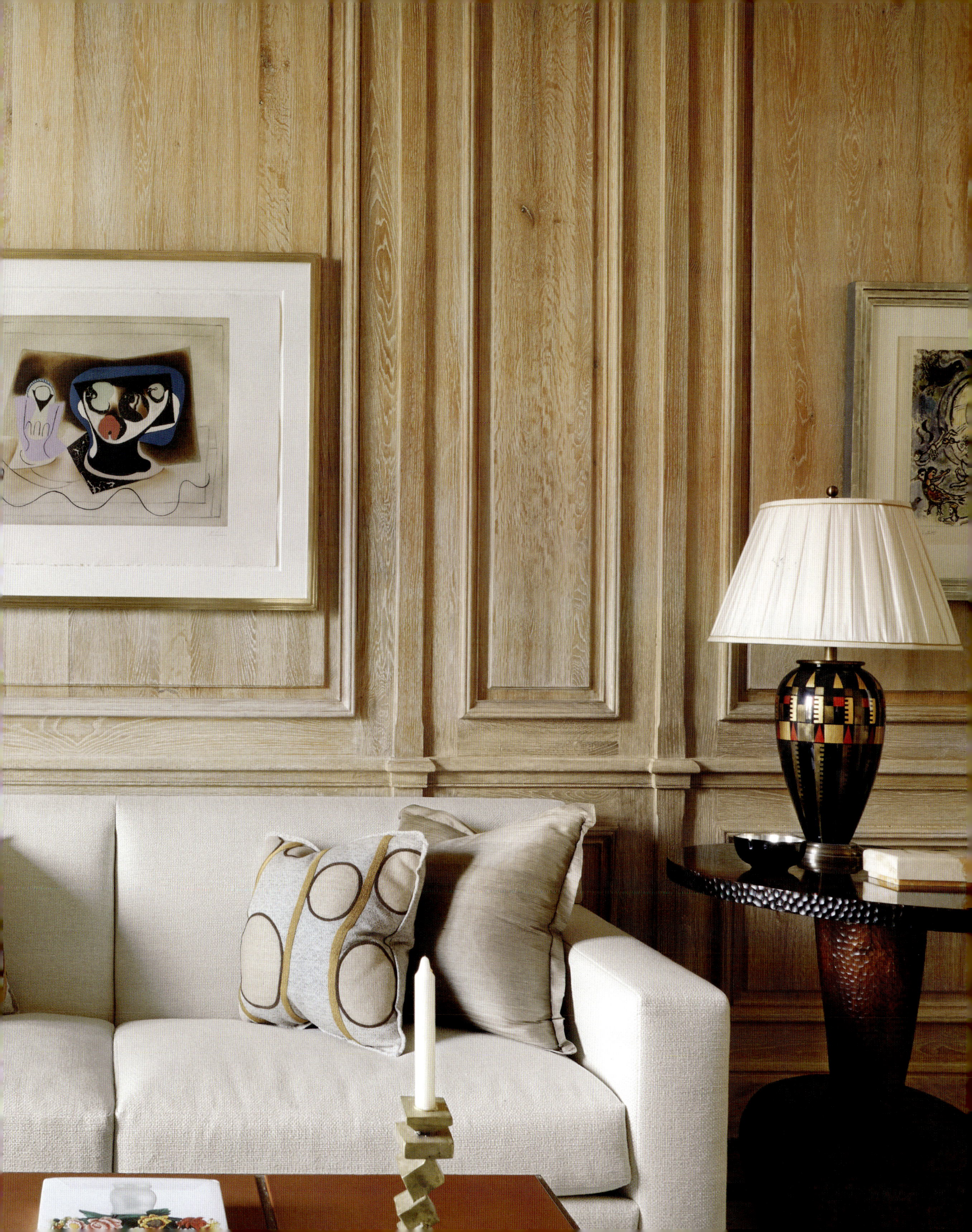

RIGHT: Even the kitchen provides the opportunity for an artful moment, with a David Hockney work hung near the window and a collection of Pippin Drysdale ceramic vessels on the marble counter. The ebonized Jouffre stools complement the black La Cornue range.

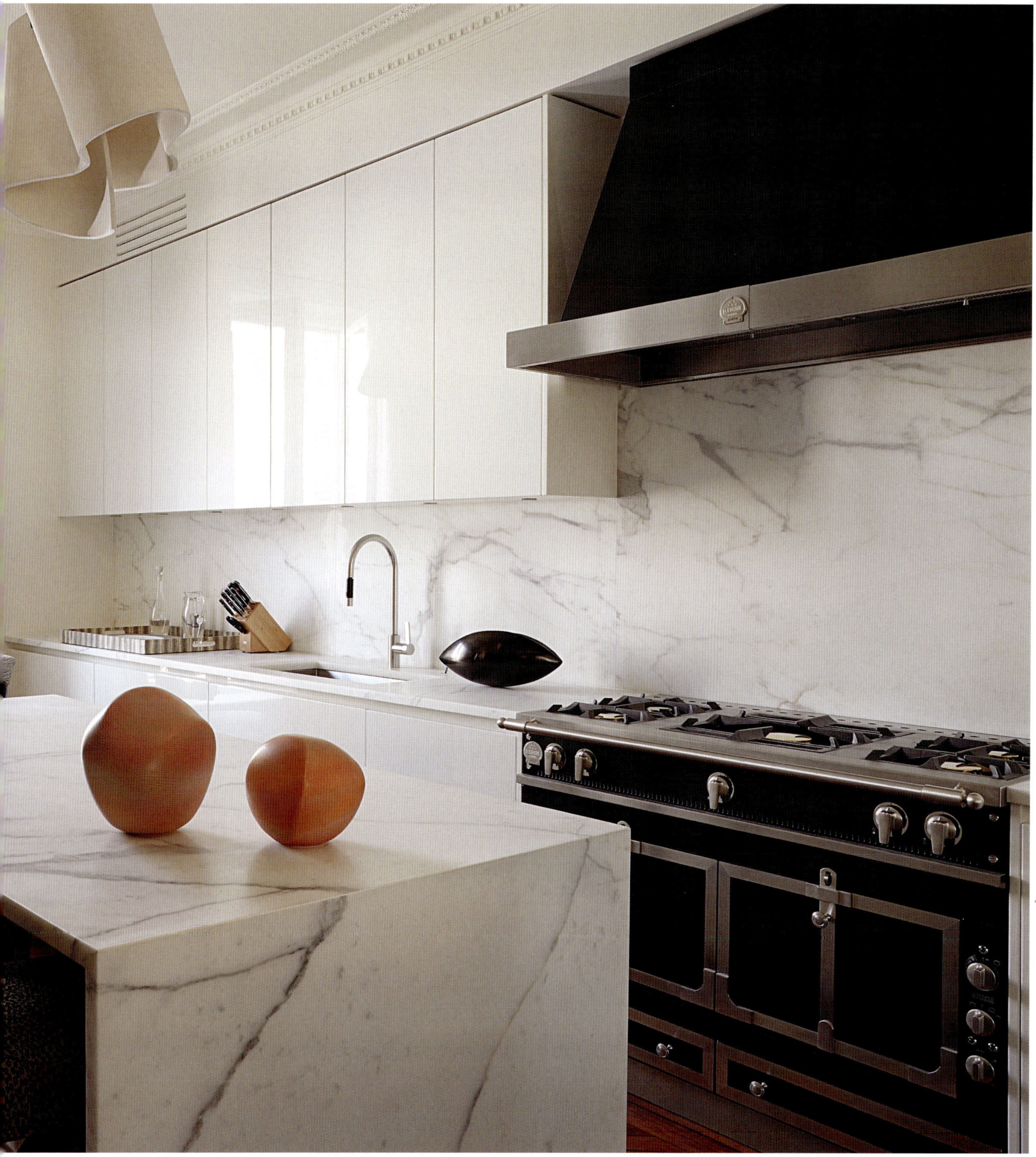

RIGHT: A sliver of a room becomes a place for children to watch television in a cozy chair by Pierre Yovanovitch or on the Tara Chapas fabric-clad sofa, above which hangs a work by Damien Hirst.
FOLLOWING SPREAD: In the primary bedroom, hand-painted de Gournay wallpaper creates elegant drama. Adding to the glamorous vibe are a chandelier by Alexandre Vossion and a bed by Vosges. A wall of mirrored closets provides much-needed storage.

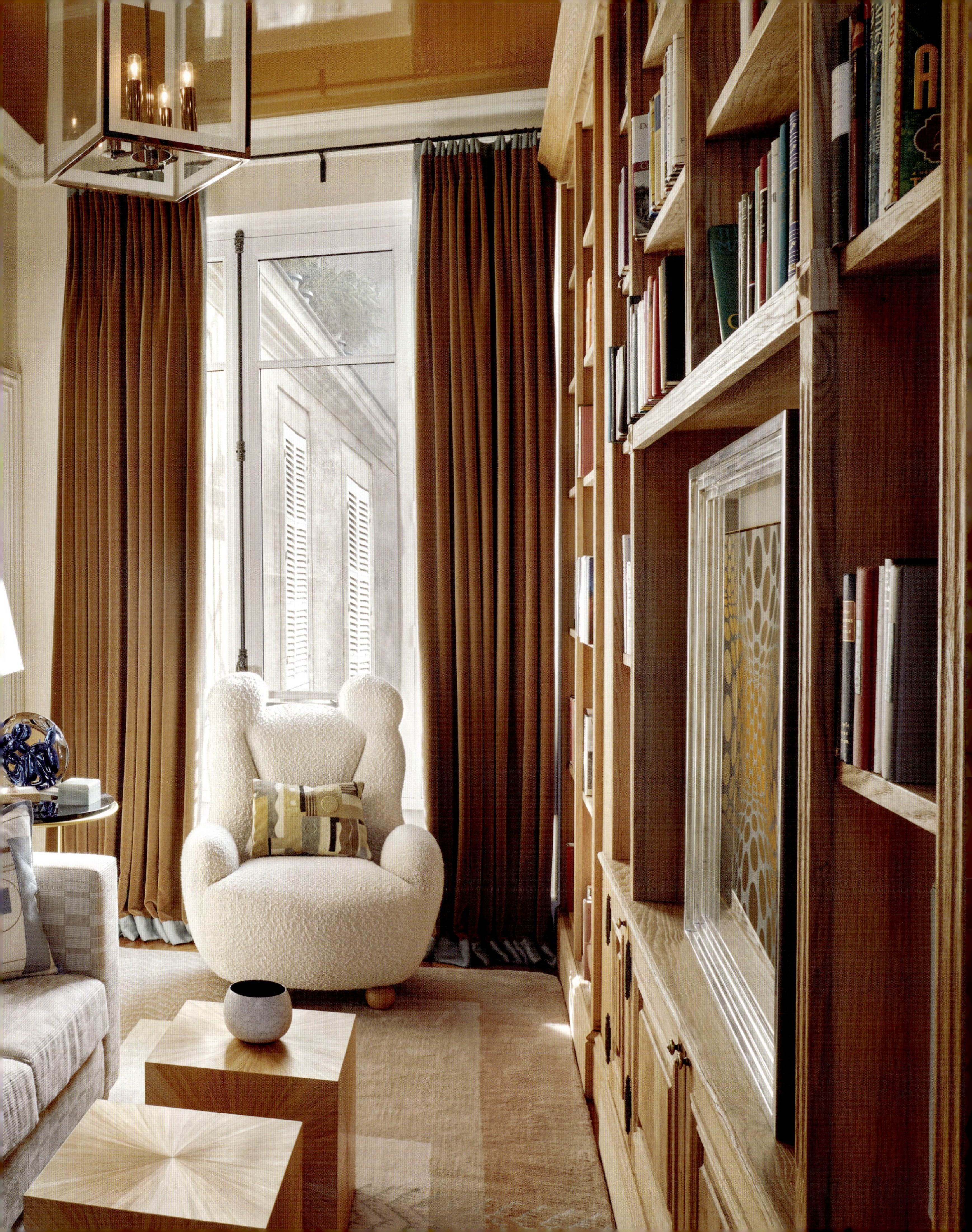

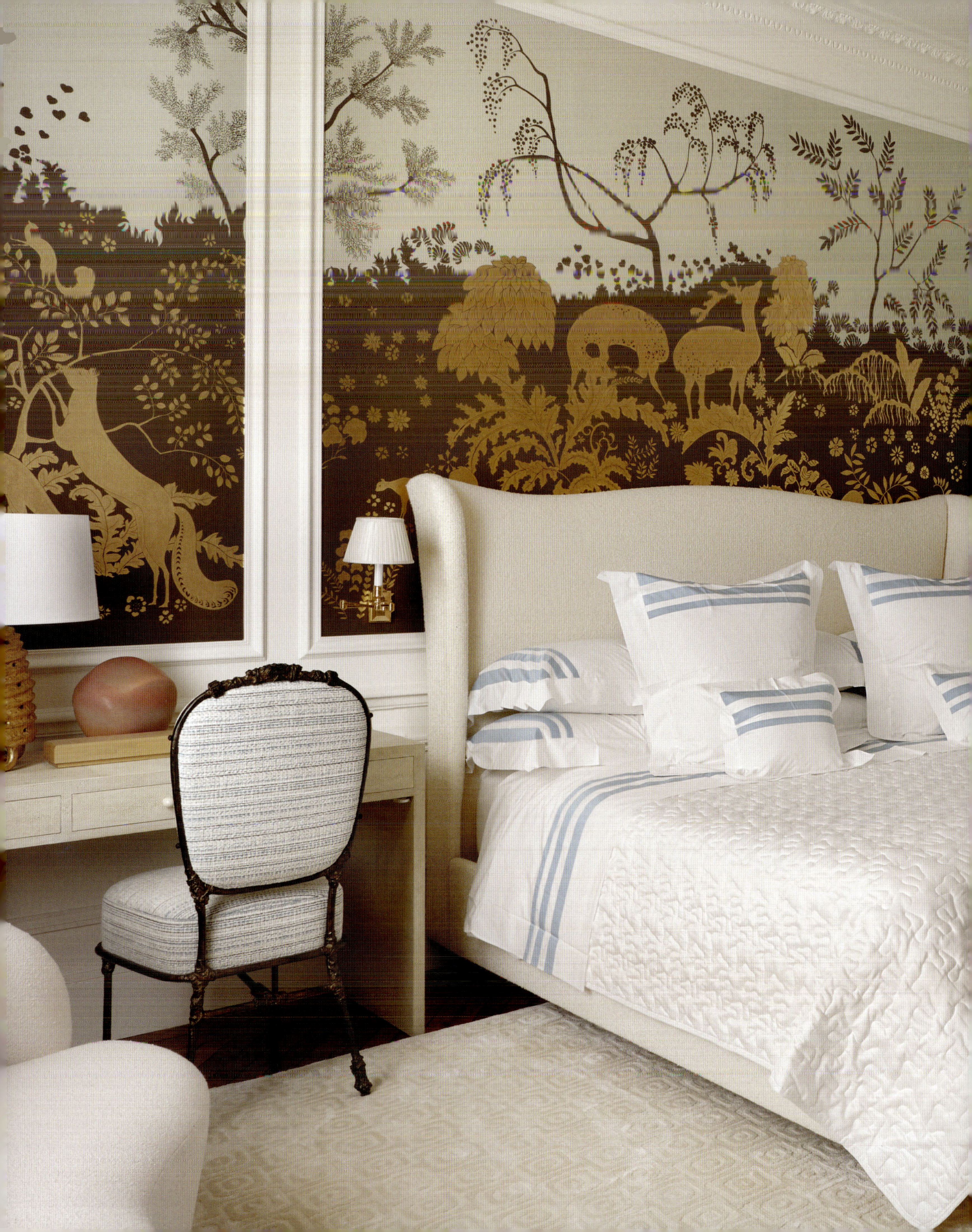

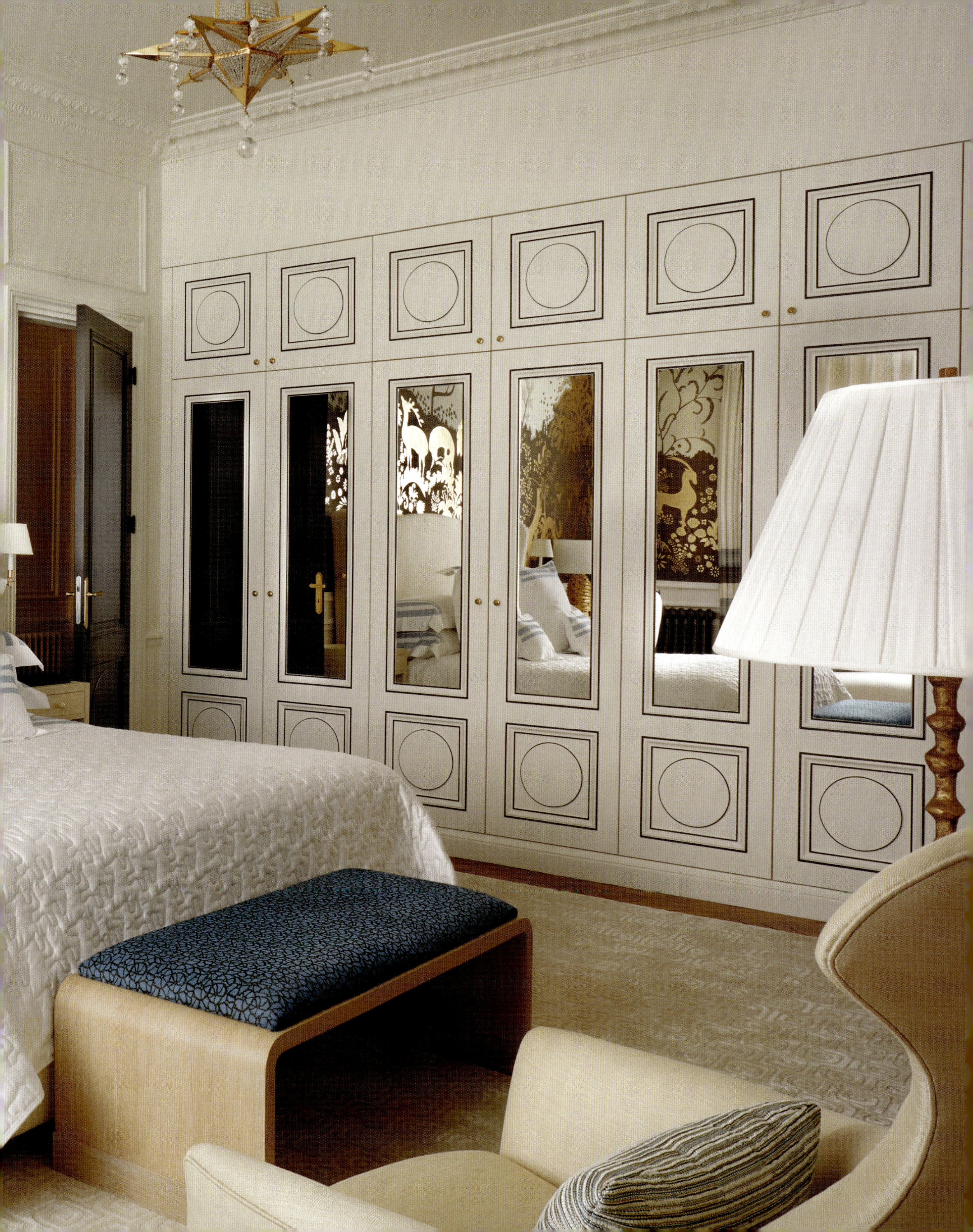

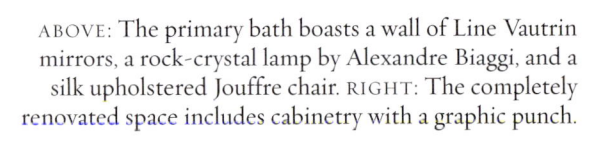

ABOVE: The primary bath boasts a wall of Line Vautrin mirrors, a rock-crystal lamp by Alexandre Biaggi, and a silk upholstered Jouffre chair. RIGHT: The completely renovated space includes cabinetry with a graphic punch.

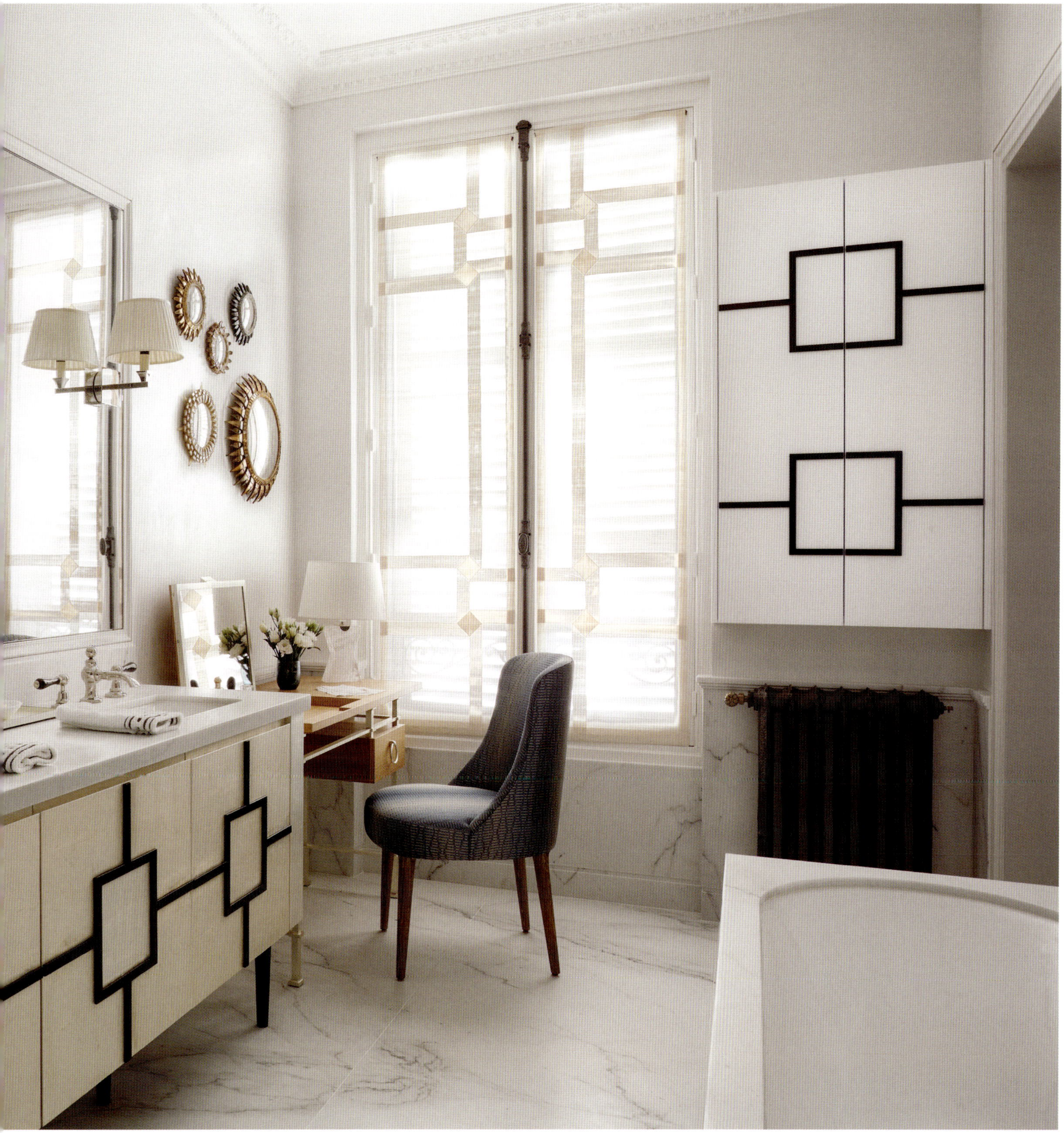

ABOVE: An artwork by Keith Haring supplies color in the son's bedroom, outfitted in shades of chocolate and beige. RIGHT: In the daughter's bedroom, a niched bed is surrounded by storage, always a plus in a cozy Parisian space.

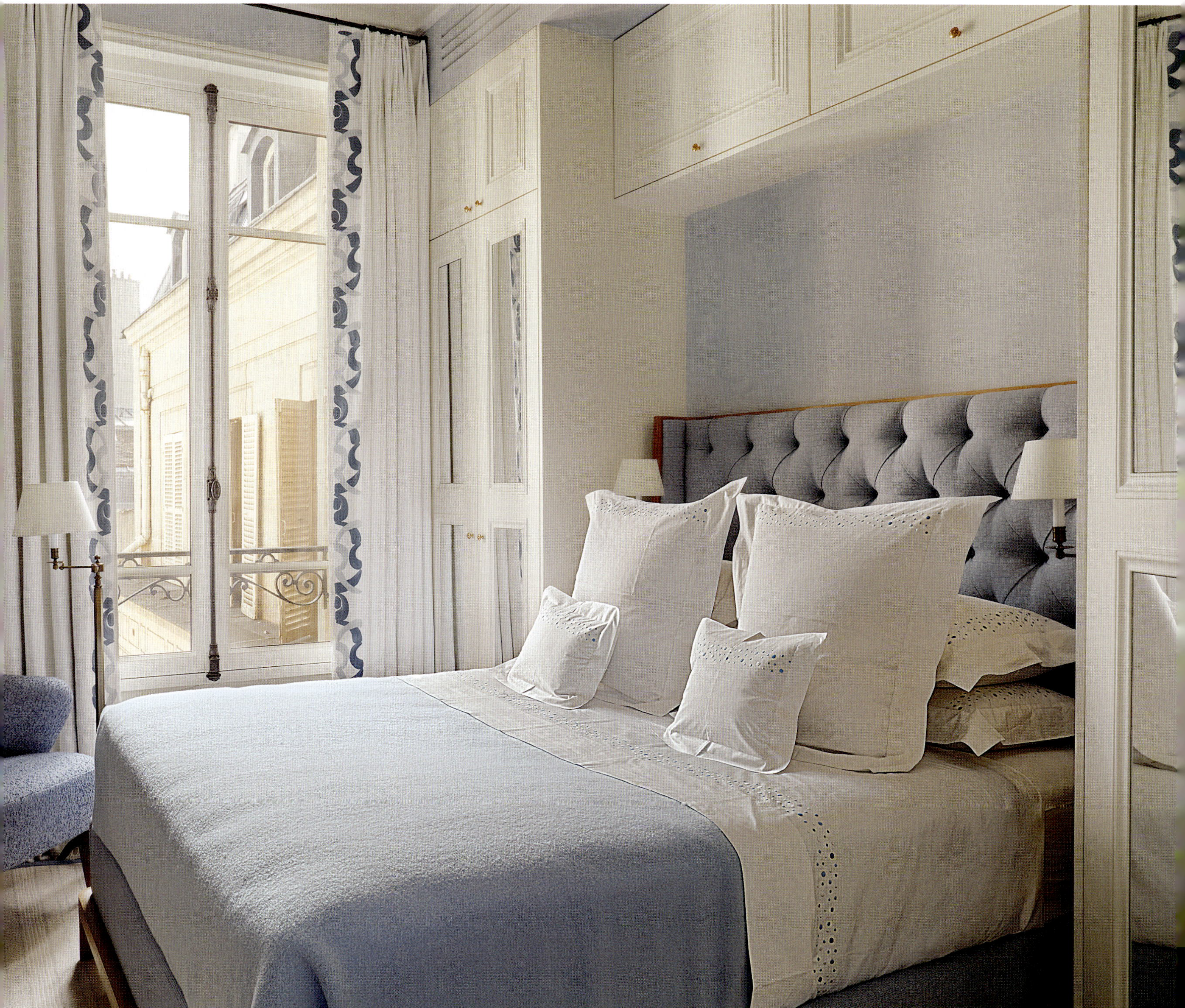

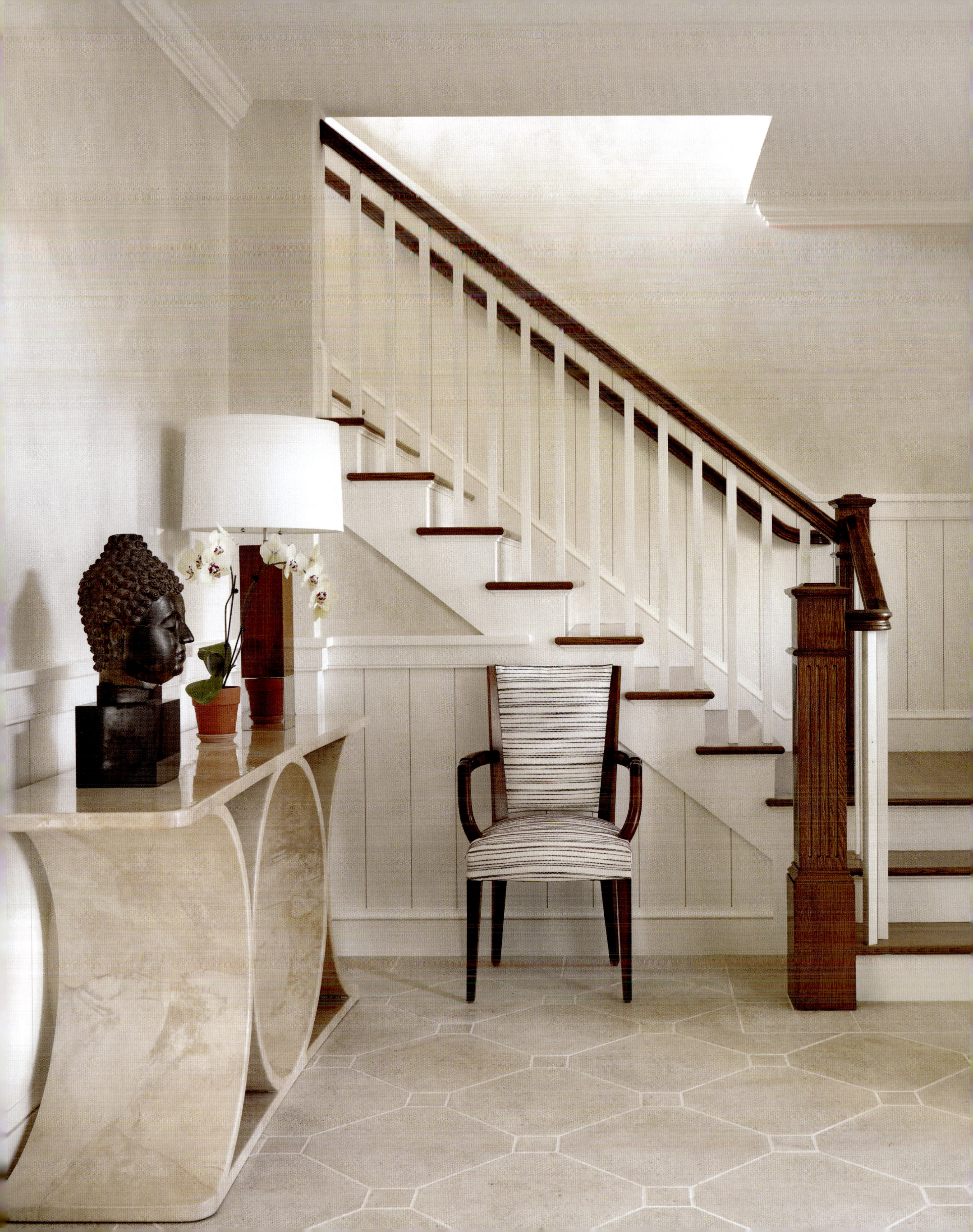

SEASIDE IN NEW ENGLAND

Although New England is rich with the architectural history of its dazzling cottages—resplendent with every type of decorative ornamentation imaginable—my clients requested the very opposite for the home they acquired surrounded by wetlands. Clear in their direction, they threw out words like *clean*, *serene*, and *tailored* as we embarked on designing their new summer getaway. Succinctly stated, overdecoration was out of the question.

In their quest to create a relaxing environment for their family of six, they had landed on the perfect parcel of land, completely removed from the traffic and activity of Cliff Walk. Surrounded by protected acreage yet with views of the ocean, the house gave me the opportunity to connect the exteriors to the interiors throughout. I wanted nothing to impede the incredible views; instead, I wanted to devise settings that seamlessly blend from indoors to out.

Upon arrival, the house conveys a tranquil tone. The new limestone-floored entry—the perfect place to put bags down after traveling from the city—has a 1940s feel with its Venetian-plastered walls, a muted palette, and a sculptural mid-century console from Lobel Modern. That same calming quality permeates the home even as more color and pattern make an appearance. Since the homeowners are nautical people with a passion for sailing, shades of blue play a major role.

The living room serves as the heart of the house with an array of comfortable sofas and chairs. I executed the furniture plan so that one's eye goes right over the sofa to the view. To add to that connection with the outside, I used curtains that are the reverse of a Clarence House geometric fabric, leaving them unlined to frame the landscape. The rug picks up another linear pattern as do the vertically striped Venetian

OPPOSITE: Creamy tones offer a warm welcome with ivory Venetian plaster walls and a limestone floor, with a console from Lobel Modern. FOLLOWING SPREAD: The living room's sweeping views of the wetlands and out to the ocean are framed by Clarence House curtains. Their geometric motif is picked up in the rug by Patterson Flynn Martin and the subtle stripe in the Venetian plaster walls, while a pair of Jonas chairs are upholstered in the perfect seaside blue.

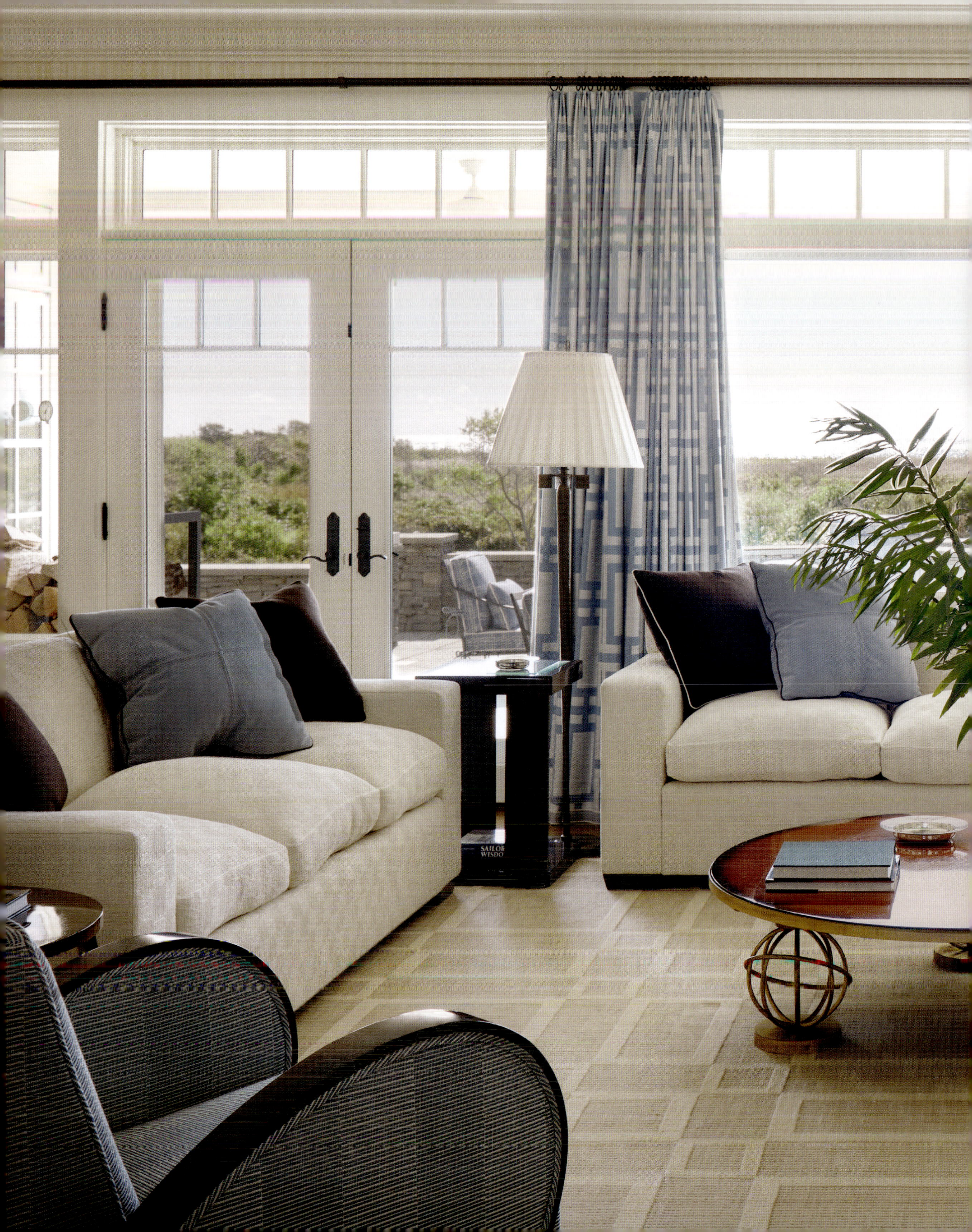

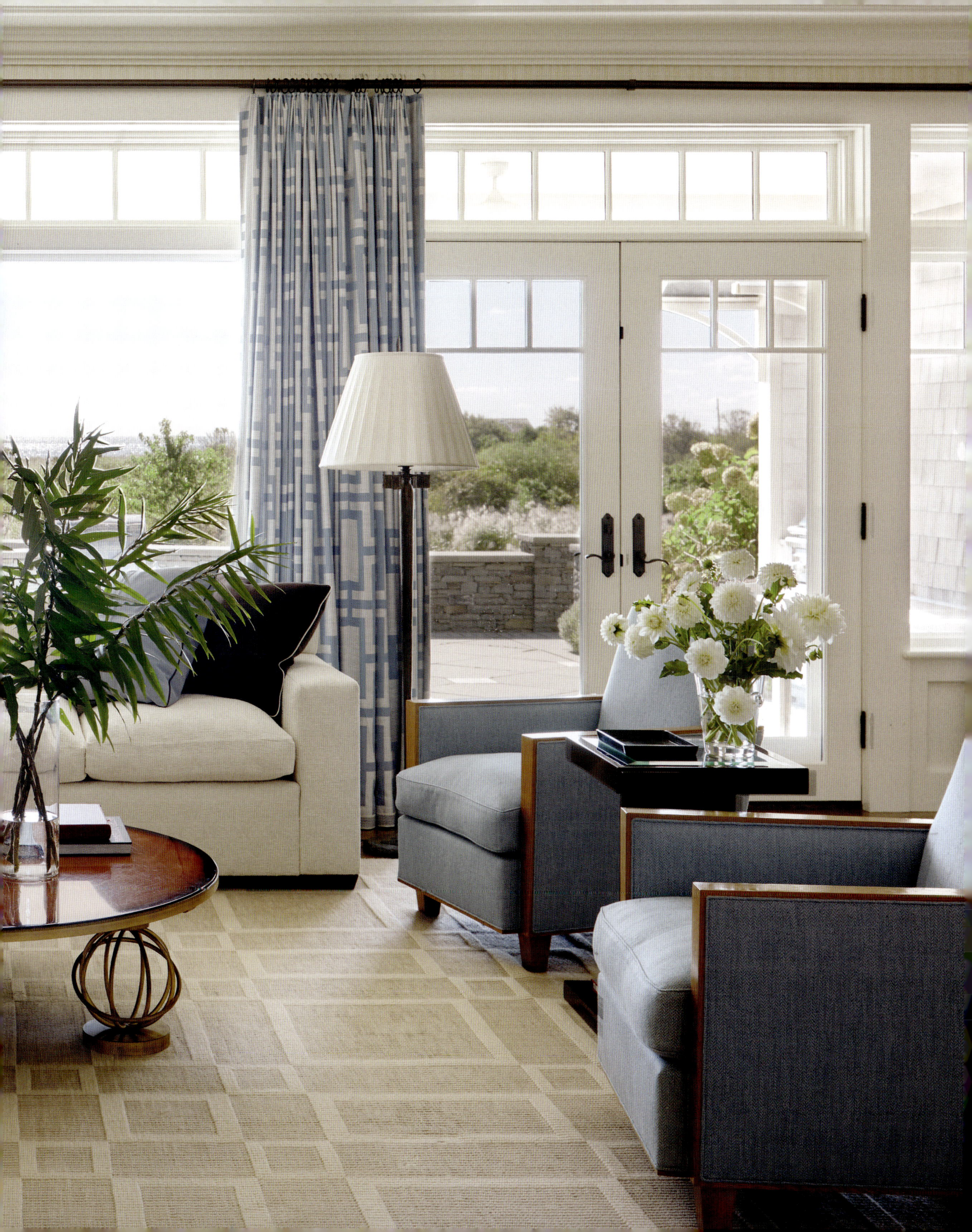

plaster walls, while both stay subdued enough not to compete. The dining room also includes varying blues—with a deep navy plaster finish above the wood paneling and similarly hued horizontal stripes on the window treatments. A 1940s Macassar dining table from a Parisian dealer reflects the view with its gleaming finish.

The library, I must admit, is a personal favorite, although when we began the project it was decidedly my least favorite. We ripped out the unattractive cherrywood paneling, which felt totally wrong for the new direction; however, we wanted to honor that cozy feeling of a wood-paneled library. Now, a faux-wood finish adds texture and charm in spades and creates the perfect backdrop for a Jean-Michel Frank–inspired sofa and chairs covered in custom-woven fabric by Tara Chapas.

Naturally, the most relaxing spaces are the bedrooms. While each is for the most part calm, there are moments that reveal the individual personality of each space. A variety of curtains, structured to block out the morning sunlight for late risers, acts as a focus with either decorative trim or an eye-catching pattern. In the primary bedroom, a thick vertical stripe was hand painted and animates the walls along with a sky-blue ceiling, while in a guest room a number of patterned pillows add a spirited layer. From these rooms on the second floor, expansive vistas open up over the trees straight to the water—offering the greatest sense of calm imaginable.

ABOVE: Surrounded by protected wetlands, the home provides a relaxing escape. OPPOSITE: A Jean Dunand framed screen from the 1940s hangs on a wall accented by a subtle tonal stripe in Venetian plaster. The vintage side table is from Karl Kemp.

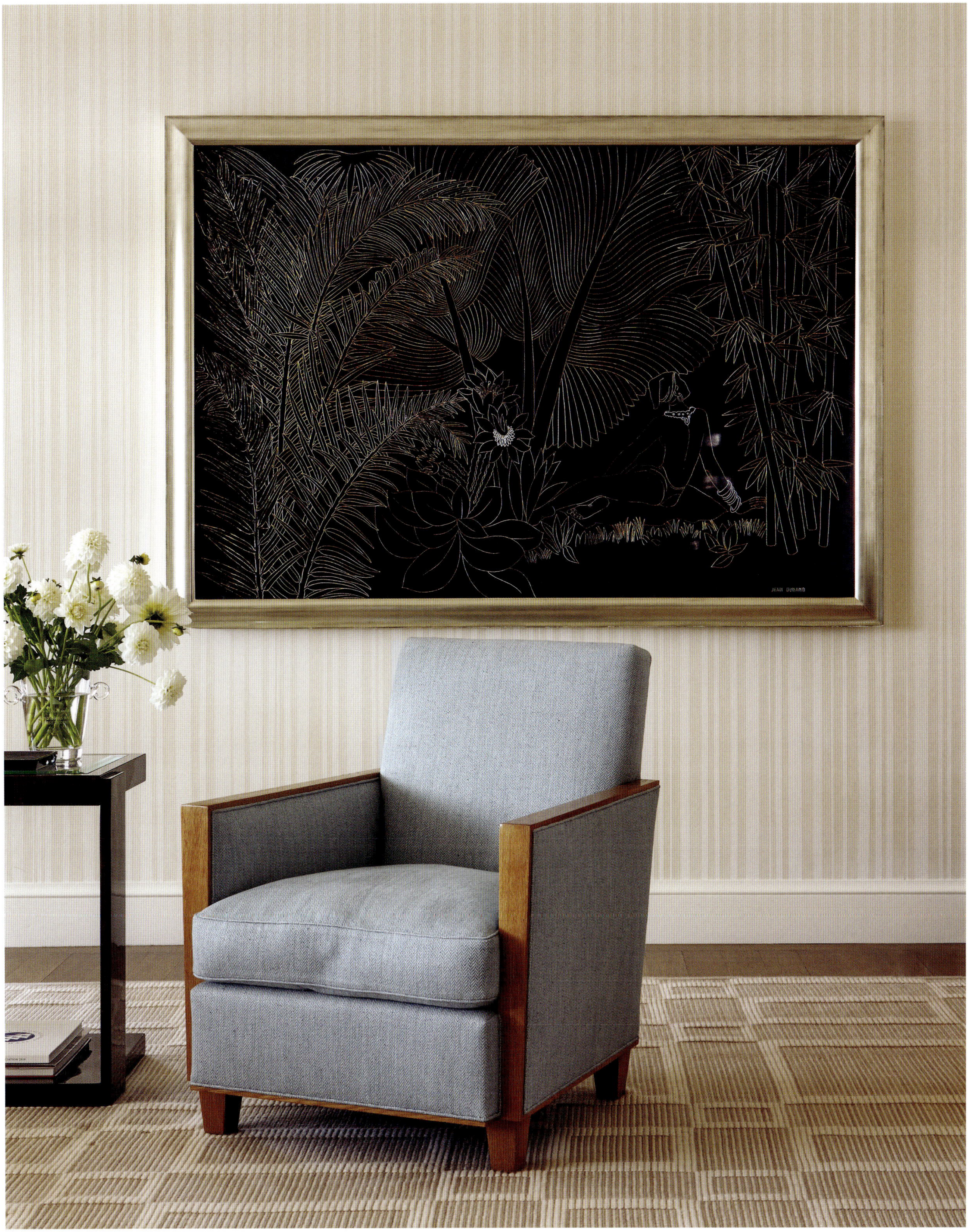
JEAN DUNAND

RIGHT: A palette of navy and white lends a nautical touch to the dining room. A 1940s Macassar table is complemented by modern, comfortable chairs from Schneller with a tight seat and back upholstered in an eye-catching pattern.

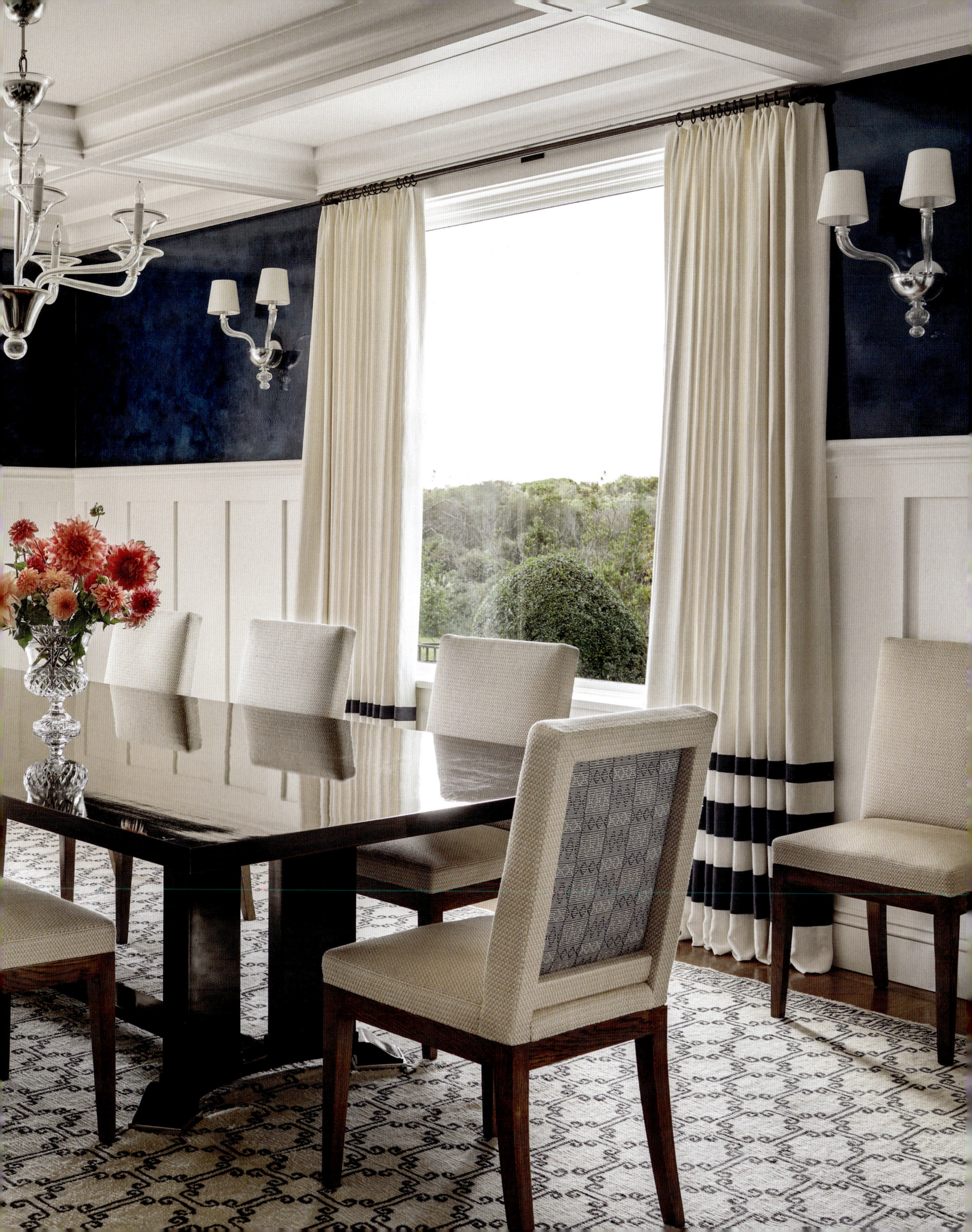

RIGHT: The faux-wood-painted finish is an unexpected play on the traditional paneled library and proves that decorative finishes can be tailored. Chairs from Jonas in a Tara Chapas fabric and a Jean-Michel Frank–inspired sofa surround a vintage chinoiserie table.

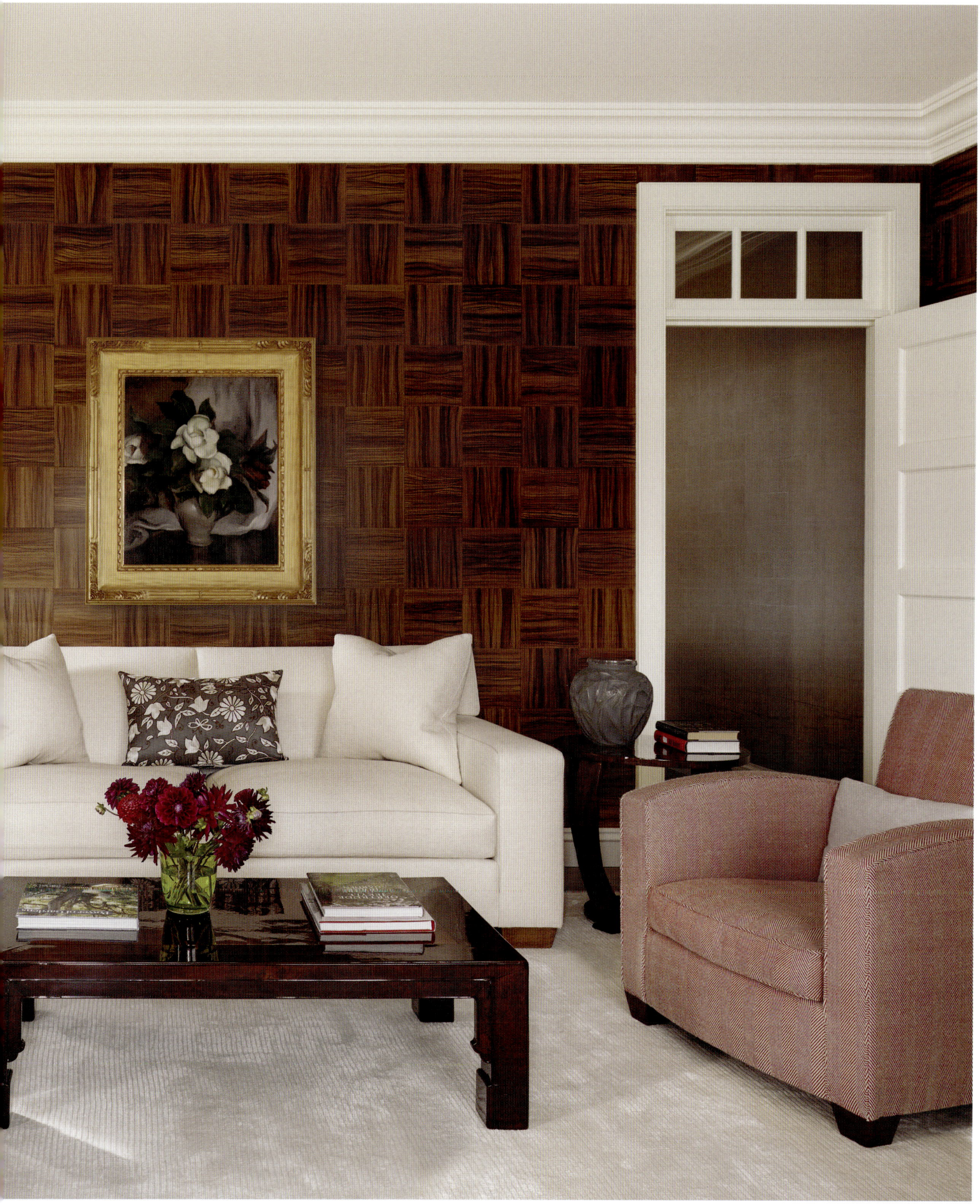

Serenity Meets Restraint

While wallpaper can bring a needed punch to a space, I prefer to utilize custom wall finishes for something more interesting and less instantly recognizable. There are almost infinite options when it comes to these hand-applied techniques, and they can quite swiftly change the entire atmosphere of a space. That bespoke quality, whether it's a subtle effect or one that's quite bold, always shines through and transforms the room into something truly special.

This home really represents the range of options. In the entry, French plaster accented with mica has the subtlest of shimmers and adds a discreet nuance to the calm space. The living room's tone-on-tone stripe creates an interesting rhythm as the eye travels across it. In the dining room, the glossy finish of Venetian plaster brings interest to the wood paneling, and the faux-wood crosshatch in the library absolutely makes the room. To complete this effect, each wall had to be taped out and then painstakingly painted in each direction. It's these types of details that not only exemplify the extra effort I go to for the perfect look, but they're also what excites me about my work.

RIGHT: Green marble countertops and backsplash bring an unexpected twist to the traditional white kitchen. A sheer curtain from John Rosselli & Associates softens the space while not blocking the views.

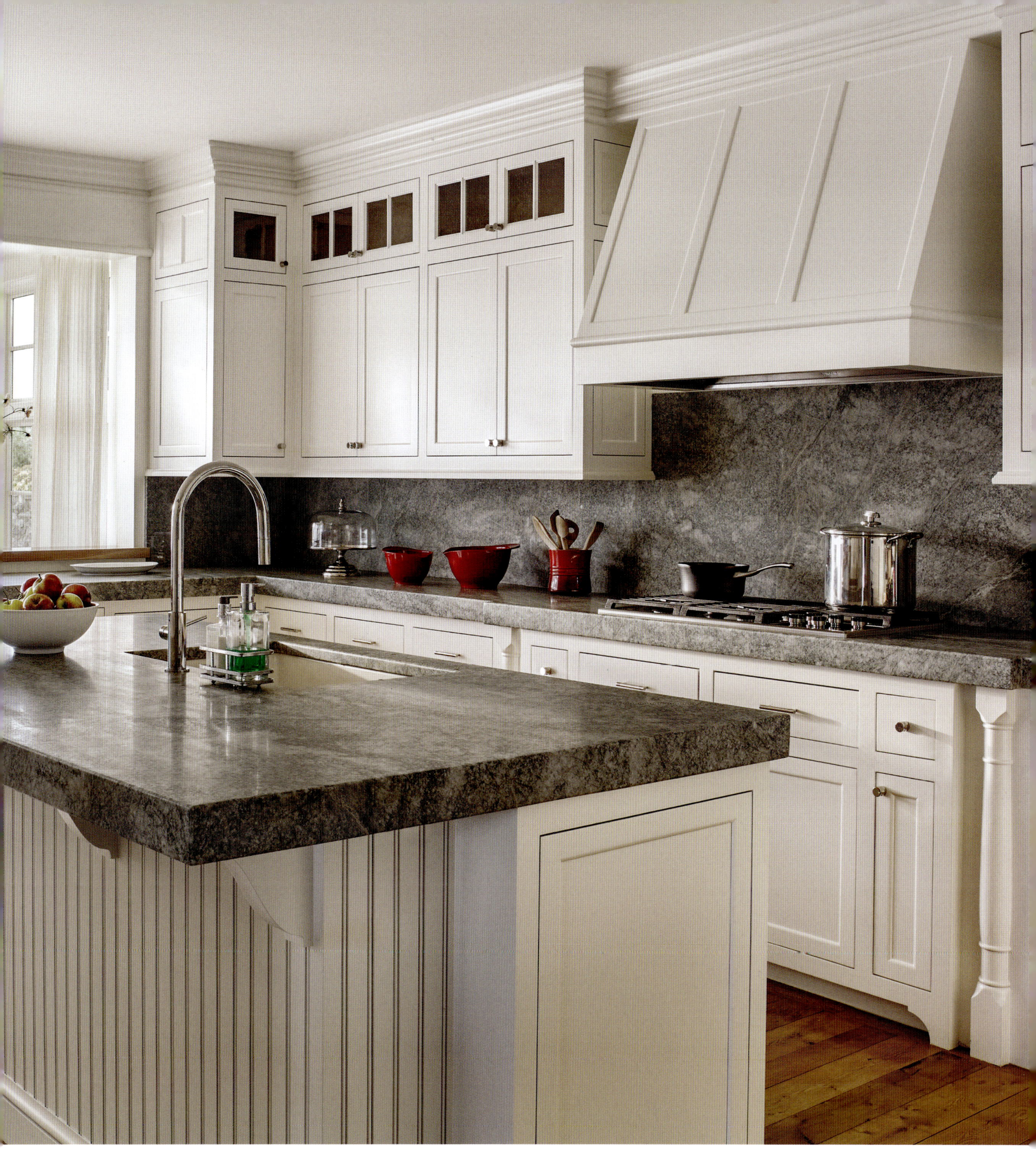

ABOVE: The primary suite is built into the roofline, so we embraced the ceiling's quirky geometry instead of masking it. RIGHT: In the bedroom, a play of patterns unfolds with hand-painted canvas striped walls, Manuel Canovas curtains, and a Brunschwig & Fils zebra print on the chair.

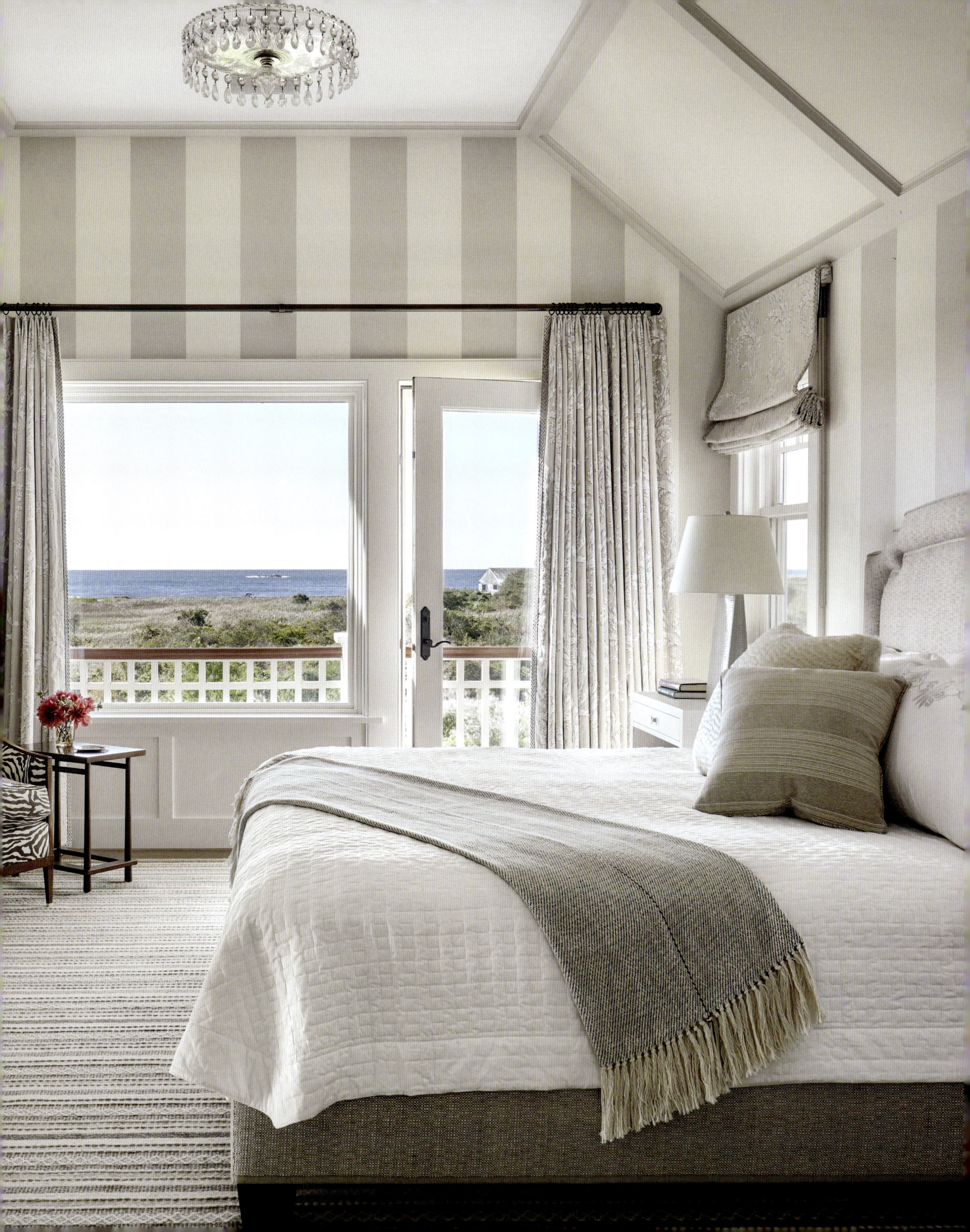

ABOVE: Curtains are hung flush to the ceiling to work around the large arched window in the son's bedroom. A drum shade helps bring the ceiling height down. RIGHT: The tailored guest room is comfortable yet not overdecorated; instead, the incredible views are the focus.

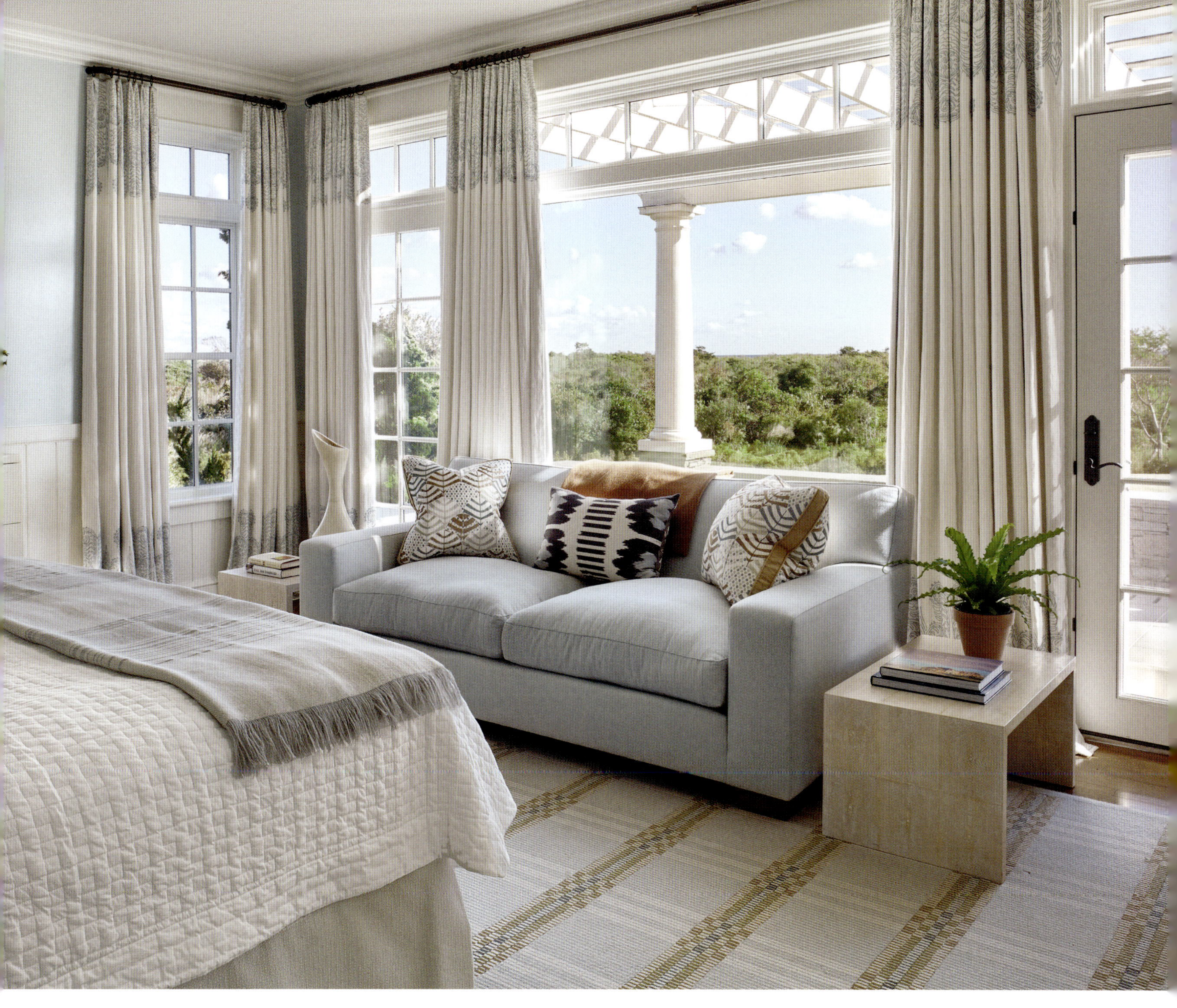

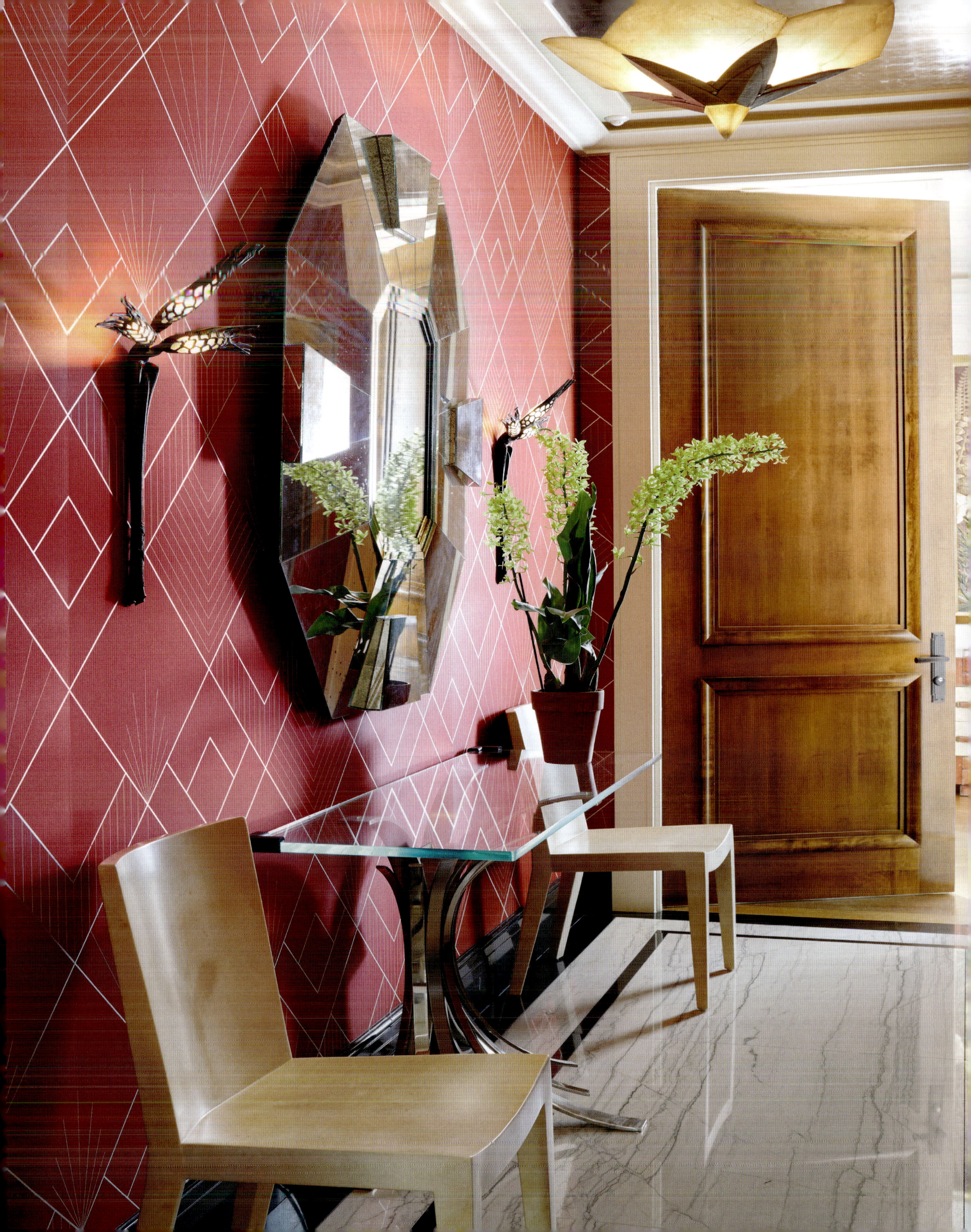

PENTHOUSE WITH CONTEMPORARY FLAIR

The decoration of a penthouse on Park Avenue, by far one of the most contemporary projects I've ever done, came about when dear friends had finished an architectural renovation and decided the results were too cold. They wanted help warming things up, so the home could display their striking collection of art while not coming off like a gallery.

In the entry off the elevator, we worked with de Gournay to create a wallpaper based on a 1940s pattern found in a book and pulled the red color from a lacquer panel just on the other side of the door. De Gournay laid out the elevations and added accents of silver leaf. A palladium-leaf ceiling also adds sparkle as people come and go. It's a small space, but it was important to keep it inviting and interesting—especially with sophisticated statement-making pieces, such as a Maria Pergay console and Serge Roche mirror—and set the tone for what's to come.

My clients gave the clear directive to keep things minimal to let the art shine. Nowhere is that more evident than in the living room, which revolves around one of the largest Yves Klein works I've ever seen. We mainly relied on white upholstery, but custom fabrics in unique textures prevent the look from reading as clinical. Additionally, Tara Chapas wove fabric in blue to pay homage to the painting, which is accompanied by a spectacular Anish Kapoor and a bold art deco two-paneled screen.

Throughout, the art and design continue to play off each other. In the dining room, the red in a Willem de Kooning canvas is echoed in the crimson panels of a Marc du Plantier sideboard. A navy wallpaper depicting reeds floating in the wind by de Gournay sets off the Jean-Michel Frank parchment cabinet, which I consider a work of art in and of itself. Living with art requires furnishings that stand up to the collection and don't just disappear in forgettable shades of beige. Together, each of these elements proves that contemporary does not have to be cold—far from it.

OPPOSITE: A custom de Gournay wallpaper in a warm red with silver accents sets the tone for the apartment as soon as one steps out of the elevator. A console by Maria Pergay, a Serge Roche mirror, and a palladium-leaf ceiling create a glamorous effect. FOLLOWING SPREAD: Although the Yves Klein painting dominates the space, the rest of the furnishings, including Diego Giacometti benches, a sofa in the style of Jean-Michel Frank, a leather console, and a Ruhlmann-inspired coffee table stand, up to its captivating presence without competing with the magnificent color.

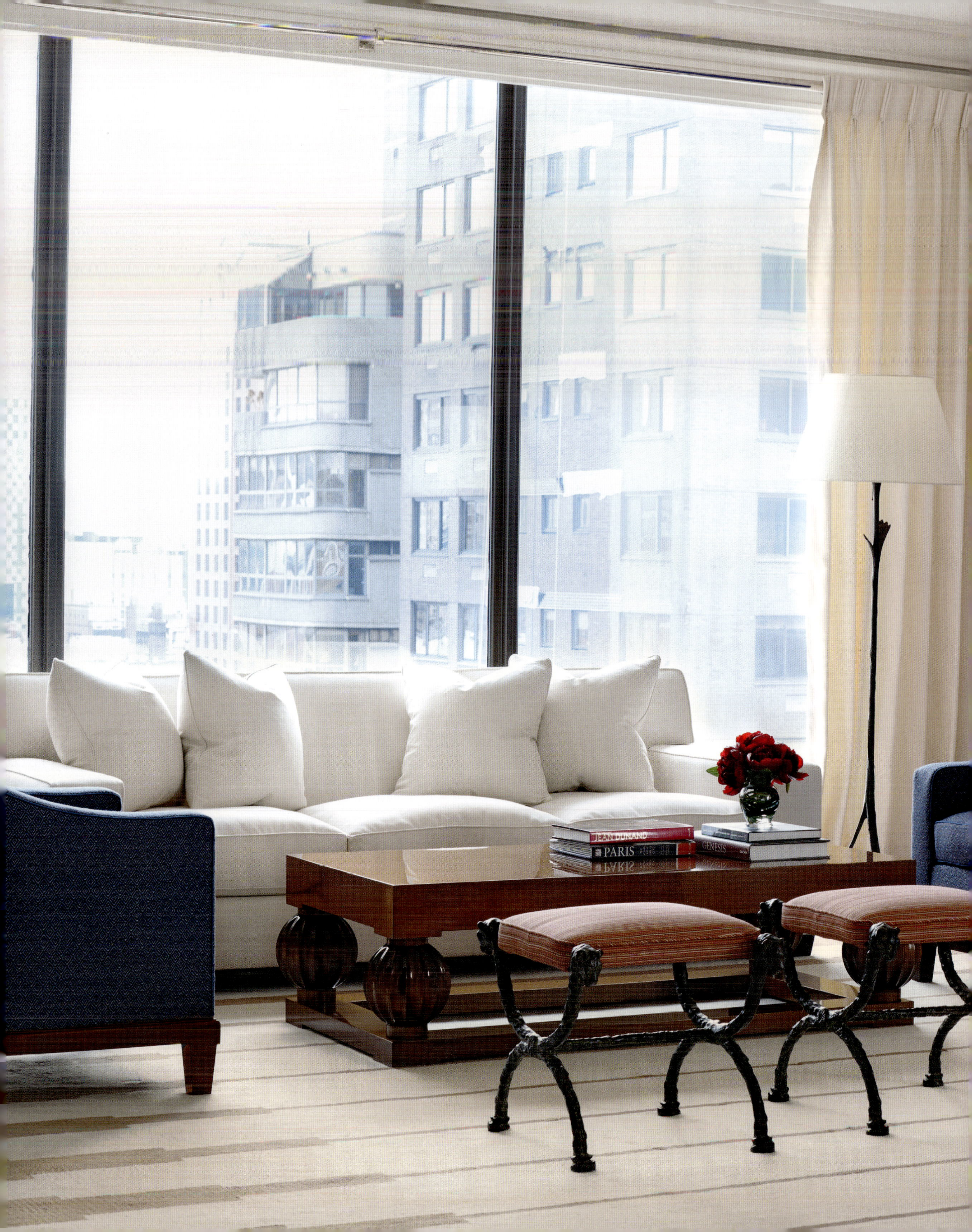
JEAN DUNAND
PARIS
GENESIS

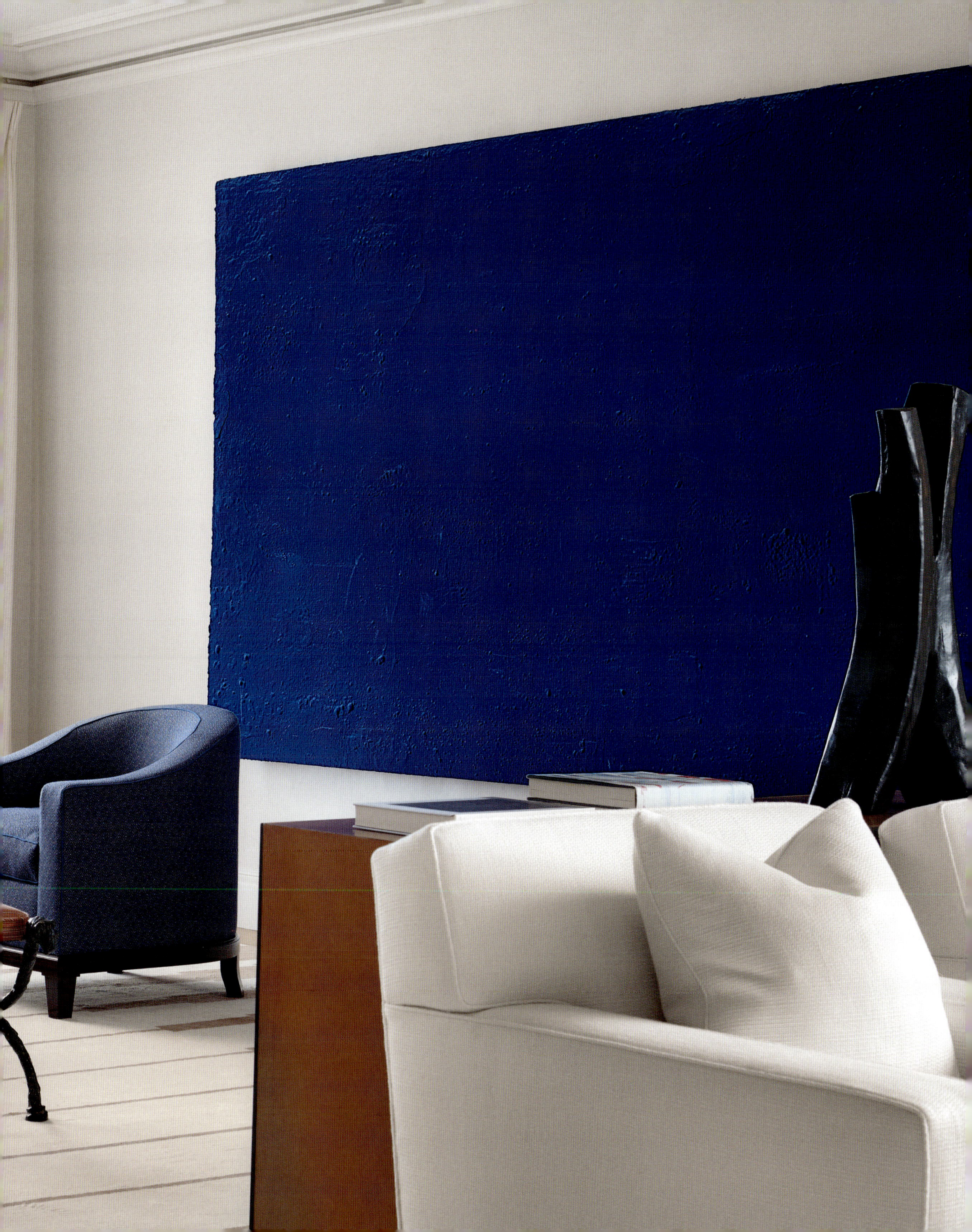

Rug Reversal

Decoration 101 says you always start with the rug and build the room around it. I learned from David Easton that everything in the room must sit on that rug. Back then, we were working primarily with antique rugs and were married to what existed. But now almost all the rugs I use are custom. By collaborating with makers such as Beauvais, I can achieve the right proportion, scale, and palette for every setting.

In this Park Avenue penthouse, the rugs were key to our goal of warming up the otherwise cool spaces. In the living room, a graphic border, which resembles the New York skyline and has an art deco sensibility, lends modernity and warmth. The rug in the dining room has a motif only around the border. The design, based on one by André Arbus, plays with the geometry of the square shape of the room and the round dining table. The moleskin color comes from the walls, and the brown from the velvet upholstered chairs. The office also features a rug with a strong border, a Greek key motif encircling a rich chocolate center, which hides every sin. With the overscale motif drawing all the attention, the rest of the room can remain relatively calm. Even though these patterns relate to the 1940s, modifying them from the original brings them decidedly into the now.

OPPOSITE: A work by Willem de Kooning presides over the dining room. The red of the Marc du Plantier sideboard complements the painting along with the André Arbus–inspired Greek key rug.

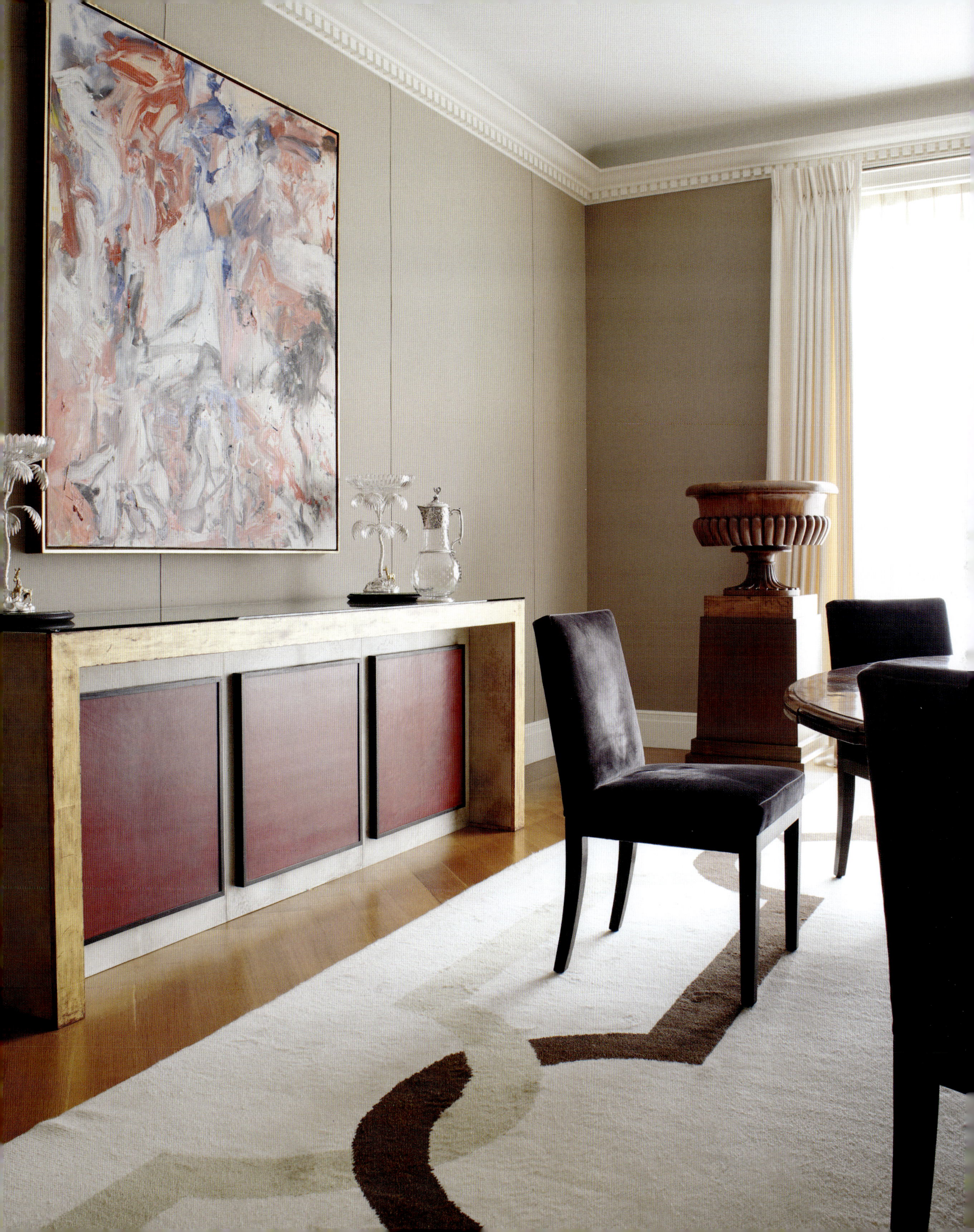

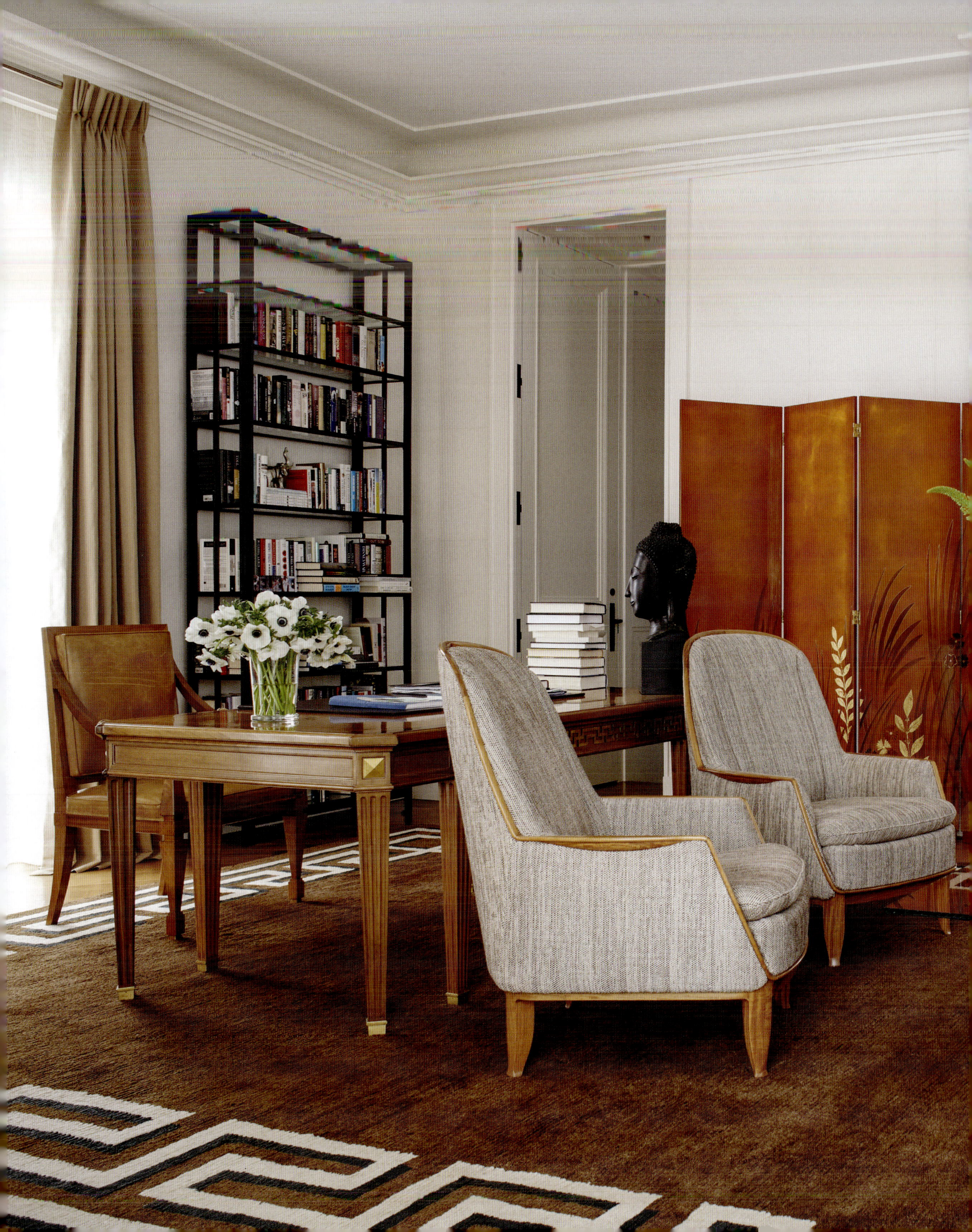

LEFT: A rich chocolate-brown rug with a Greek key border adds warmth to the office, which boasts a suite of Ruhlmann furniture purchased at auction, a lacquer screen by Anne Midavaine, and a Giacometti floor lamp.

RIGHT: The strong minimalist fireplace is flanked by a pair of art deco chairs by Edgar Brandt, while a framed, two-panel red-and-white screen from the 1930s hangs above.

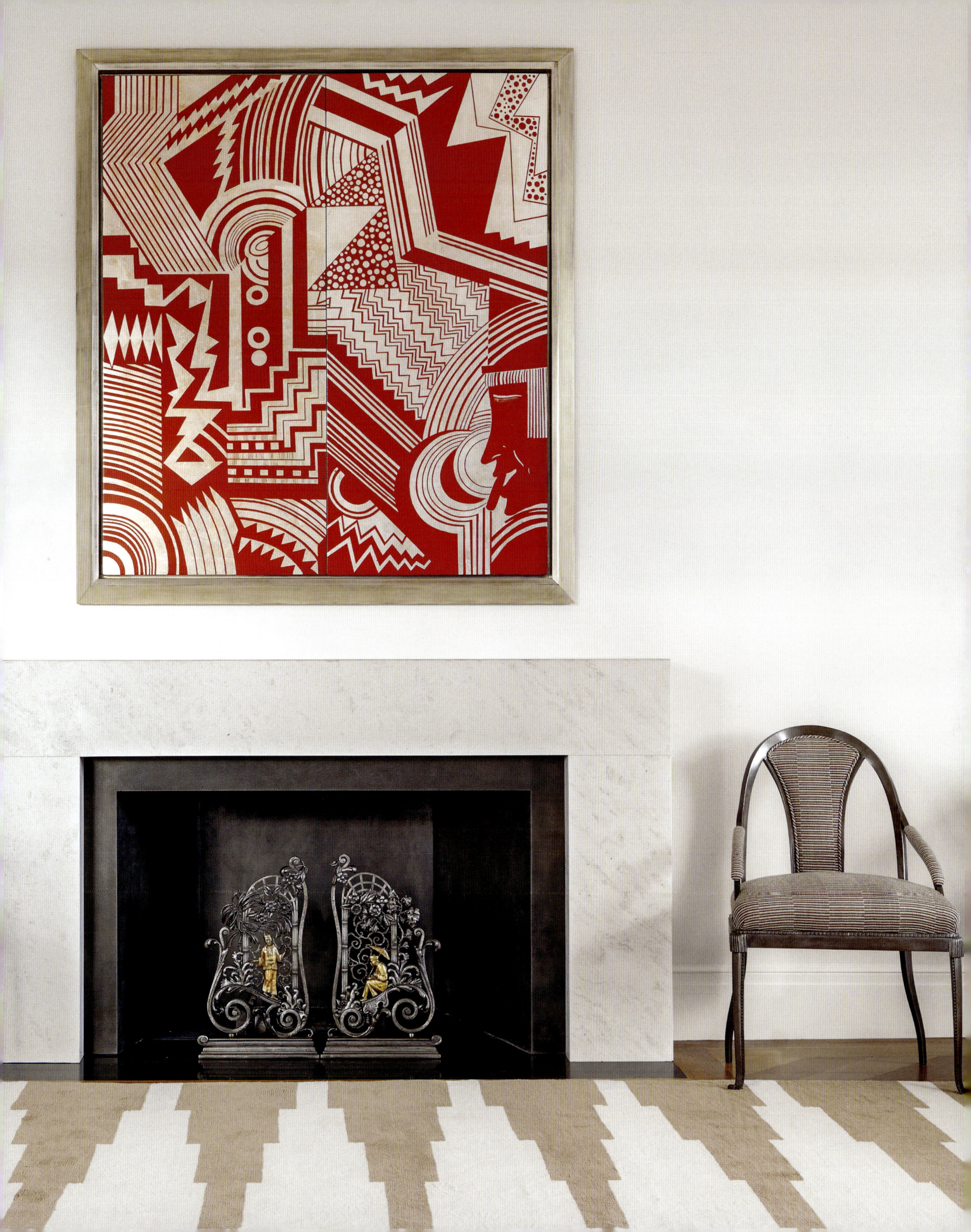

RIGHT: The subtle palette of the living room allows for a large work by Anish Kapoor to reflect a range of beige tones. A curvy Pierre Chareau bench plays off the walnut doors.

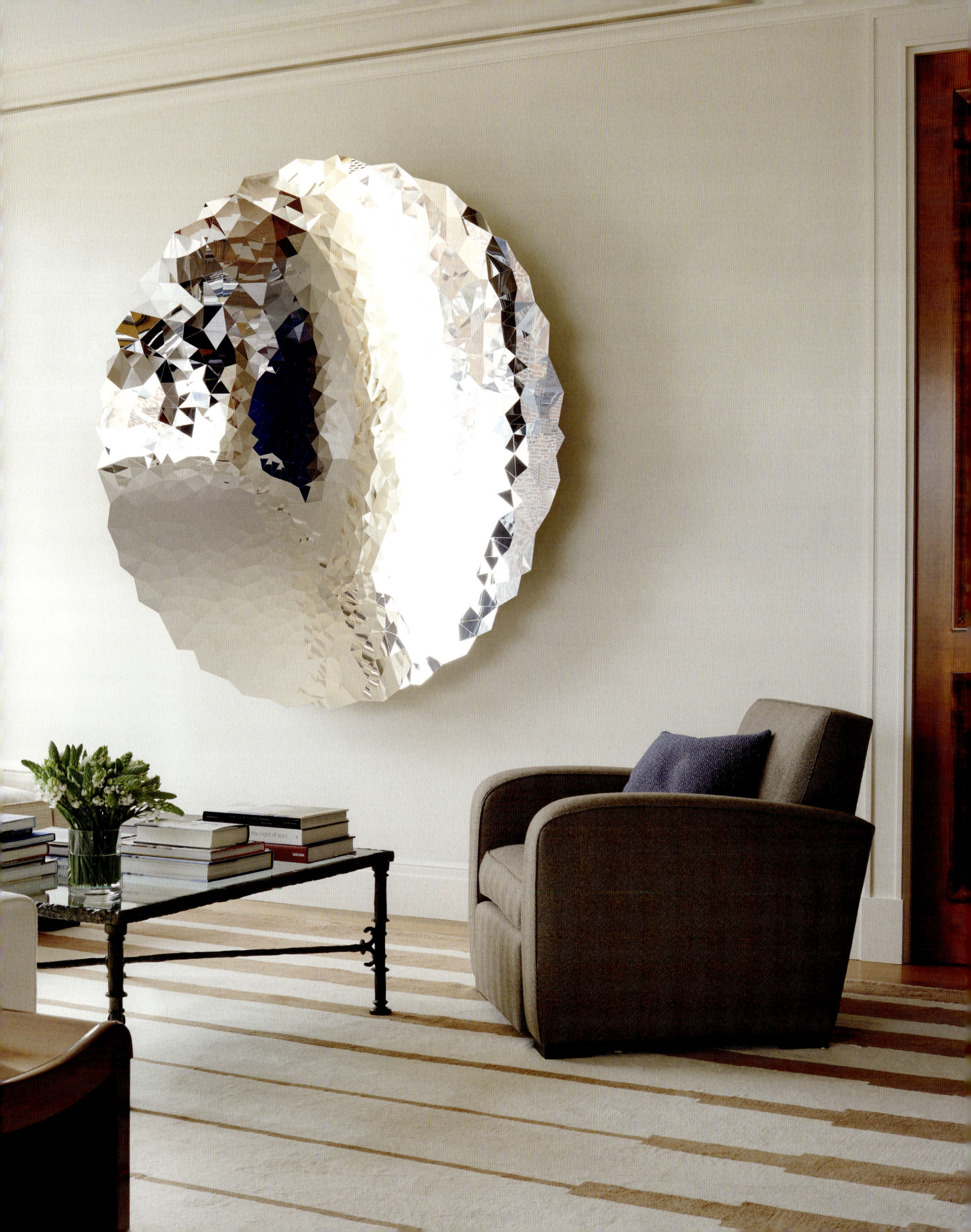

ABOVE AND RIGHT: In the primary bedroom suite, a hand-painted bamboo scene by de Gournay creates movement. A straw marquetry bed and side tables rest on wall-to-wall carpet, which keeps things cozy. A goatskin cabinet by Jean-Michel Frank acts as both storage and a work of art.

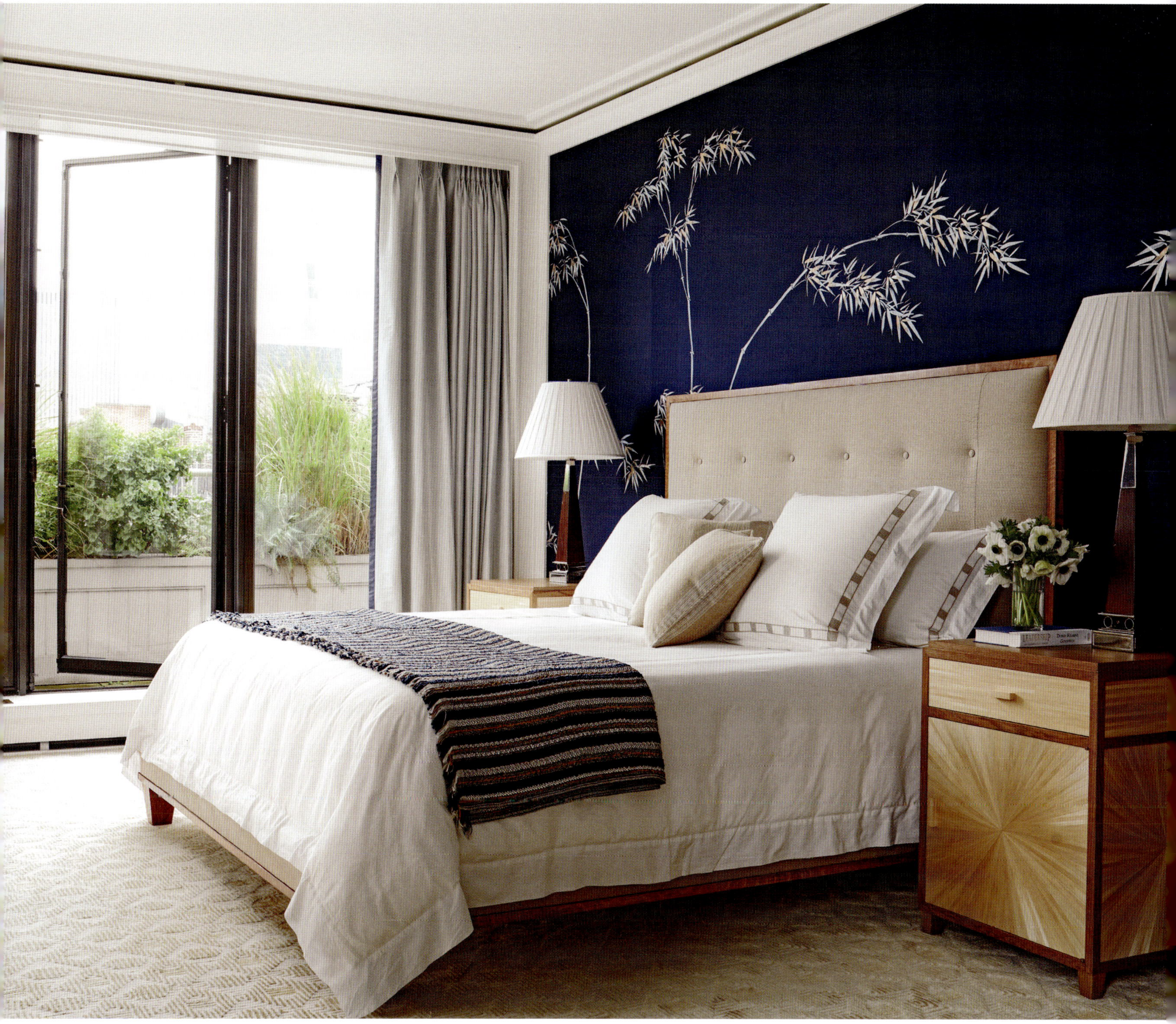

ABOVE: A guest bath offers sweeping views of the city from the shower. OPPOSITE: Touches of green run through several elements of the guest bedroom, including the Gracie scenic wallpaper, shagreen side table, and bed linen embroidery. The Georges Jouve lamp is a personal favorite.

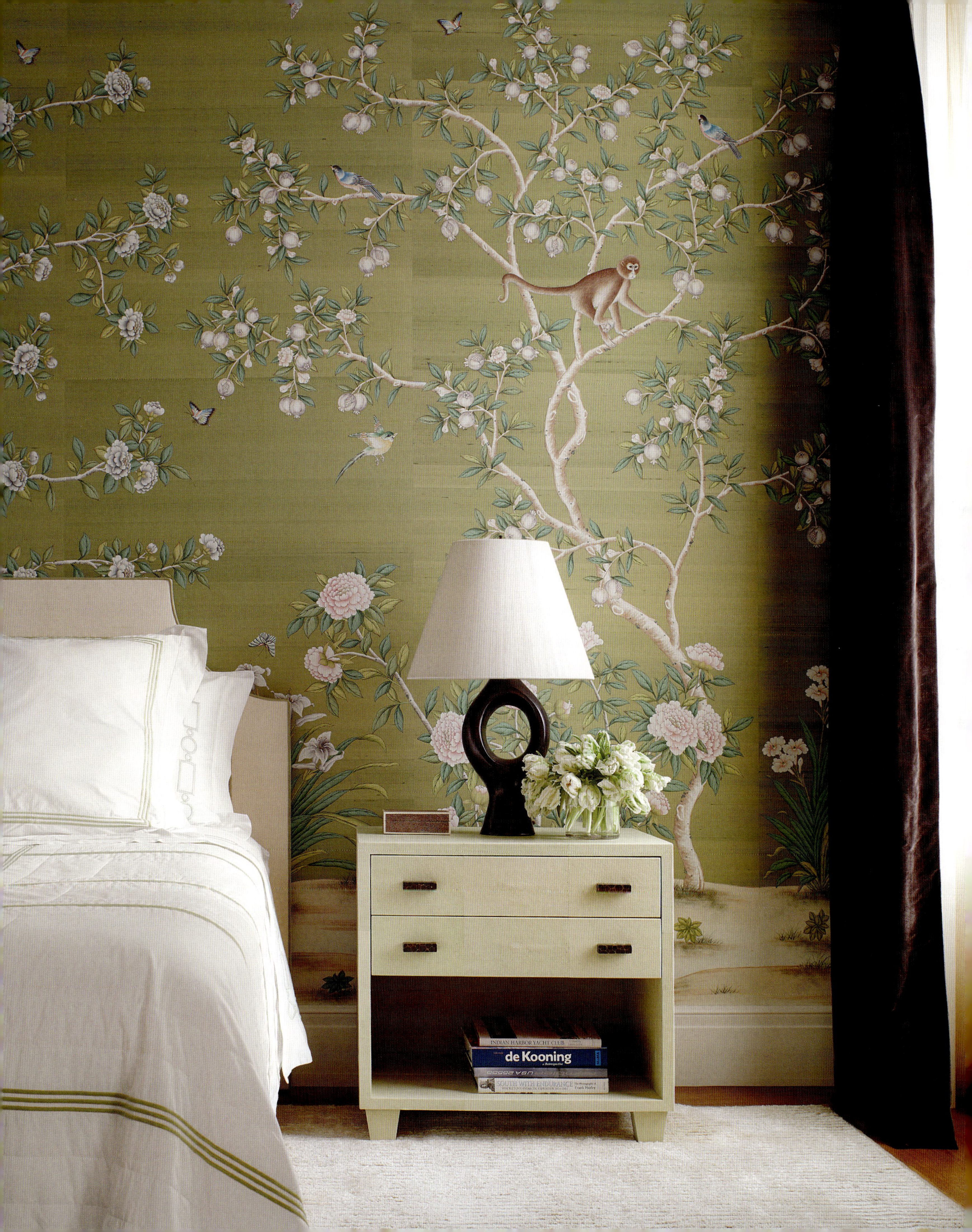
INDIAN HARBOR YACHT CLUB
de Kooning
SOUTH WITH ENDURANCE

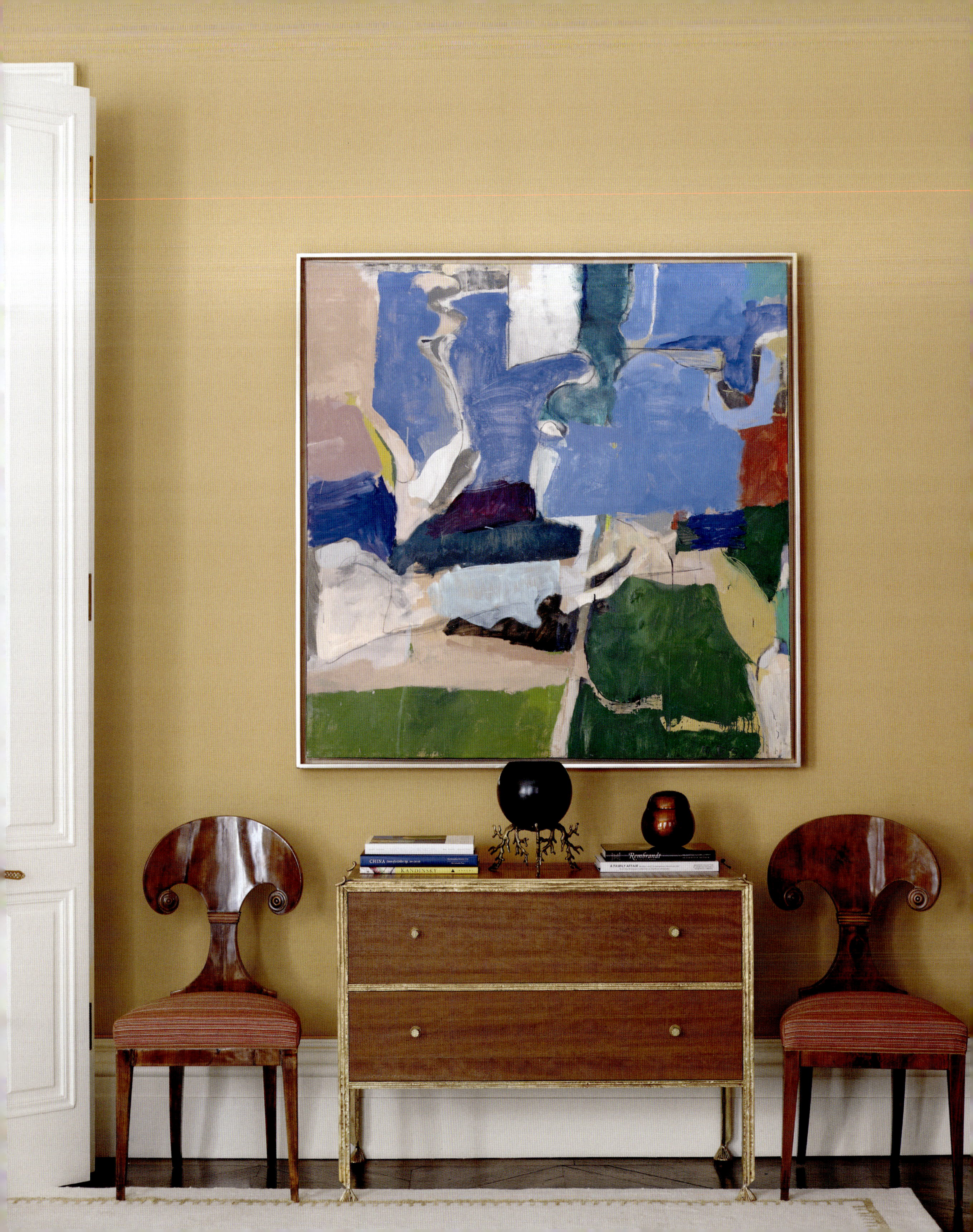
CHINA
KANDINSKY
Rembrandt
A FAMILY AFFAIR

NEW ART COLLECTION
SPARKS REDESIGN

It's always exciting when clients call in need of a refresh, but there's nothing more inspiring than when the catalyst is a new collection of art. In this case, the couple had just purchased a lively Gerhard Richter painting, and it just wasn't showing well in the existing space. I headed over to their Upper East Side town house to assess and discovered they had also acquired a Wayne Thiebaud and a Richard Diebenkorn, as well as a few other works. In this case, the clients were right: the furnishings weren't standing up to the artwork. Although we had to transform the living room to support the blue-chip collection, the homeowners still wanted to keep things stylish and comfortable. Letting the collection be my guide, I chose furniture of impeccable quality, oftentimes directly sparked by an individual work. For example, the red in the Richter led to the Fortuny chairs, the *dégradé* curtains, and the new fabric for Biedermeier chairs that the residents already had. The Diebenkorn led to a Louis Cane commode, since the piece was so strong and so architectural that it wouldn't fight with the art. Jouffre-curved sofas for Schiaparelli, a Marc du Plantier table with a shagreen top, and a LaVerne cocktail table are among the other artful additions.

The walls called for something warmer than typical gallery white. A fabric from Old World Weavers in wheat gold became a universal backdrop for the graphic Richter, the bright blues of the Diebenkorn, and the creamy whites of the John Chamberlain wall sculpture. I relish opportunities like this when I get to create a backdrop as timeless as the art itself.

OPPOSITE: A painting by Richard Diebenkorn pops off a caramel-colored upholstered wall. Below, a Louis Cane commode is flanked by Biedermeier chairs with an objet by Hervé Van der Straeten.

RIGHT: A large canvas by Gerhard Richter presides over the living room, where an array of furniture with curving lines, including a Jouffre sofa, a pair of chairs covered in Fortuny fabric, and a Louis Cane table, comes together.

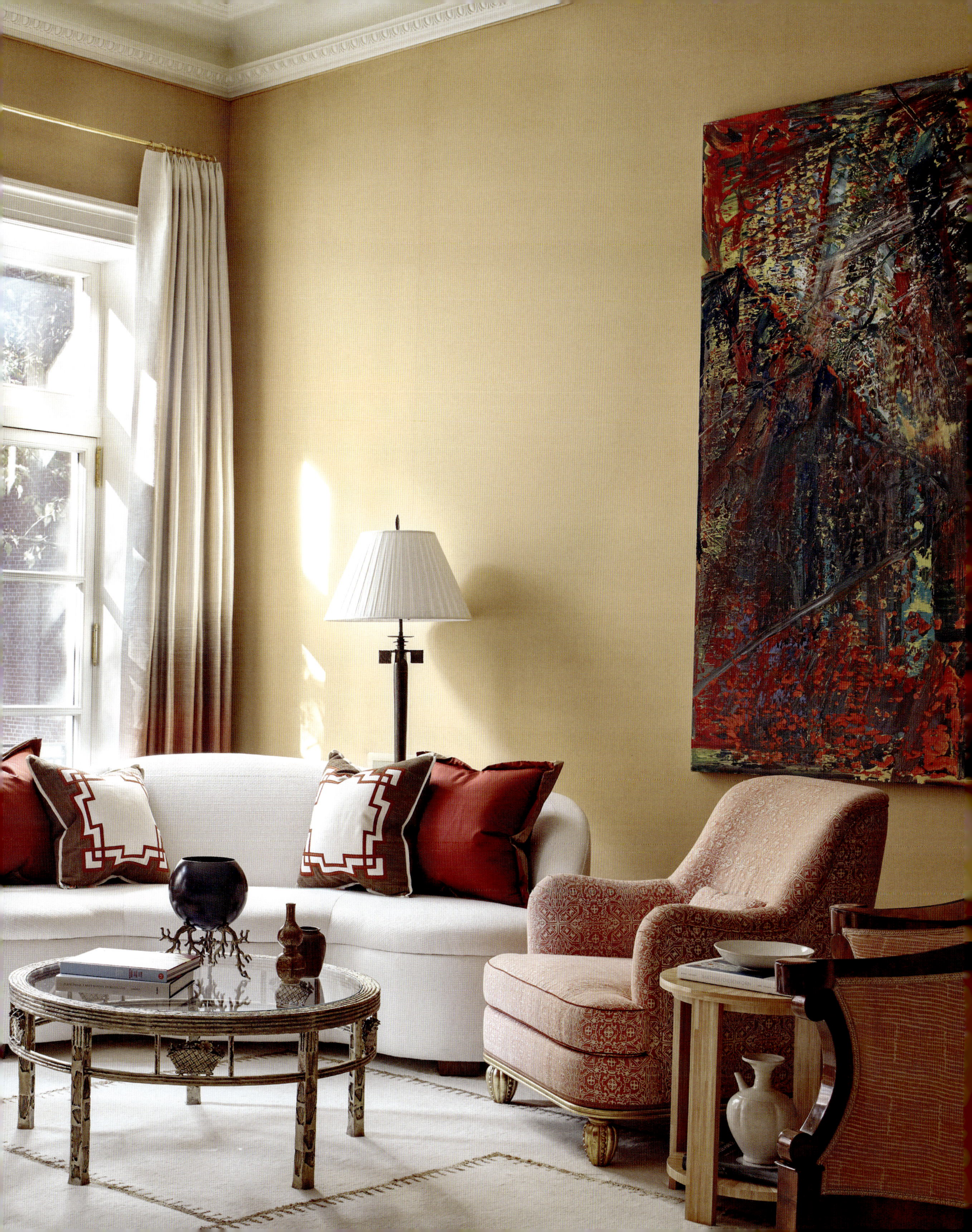

Mixing Contemporary Art with Traditional Architecture

For me, contemporary art looks best when hung in a traditional envelope. The tension between the two creates sparks. The paintings and sculptures look all the more daring in contrast, while the architecture comes across as timeless. In many ways, this mix conveys a life well lived—someone who appreciates the ever-changing cultural landscape while staying grounded with classical foundations. I love how a molding can set off a frameless canvas just as much as how an avant-garde sculpture can disrupt the precision and symmetry of a space.

This project captures that exact kind of magic, and it was thrilling to reimagine the space with my clients after they had decided to go more contemporary with their collection. The difference is incredible. I simply love the way that the John Chamberlain and Wayne Thiebaud works interrupt the rhythm of the French doors. Additionally, the sheer scale of some of these canvases requires substantial walls. Gracious proportions benefit from having one large work, and these types of paintings generally need some breathing room to truly show well.

RIGHT: Towering, *degradé* curtains by Pietro Seminelli separate works by Wayne Thiebaud (left) and John Chamberlain (right). The white Beauvais rug with minimal pattern intensifies the rich color on the walls.

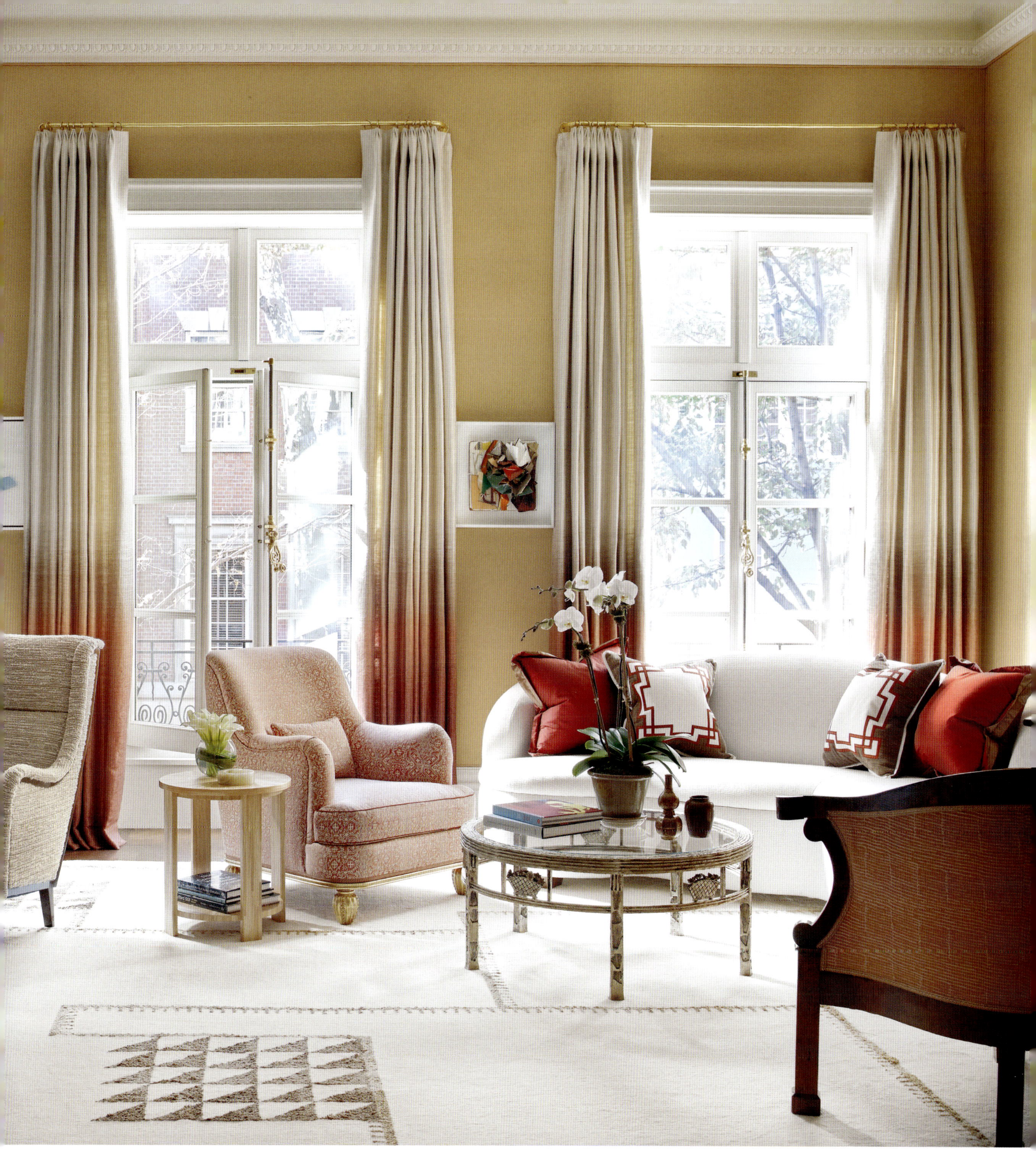

A POLISHED LONDON TOWN HOUSE

When longtime clients announced they were planning a move to London, I couldn't wait to start the process of creating their new home. Their tastes had evolved dramatically since I had designed their Sutton Place apartment in New York City, and it was exciting to set the stage for the next chapter of their lives while continuing their break with the strictly traditional. Once they purchased a nineteeth-century Kensington town house, I knew much of the design work would center on merging its Georgian architecture with their ever-growing collection of twentieth-century art and design. Since the five-story residence with its gracious columned portico had recently been completely renovated, I could immediately dive into the project without worrying about having to make updates.

Although rather spare, the main entry sets the stage for how the language of traditional could harmonize with contemporary. Classical crown moldings, limestone floors, and paneling became a clean envelope in which standout pieces could take center stage. Patrice Dangel conceived a custom white plaster and bronze cabinet, while W. P. Sullivan crafted a gilded mirror, both based on age-old artisan techniques. These pieces blend seamlessly with the architecture, while adding another dimension of interest. Additionally, the glossy black door plays off the iron railings, the Jamb lanterns, and the hard-edge style of a Leon Polk Smith artwork.

OPPOSITE: A group of four paintings by Günther Förg provides an artful welcome in the stair hall.

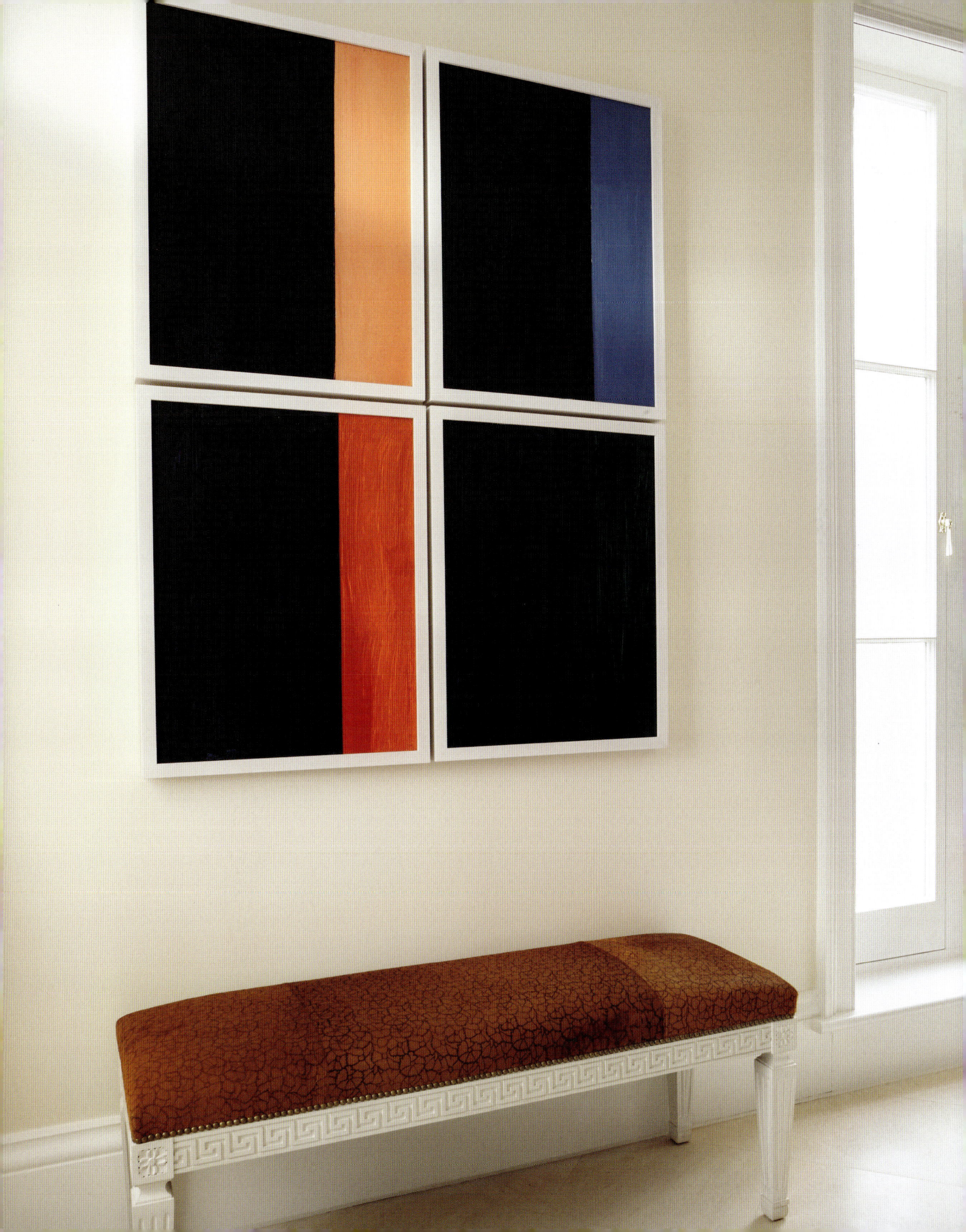

ABOVE: In the entry hall, a Louis Cane commode in bronze and plaster plays host to a lamp by Christopher Spitzmiller, while a W. P. Sullivan mirror hangs above.
RIGHT: Jamb lanterns and sconces play well with the town house's late nineteenth-century Georgian architecture in the limestone-paved entry hall. We warmed up the space by adding wainscotting and keeping the existing crown molding.

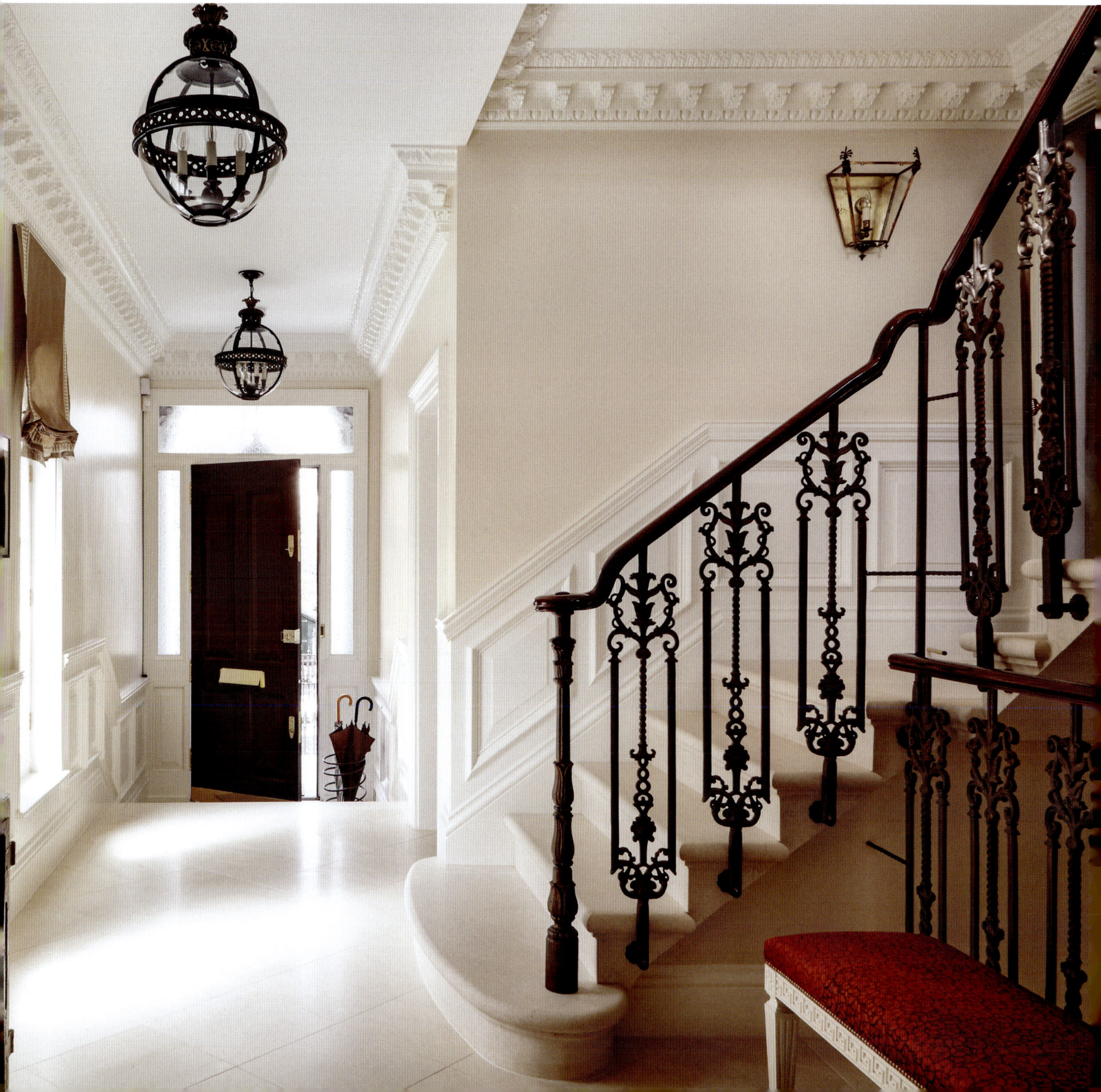

RIGHT: The living room's palette of soft tones creates the perfect backdrop for showcasing an impressive collection of contemporary art and design. A Sigmar Polke artwork hangs above the Chesneys mantel, where a François-Xavier Lalanne Monkey perches. A Günther Förg painting, a Claude Lalanne Gingko side table, a Jean-Michel Frank cocktail table, and Line Vautrin sunburst mirrors create a spirited dialogue.

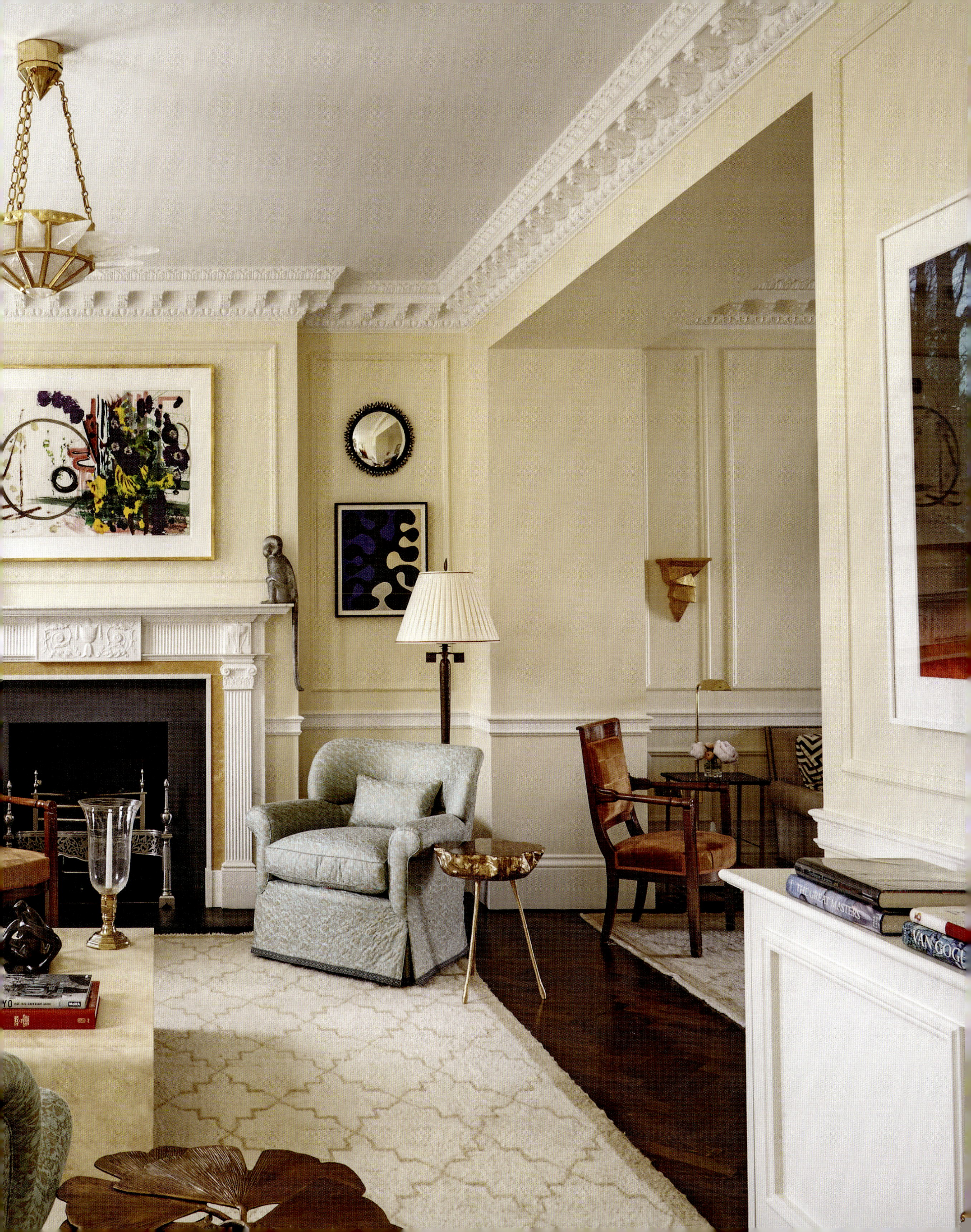
THE GREAT MASTERS

Building a Sophisticated Collection

Passionate collectors are some of the most fascinating people I know. Not only do they have particular individual tastes, but they also possess a deep knowledge of periods and styles, techniques and mediums. Collaborating with these London homeowners and their art adviser was such a fulfilling process for me. My clients' interests are so vast, and it's incredible to watch their collection grow—from painters such as Günther Förg, Sigmar Polke, Per Kirkeby, and Robert Motherwell to collectible design from François-Xavier Lalanne, Pippin Drysdale, and Line Vautrin. Looking back, it's so exciting to recall how they acquired some pieces at just the right time. For example, the Frank Bowling canvas in the family room was purchased just before his retrospective at the Tate was announced.

In addition to working with galleries and auction houses to find just the right works, there's an unparalleled joy in the process of commissioning pieces. We tapped Louis Cane to create a commode in the exact red from a Milton Avery work. Alexandre Vossion knew exactly what was needed to devise a modern take on a crystal chandelier that captures our theme of youthful sophistication. And custom ceramics by Kate Malone depicting the four seasons are as timeless as they are temporal.

RIGHT: On the opposite side of the room, a chair upholstered in Fortuny and the Lee Jofa silk curtains recall the rich but muted tones in a collage by Robert Motherwell.

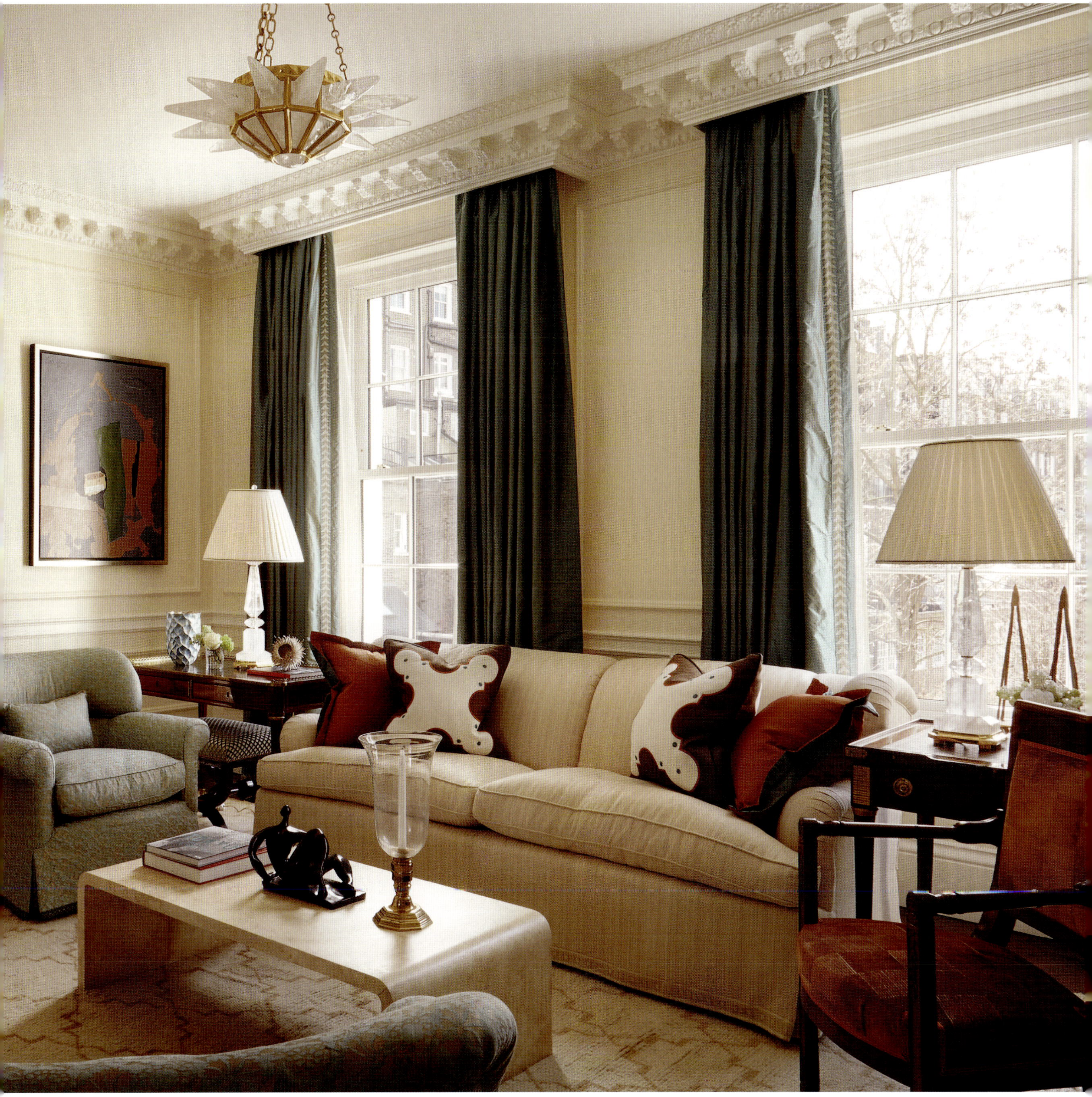

ABOVE: A Milton Avery surmounts a bright red commode by Louis Cane on which two sculptures by Lucio Fontana are displayed. OPPOSITE, CLOCKWISE, FROM TOP LEFT: Details of the room include a rock-crystal chandelier by Alexandre Vossion, as well as a Claude Lalanne Ginkgo side table and Carp sculpture in front of the Jasper Johns print and a François-Xavier Lalanne Monkey sculpture.

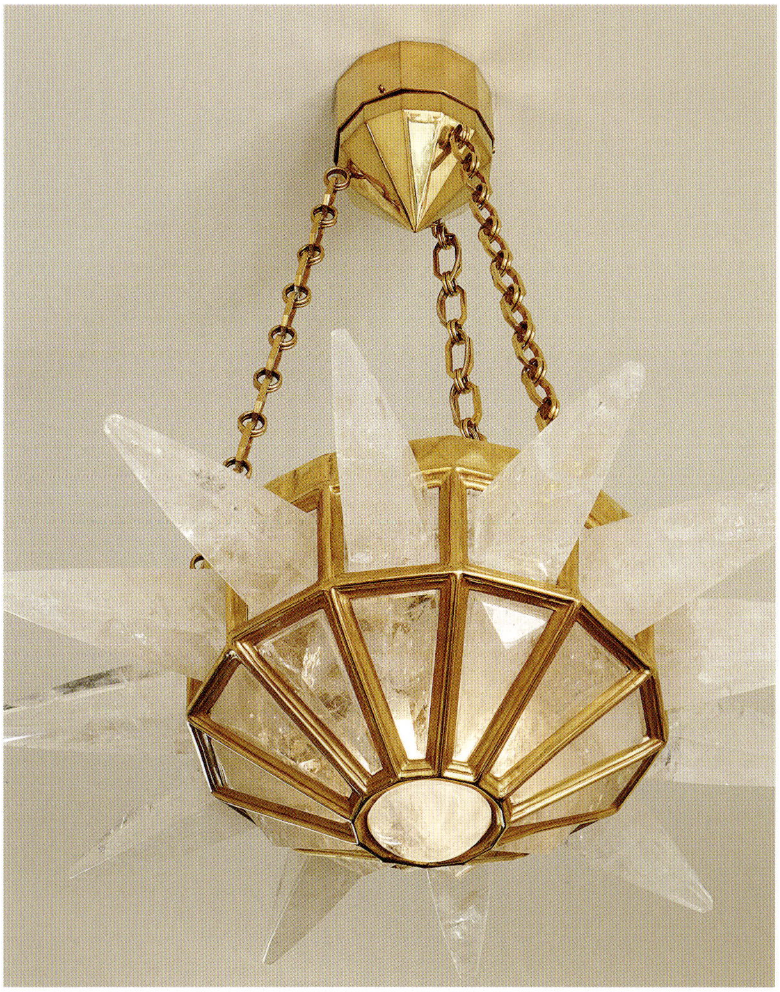
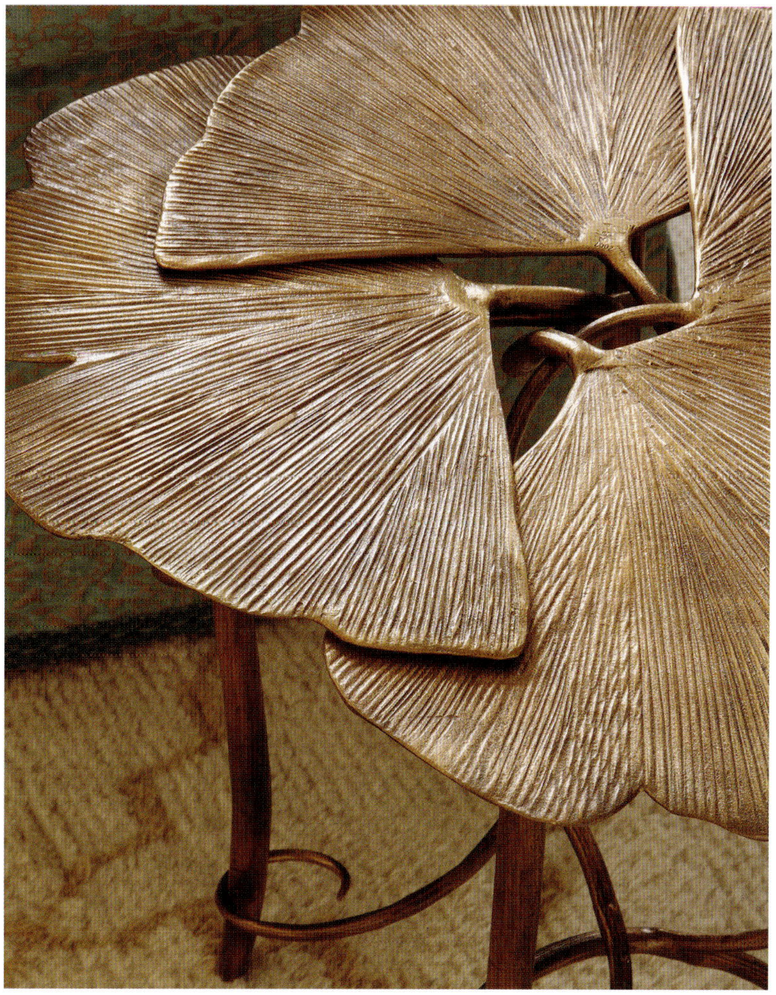
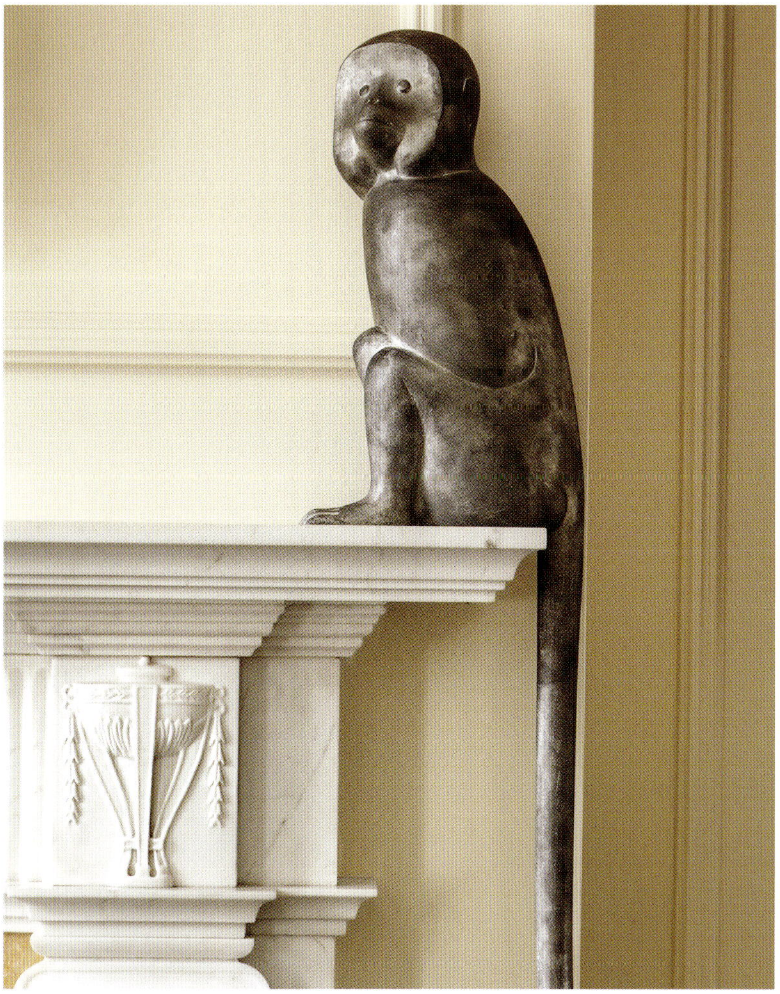
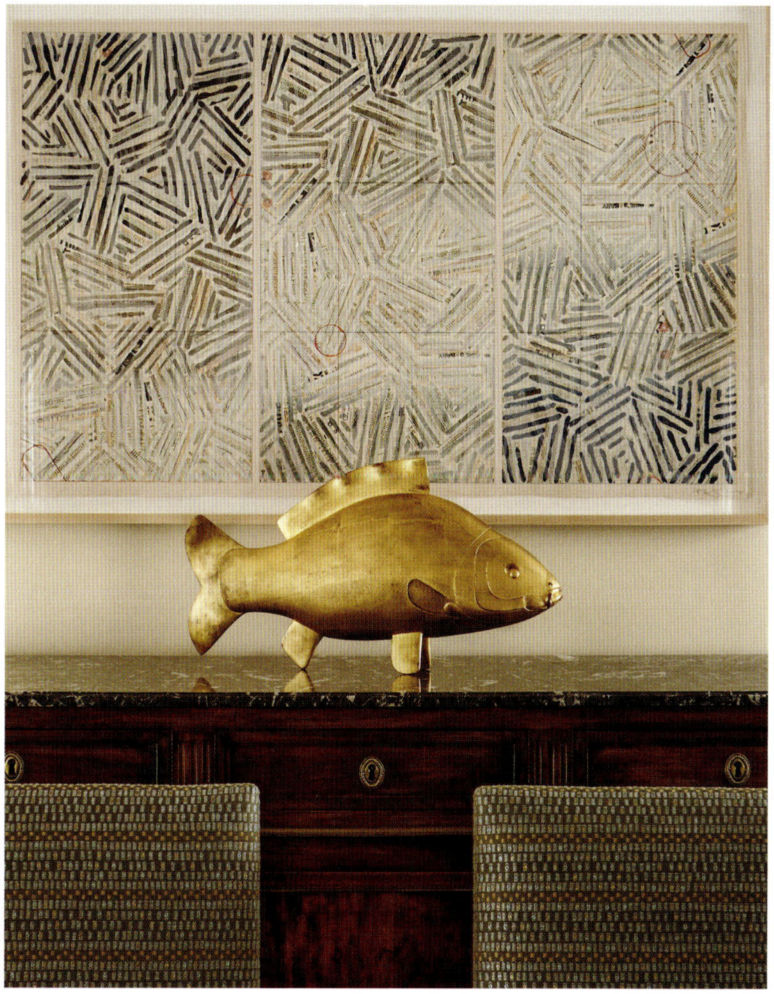

RIGHT: A striped wallpaper by Claremont adds whimsical flair to the layered library, which features a pendant by Patrice Dangel, a mirror by W. P. Sullivan and an Atelier Viollet desk paired with a Jules Leleu chair.

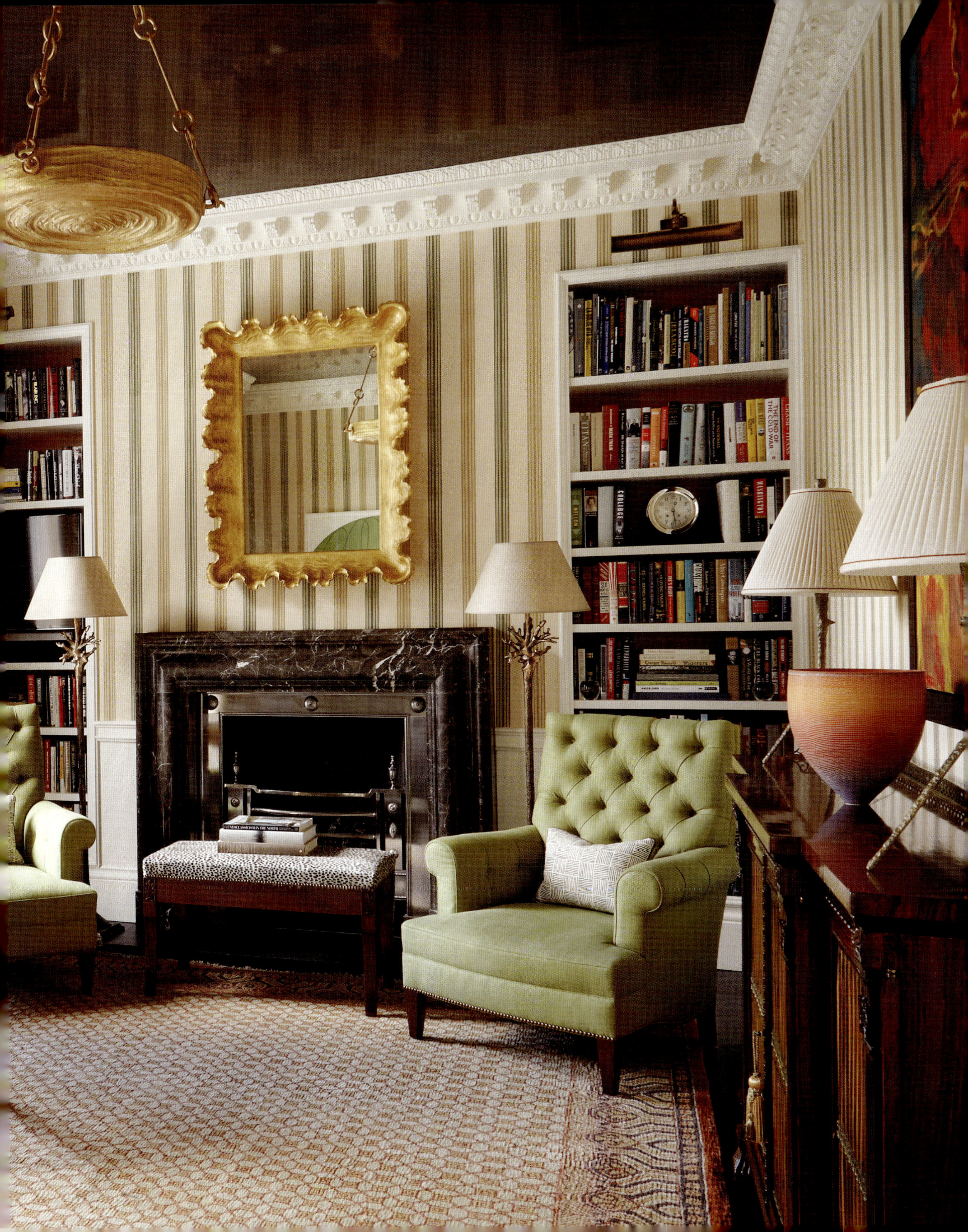

In the living room, a neutral palette of furnishings allows the stellar collection of art and design to shine. Magnolia hued walls, a creamy cocktail table in the style of Jean-Michel Frank, and informal Moroccan rugs build the perfect backdrop for a Sigmar Polke painting depicting a dancing woman in a hula skirt against the moon paired with a François-Xavier Lalanne Monkey on the mantel. A pastel by Günther Förg and a Leon Polk Smith abstract work take on another dimension when sunburst Line Vautrin mirrors are hung above. The traditional side tables and Chesneys mantel tether the room to tradition.

Another extraordinary aspect of the house's floor plan are the soaring twenty-foot windows in the family room. Unlike many town houses, here, light floods into the house, which also has the unique benefit of three sides of windows. Above, in a mezzanine overlooking the space, the formal dining room keeps things very classic with a three-pedestal Georgian table while more contemporary elements veer toward the youthful. In the library, those types of complementary contrasts continue—a Per Kirkeby painting hangs against hand-blocked striped wallpaper. A Wolfgang Tillmans photograph is accompanied by a mahogany Jules Leleu desk chair. Mixing the traditional with the contemporary can be tricky—but having confidence in every decision is crucial to a design's overall success.

OPPOSITE: A powerful work by Per Kirkeby appears delightfully unexpected on the library's striped walls. Below, a ceramic vessel by Pippin Drysdale feels equally surprising on a traditional cabinet.

Charlie D.
ALEKSANDRA SHATSKIKH BLACK SQUARE
HOUSE of CARDS
WILLIAM D. FORAN
barbican
CONSTRUCTING WORLDS
PRESTEL
Biedermeier
Art and Culture in Central Europe 1815-1848
INVENTING ABSTRACTION 1910–1925
CCCP
COSMIC COMMUNIST CONSTRUCTIONS PHOTOGRAPHED

ABOVE: At the rear of the house, a double-height family room plays host to a work by painter Frank Bowling. RIGHT: The lofted space above acts as the dining room with a dramatic C. L. Sterling & Son crystal chandelier suspended over the table.

MARK ROTHKO
SIGMAR POLKE
de Kooning
BAUHAUS
SAINT PETERSBURG

RIGHT: An Hervé Van der Straeten chandelier hangs above the family room, which is anchored by a custom-designed sofa by Schneller in the style of Jean-Michel Frank, a pair of Christopher Spitzmiller lamps, and a hide rug.

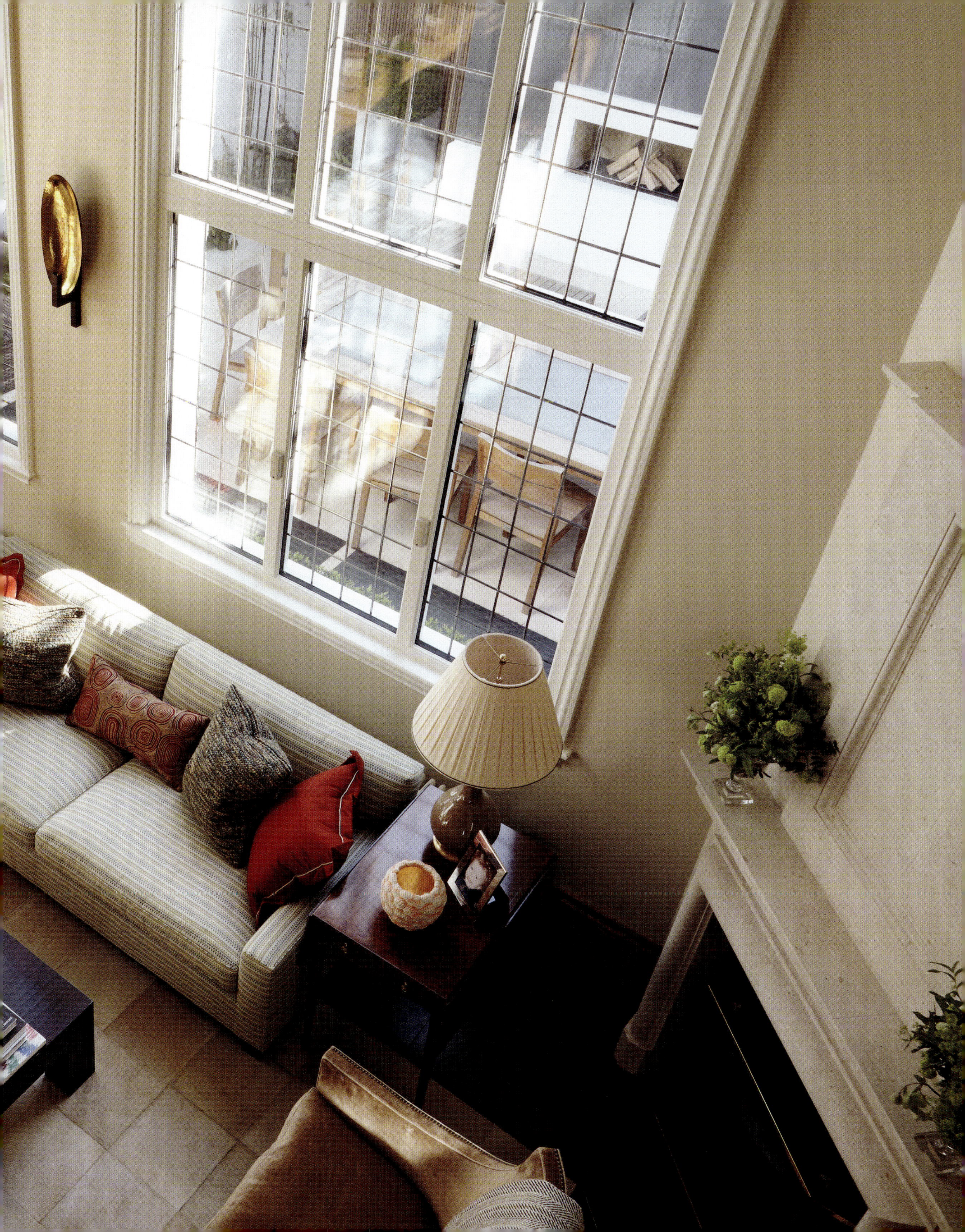

ABOVE: A cabinet commissioned from Hubert Le Gall lends a contemporary twist to the more traditional bedroom. RIGHT: A needlepoint rug by Patterson Flynn Martin adds charm and warmth under the bed, which is covered in a John Rosselli & Associates fabric.

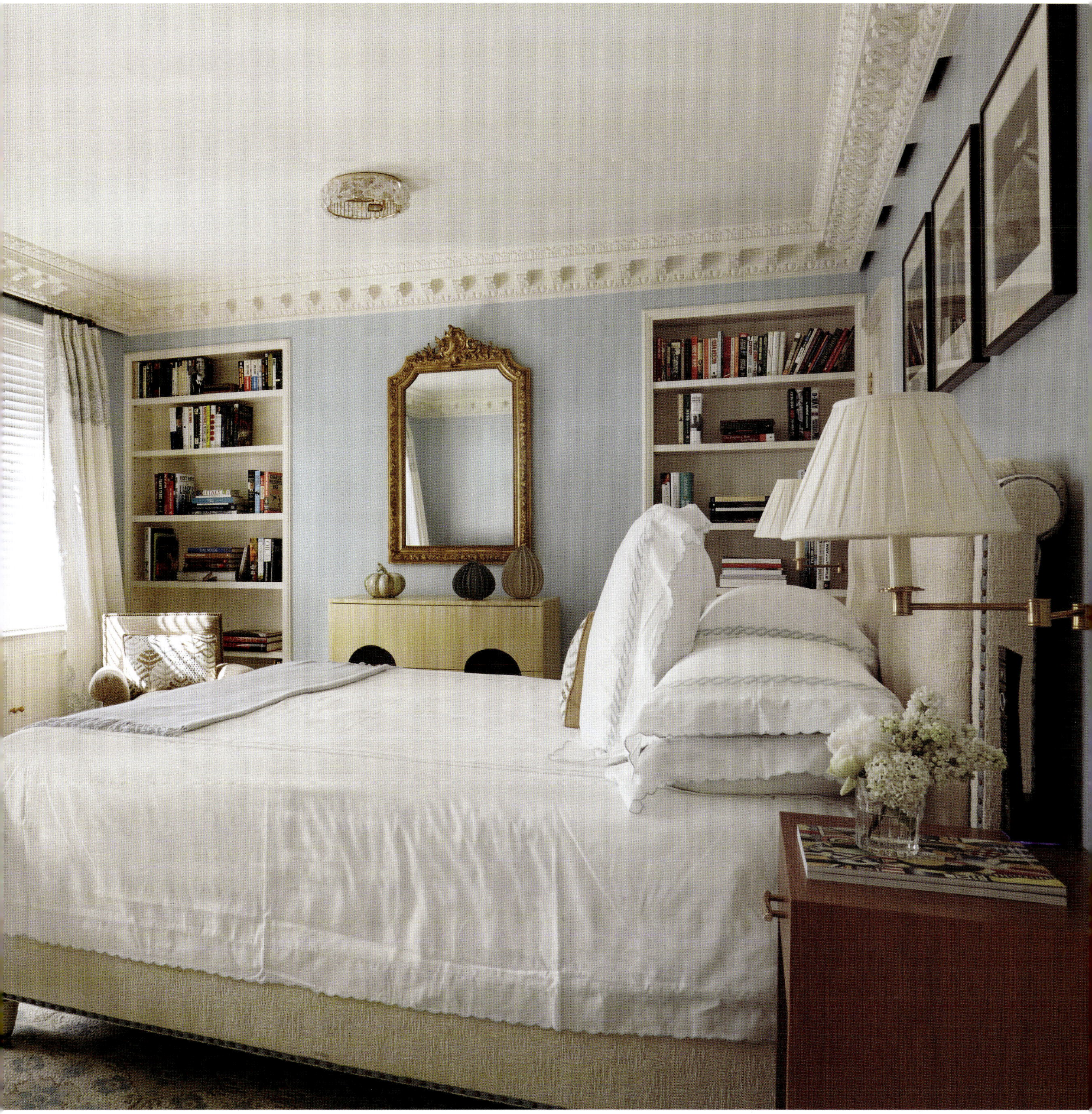

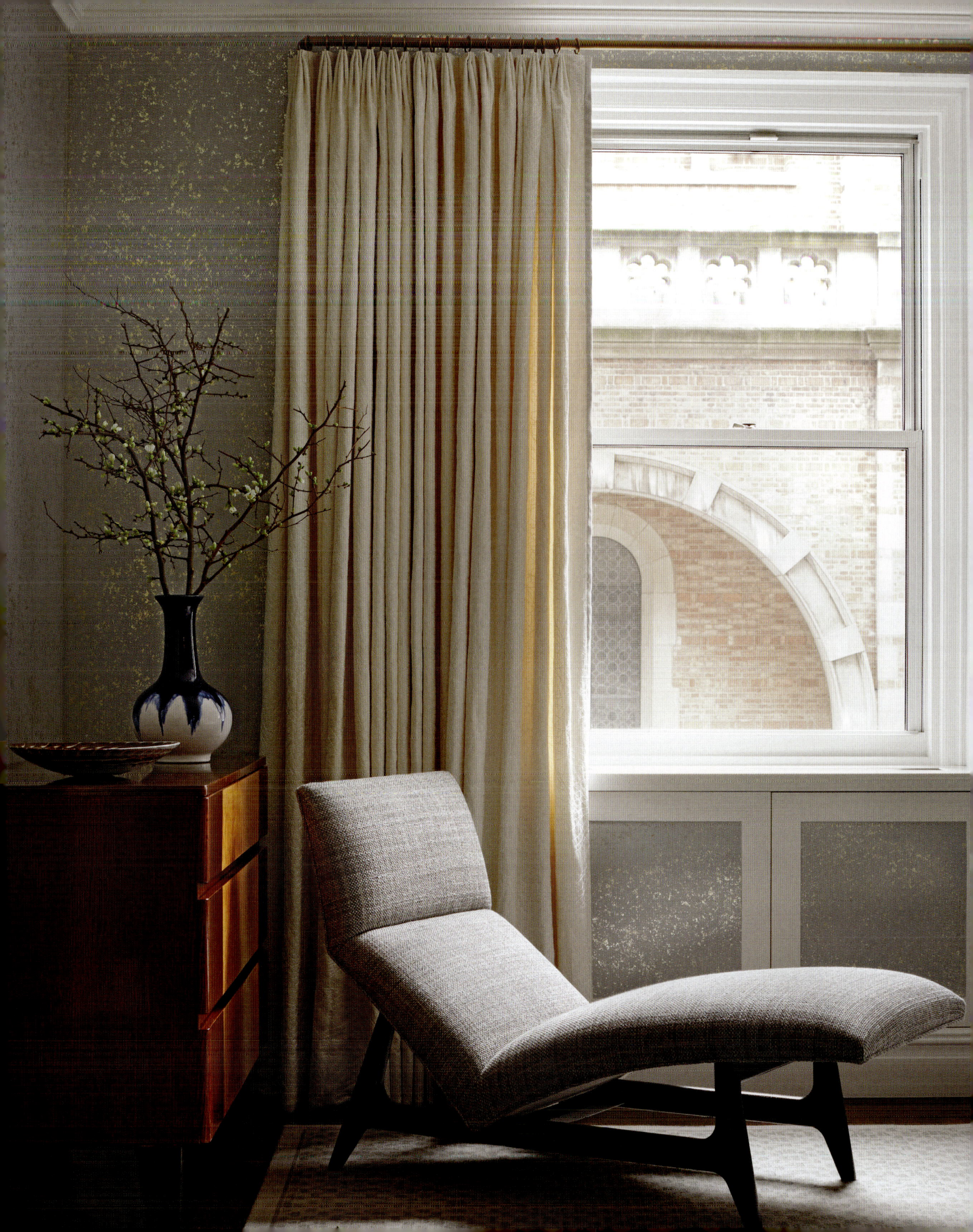

YOUTHFUL URBAN CHIC

Sometimes clients call on you to reimagine just a few rooms of a home to fit their needs. A young family, who loves to entertain, wanted public spaces to be more aligned with their vision of how they wanted to host their guests. The large living and dining room called for a youthful yet still sophisticated approach, and the layout of the spaces required that they flow from one into another in a cohesive manner without feeling too matchy.

In the living room, I carved the large space into two seating areas. The wife was drawn to a soothing color palette of gray and white, so I relied on the artwork to bring in most of the color and looked to patterned fabrics and rugs to insert a bit of zip. Giraffe-printed leather around the games table, where the children like to play backgammon, and swirly optic stripes on Ruhlmann-inspired chairs add energy to the otherwise serene space. A mix of low coffee tables and higher side tables provide options for both the hosts and guests to rest their glasses, while a tonal patterned rug unifies the look.

Continuing the directive to keep things calm, I had the dining room's walls finished in a silver leaf and mica glaze. Artisans worked to create the mesmerizing, glistening effect that defines the elegant room. In its previous incarnation, the space had a long rectangular table that the clients never thought really worked. Now, a circular table seats eight or ten—and makes for much more convivial conversation. Overall, the goal was to keep things soothing, so it seemed like the perfect final note to position a sculptural chaise longue in the corner—an invitation to read the paper on quiet Sunday mornings once all the guests have left.

OPPOSITE: A vintage chaise in the dining room gives another purpose to the space on Sunday mornings, when it becomes the perfect place to relax with the paper and a cup of coffee. FOLLOWING SPREAD: Multiple seating areas allow for gracious entertaining along with myriad ways for the family to spend time together. A cool palette of whites and grays per the client's request is punctuated with subtle uses of pattern on various chairs.

PATEK PHILIPPE
DOISNEAU
PHOTOGRAPHY
the Hermitage collections

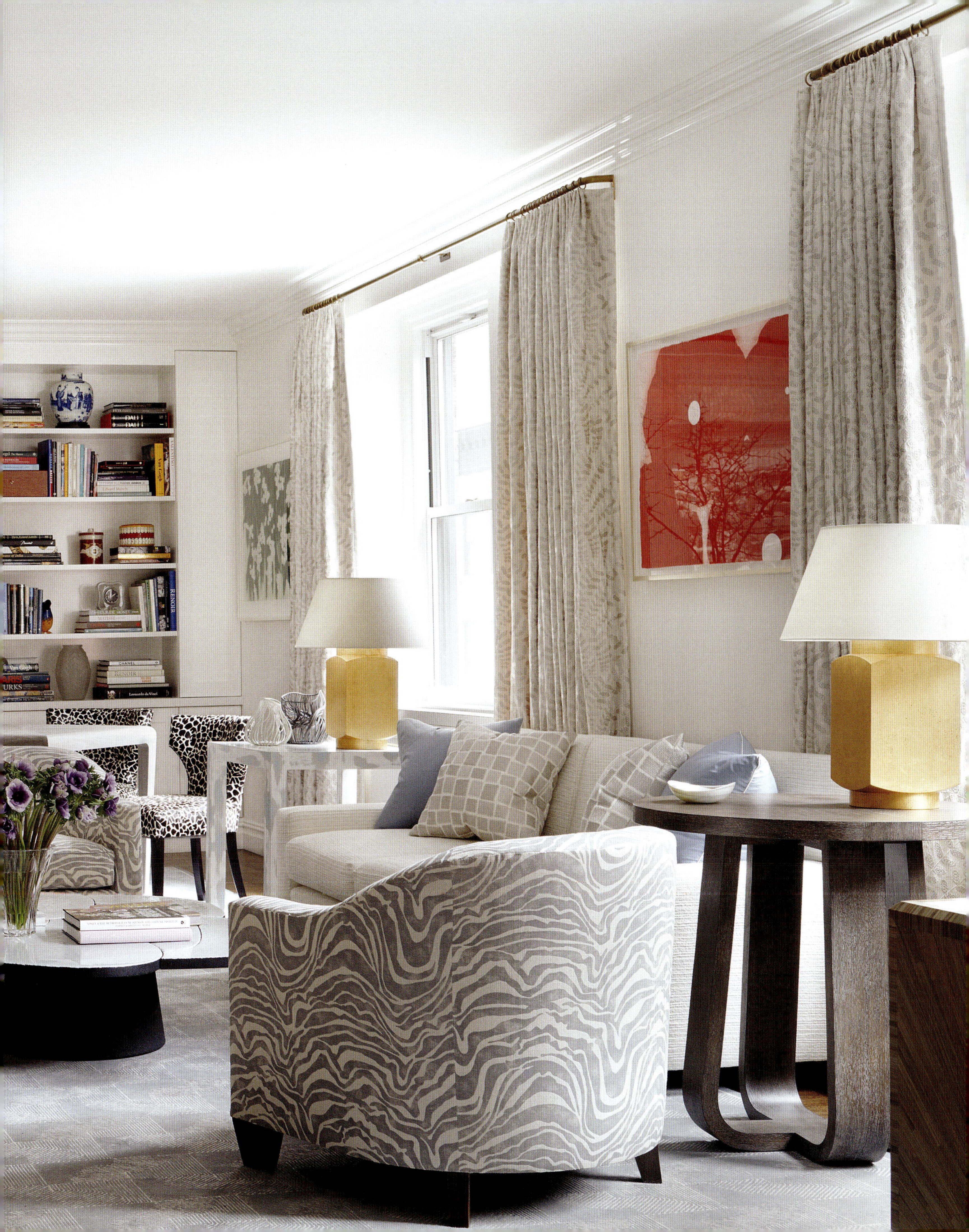

RIGHT: The living area flows freely into the dining room without being a totally open space plan. Straw marquetry cabinets, which provide extra storage, are surmounted by works such as a photograph by Candida Höfer and a painting by Hunt Slonem.

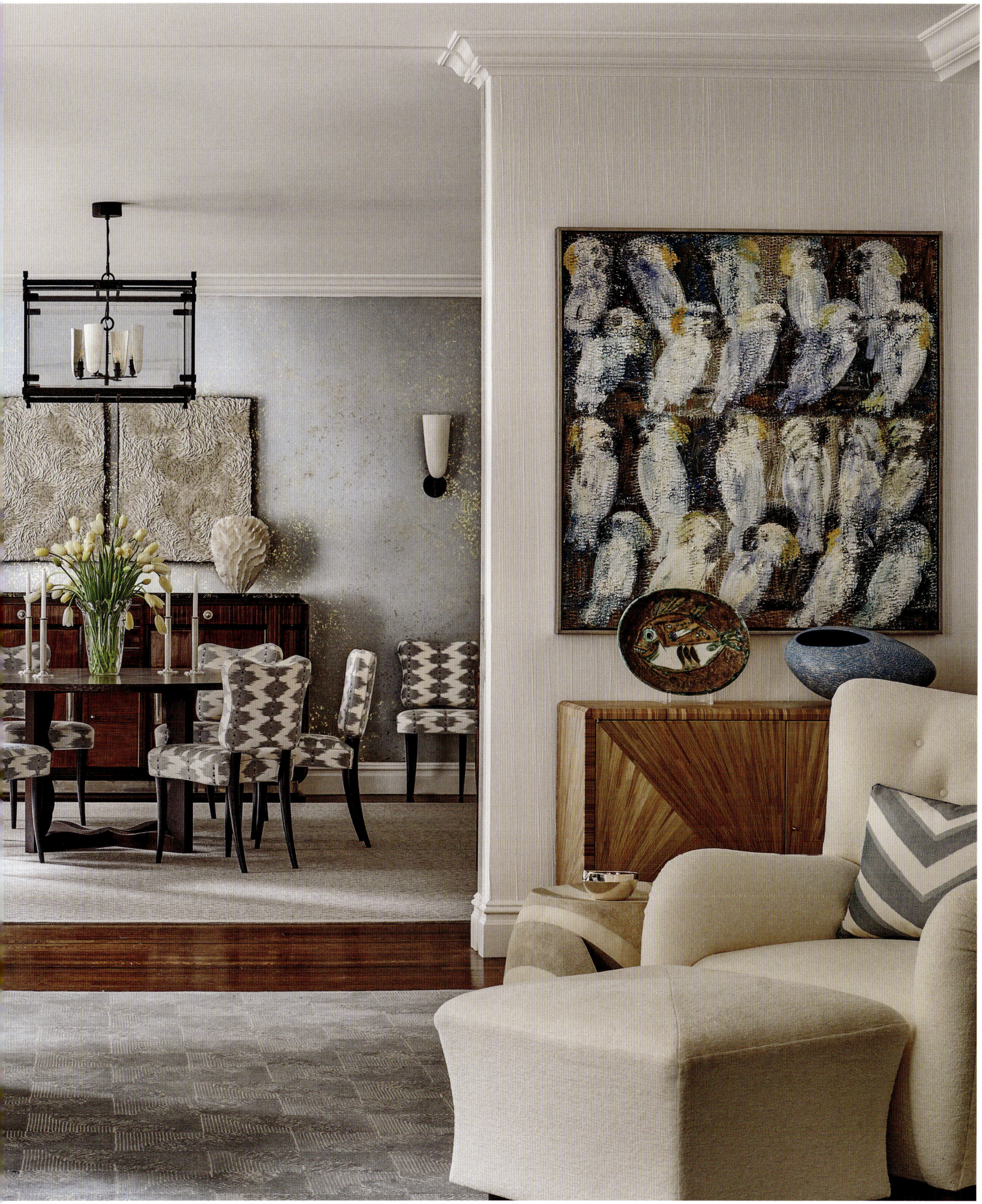

An Unexpected Mix

I firmly believe in buying the best when you can, but what's equally important is how one puts it all together. Designers love talking about the mix—old with new, high with low, curves with lines, and the list goes on. Unexpected combinations create conversations between pieces of furniture, objects, and art. Just like a perfectly seated dinner party, there needs to be a common thread to link everything but from there the more unpredictable the better.

For this Park Avenue apartment, celebrating these combinations brought a breath of fresh air that aligned with the sensibility of a young family while still fitting in on the Upper East Side. In several cases that came from taking a traditional piece of furniture and upholstering it in a bold print. For example, the Ruhlmann-style barrel back chairs in the living room become more youthful in a zippy, undulating stripe. Additionally, faux giraffe hide really peps up a standard games table. The collection of other tables in the living room also proves the power of the mix. The low coffee tables aren't a pair—if anything, they're opposites, and the side tables are just as different. As a whole, it's this variety of pieces that shapes the personality of the space into something wonderfully unexpected.

OPPOSITE: A seating area is assembled around an ivory-lacquered low table from Bernd Goeckler Antiques. The fabric on the chair is Cowtan & Tout, and the bookshelf is part of the renovation.

Venice
PATEK PHILIPPE
DOISNEAU
SULTAN
PHOTOGRAPHY
Toulouse-Lautrec
the Hermitage collections

RIGHT: Bold artworks punch up the serene palette. A variety of tables, including a coffee table by India Mahdavi, provide interest. The lamps are a scaled-up version of ones by Jean-Michel Frank.

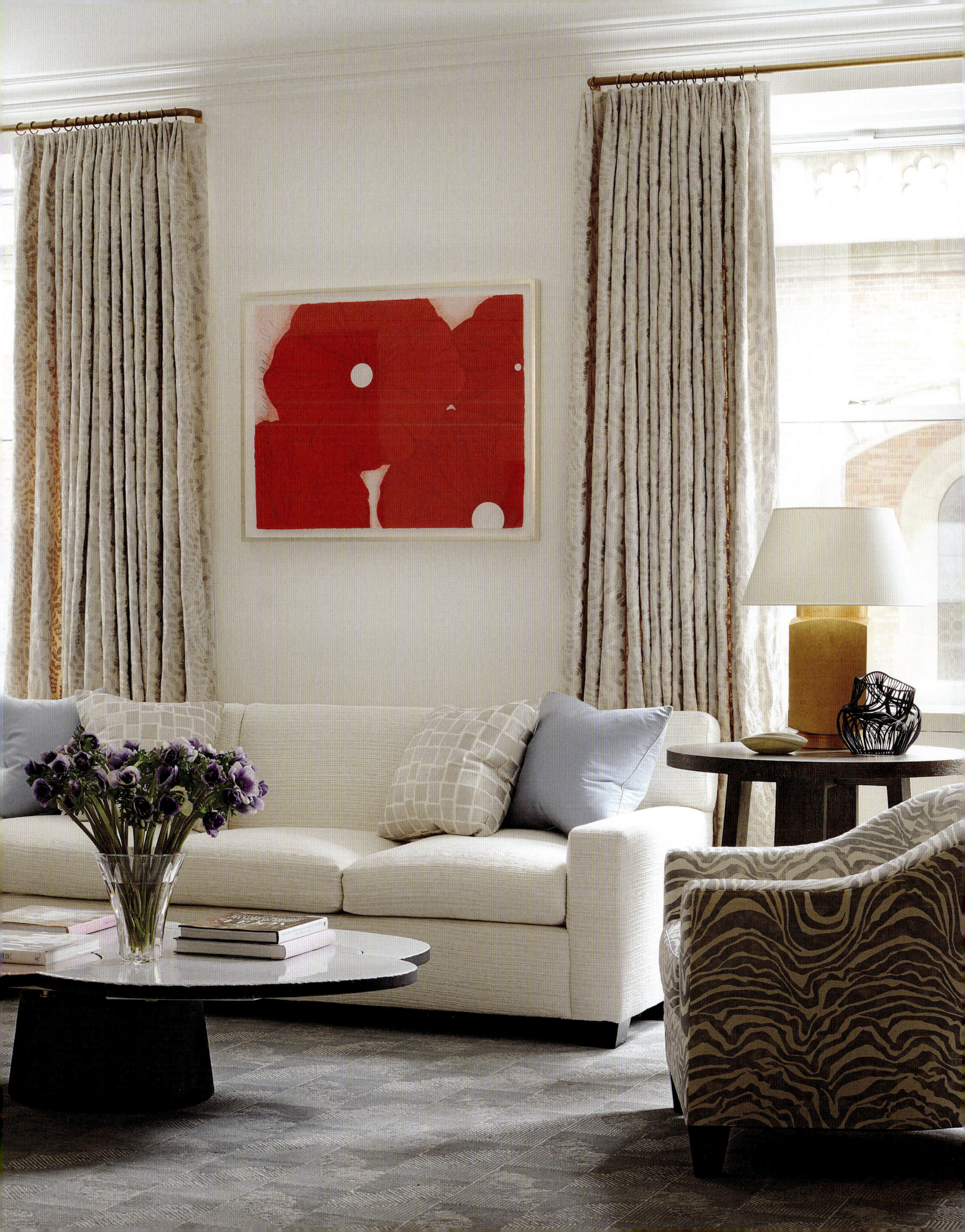

RIGHT: A shimmering mica finish brings a subtle glamour to the dining room, which is decorated with a vintage sideboard, Royère-inspired cartouche back chairs with fabric from Cowtan & Tout, and a Patrice Dangel light fixture and sconces.

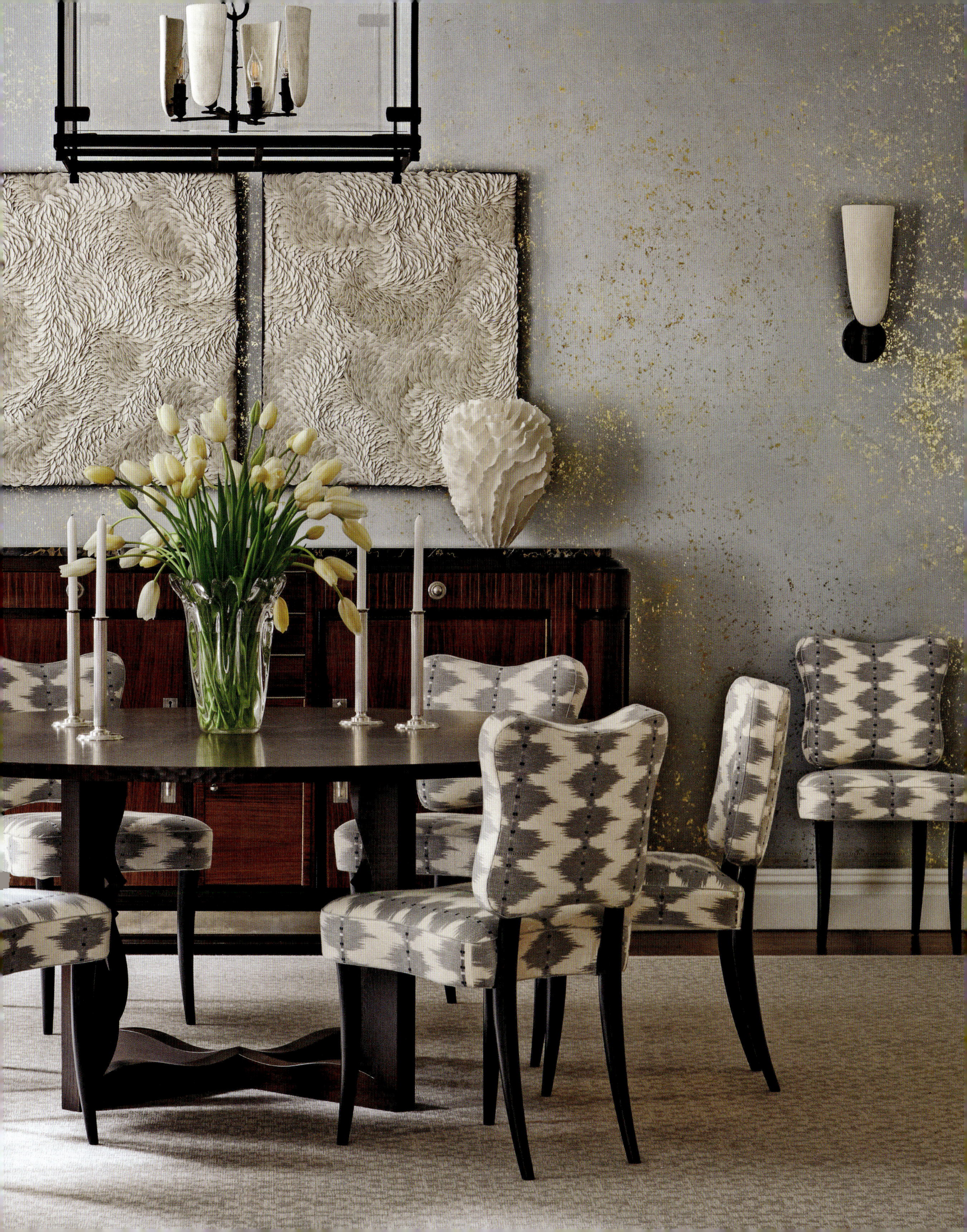

PRESERVING A SCOTTISH CASTLE ON THE NORTH SEA

When longtime clients called me to ask what I was doing that weekend, I had no idea that being available would lead to a four-year renovation of an 1860s historic stone house on the Scottish cliffs. We proceeded to spend that weekend walking around North Cliff, talking about their love of golf, and plotting how to fully update this charming Victorian without losing its architectural bones. Having been in the same family since World War II, the house was ready for a full-scale intervention.

Working with a local architect, we unpeeled layers of additions and modifications that had happened over the decades and decided which were worth keeping, such as the Robert Adam–inspired dining room. We reconfigured the entry, powder room, and kitchen as well as paired all the bedrooms with en suite baths. In the end, we took down every wall to put everything back together to look as if it had always been that way. In the process, we seized the opportunity to install new fireplace mantels and add a staircase off the breakfast room that leads out to the magnificent garden and the North Sea.

For the interiors, the clients gave me the directive of English country house. In the living room, the view out the double bay windows needed to be the star, so we did the curtains in blue to frame the setting. Although the scale of the space is quite grand, we needed to bring it down to feel comfortable. Upholstered sofas and chairs soften the room, while a collection of brown furniture lives up to the architecture. Upholstery serves a completely different function in the dining room, where a claret-red fabric on

OPPOSITE: Upon entering this historic Scottish house, there's a feeling that it has always been this way, although the renovation took four years. We replaced the existing floor with new limestone to give a timeless effect, while we swapped the Victorian railing for a 1900s design. An eighteenth-century chinoiserie mirror hangs over an English card table.

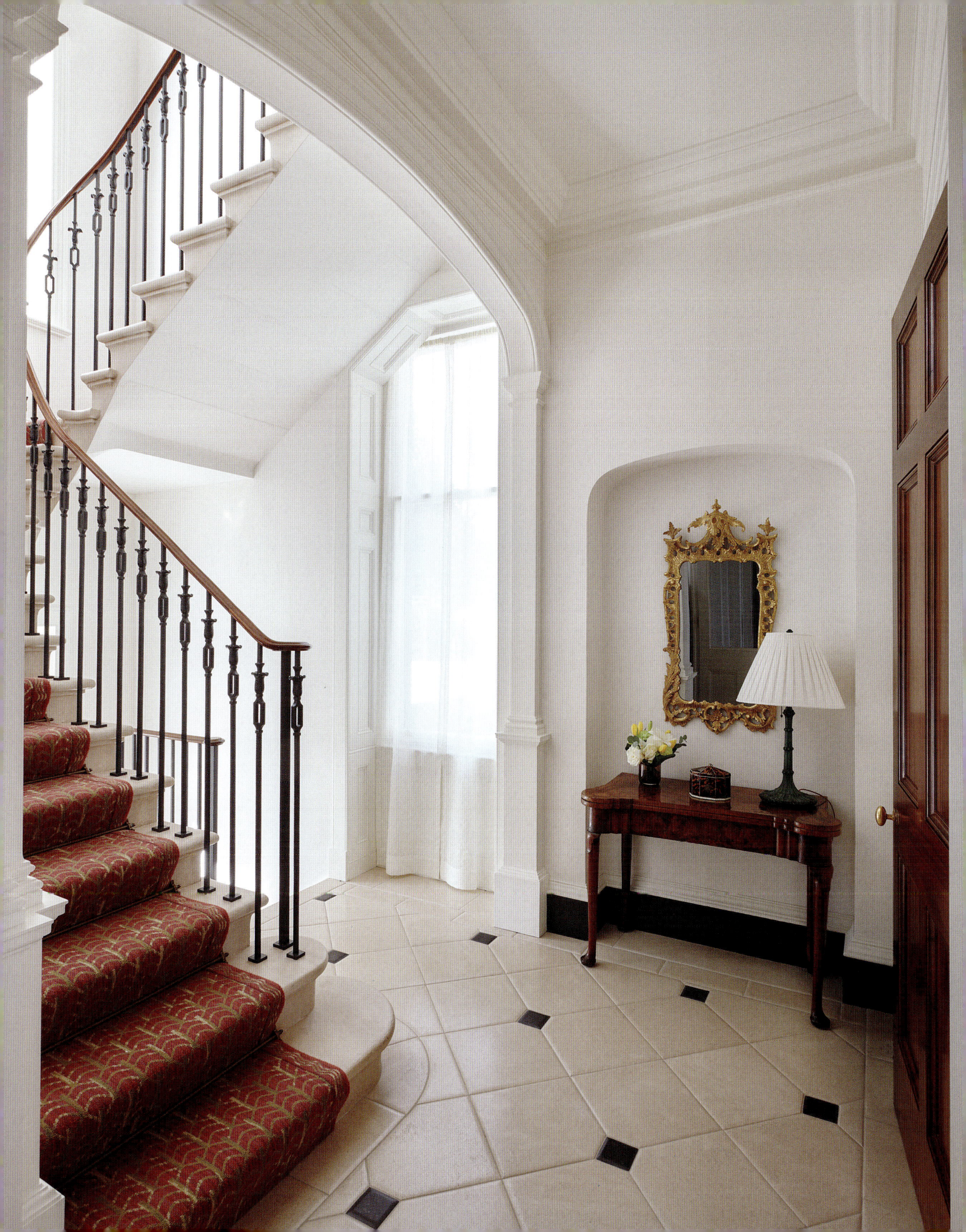

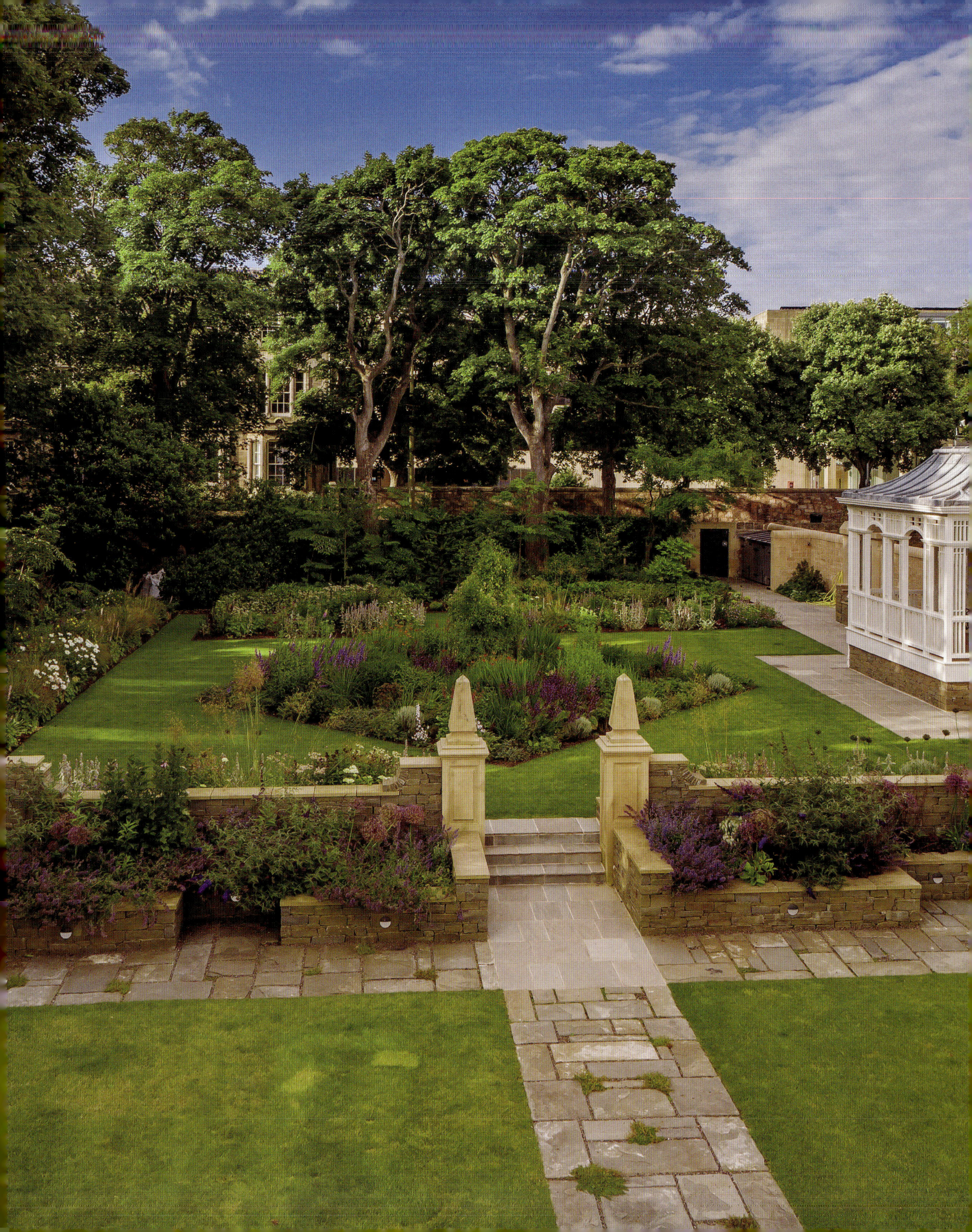

the walls nods to the Mark's Club in London and heightens the drama of the neoclassical cove ceiling and architectural detailing.

On the ground floor, a rabbit warren of staff and mechanical rooms was transformed into a billiards room. Paneling the entire space recast it into the perfect place to unwind after a day of golf or for after-dinner drinks. All the woodwork is new but designed to architecturally match, so the space feels like a fluid part of the entire residence—not tacked on.

I love plaids and tartans—but by avoiding those Scottish clichés, we created a weekend home with all the modern comforts that's perfectly suited to the history of the house while reflecting its sublime location.

OPPOSITE: The garden was completely replanted, and the conservatory rebuilt. ABOVE: The cliffside location on the North Sea makes for dramatic views from the interiors. FOLLOWING SPREAD: In the living room, an array of antique brown furniture—the secretary, the Empire chairs, the sofa table, and the bench with vintage needlework—recalls the collected feeling of an English country house.

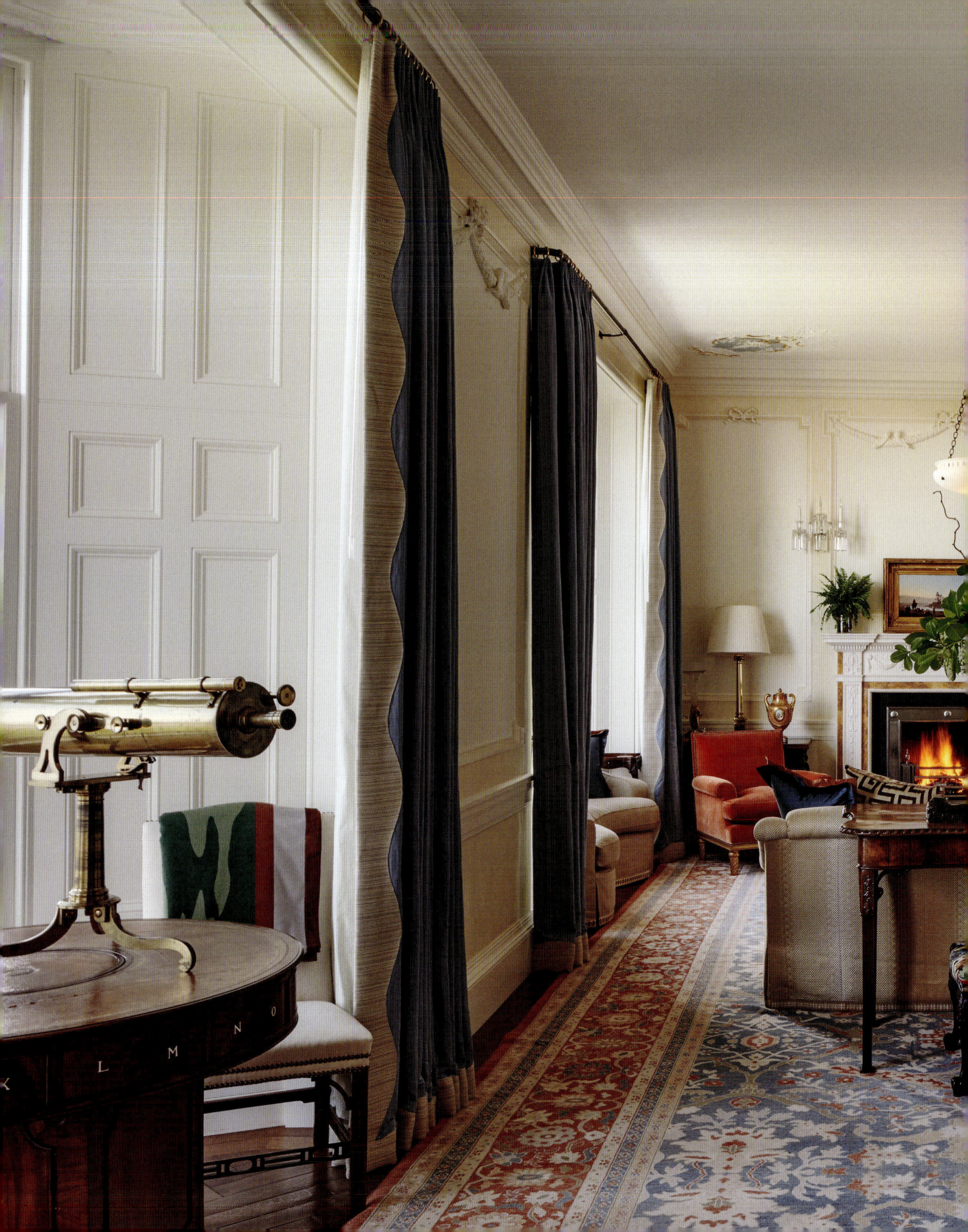
L M N O

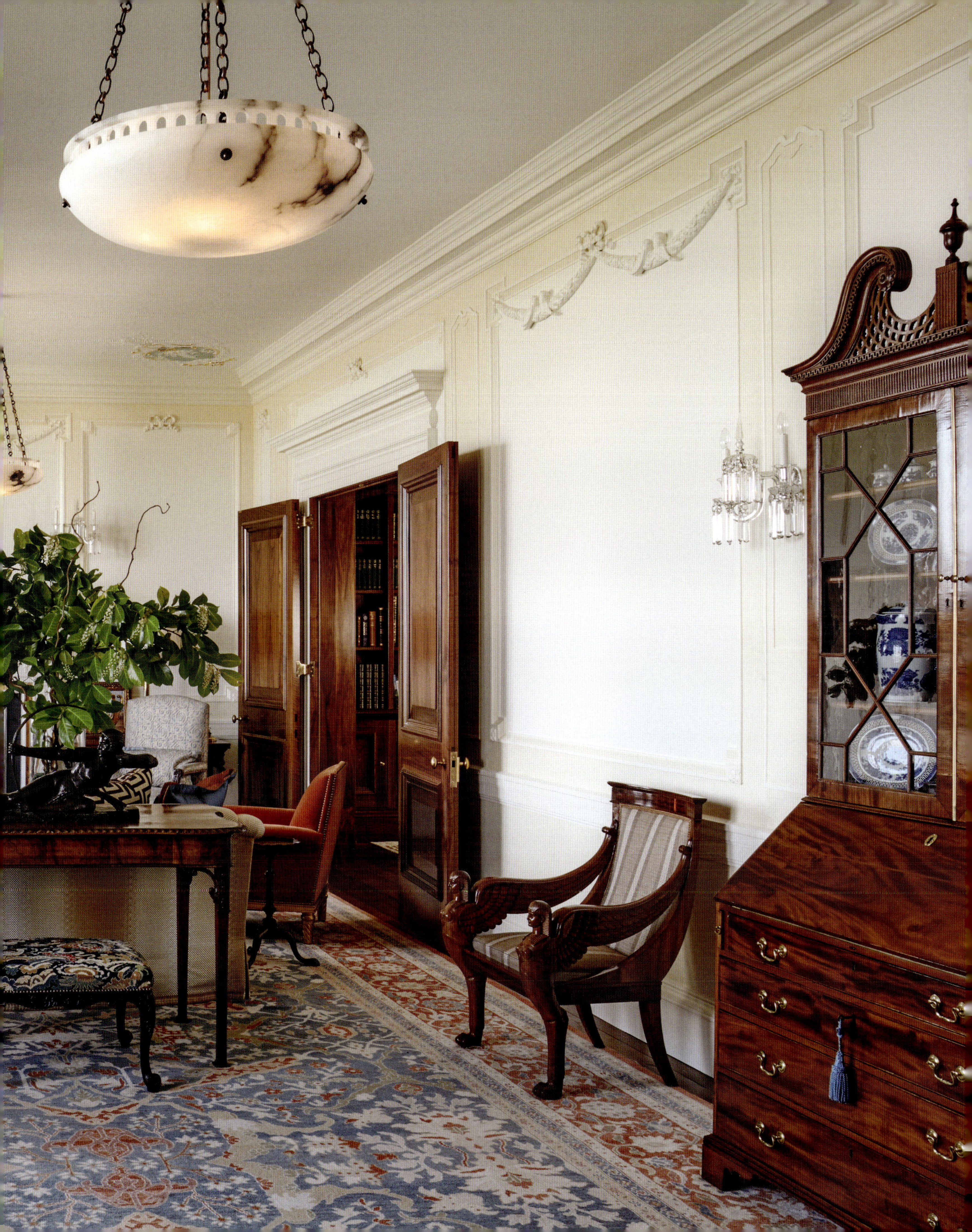

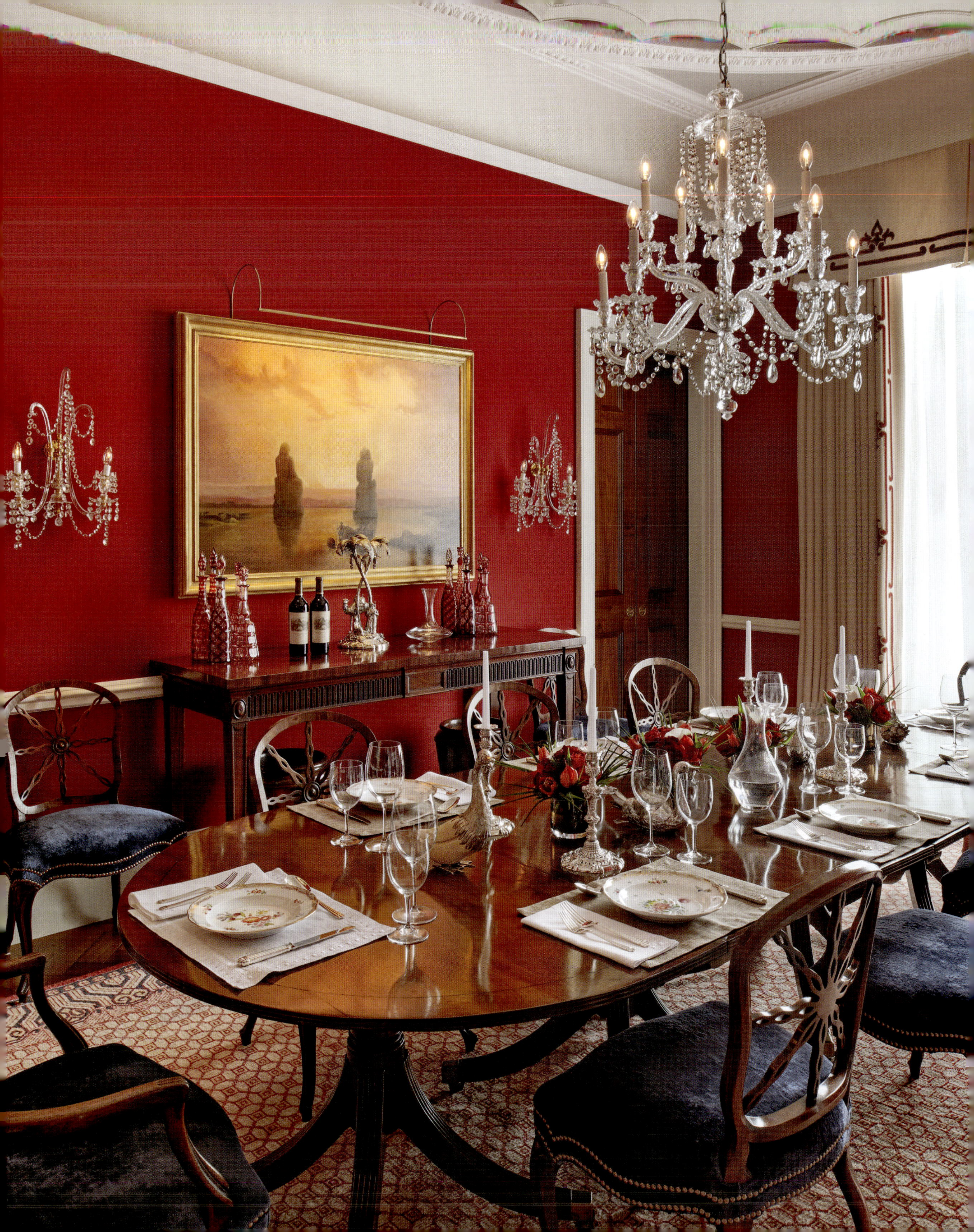

No Substitute for Brown Furniture

Some may turn up their noses at brown furniture, believing it's decidedly out of style. But for those in the know, there's never been a better time to purchase quality antique pieces made of wood. Since the market has a surplus of these designs, now is the time to buy while prices are negotiable. Once-coveted pieces with names like Chippendale and Gainsborough are more attainable than ever now that the fashion has veered away from these classics—making buying the very best within reach.

The classical architecture of this Scottish country house along with its wood doors and frames gave me the opportunity to hunt for all manner of wood furnishings—from a George III three-pedestal table to a Robert Adam sideboard.

The dining room has long been a place to show off a suite of furniture, but I prefer to mix from different periods for a more personal approach. By using their lines to connect various periods and styles, the pieces work together as an interesting mix with different points of view, like a well-seated dinner party.

Bringing in a touch of mahogany and walnut pieces—an excellent way to add character to a room—keeps the space from looking like a showroom. They possess an air of distinction and can be repurposed into different spaces for decades to come, plus it's interesting to mix up objects from their original function. Timeless and elegant, quality workmanship never goes out of fashion.

OPPOSITE: The dining room speaks to tradition with a set of cartouche-shaped mahogany chairs bought at auction surrounding a three-pedestal mahogany table. A mid-century English crystal chandelier as well as Holland & Sherry embroidered curtains further enhance the formal space.

RIGHT: A cozy American walnut–paneled library makes an ideal space to gather in winter. Warm golds are carried throughout the room, including the embroidered fabric by Pierre Frey, the sofa covered in Lauren Hwang velvet, and the chinoiserie mirror.

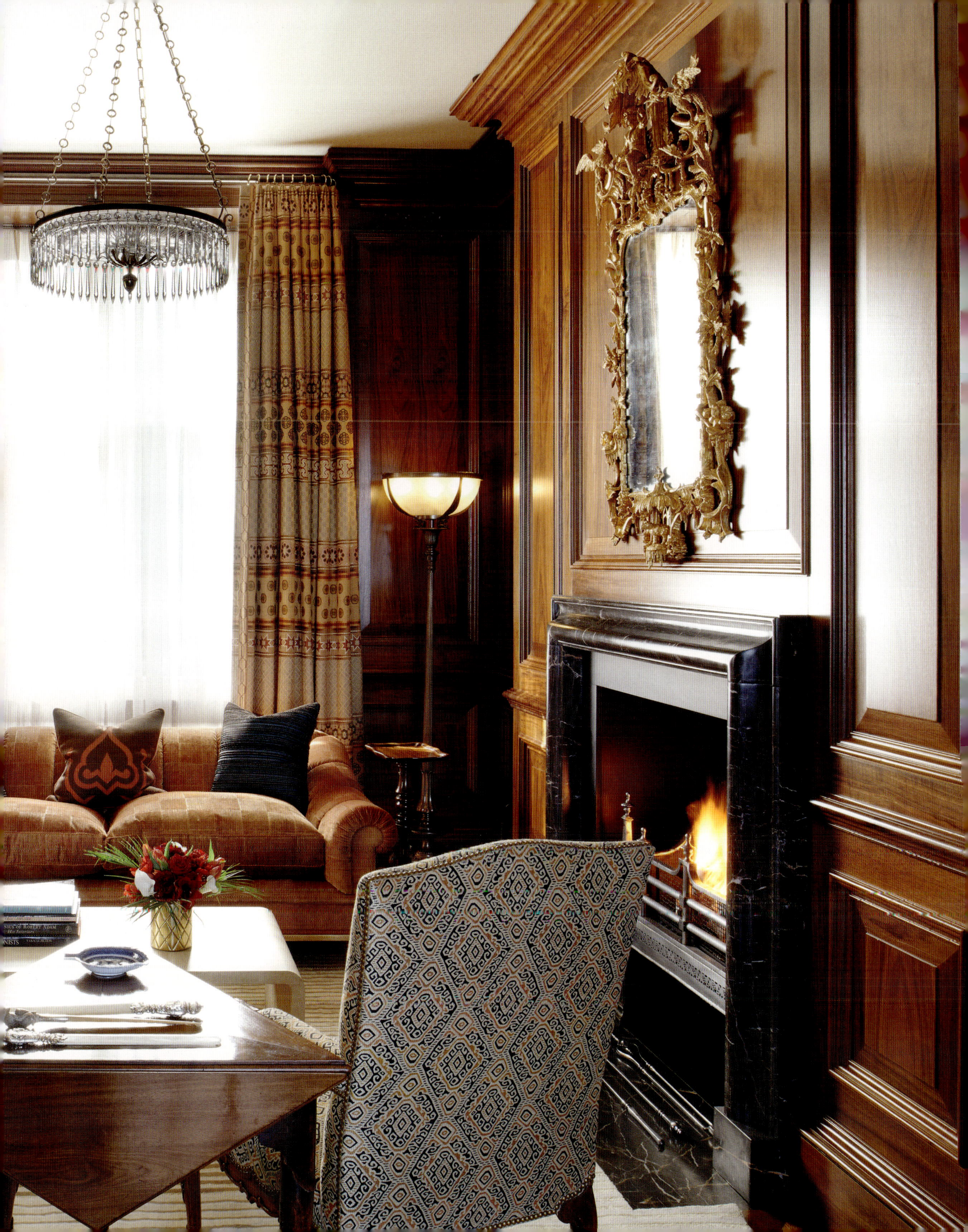

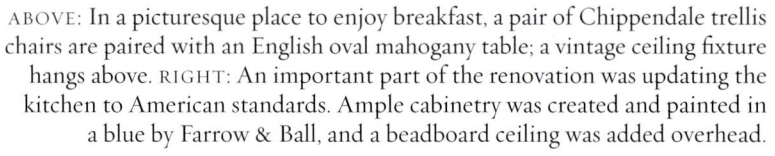

ABOVE: In a picturesque place to enjoy breakfast, a pair of Chippendale trellis chairs are paired with an English oval mahogany table; a vintage ceiling fixture hangs above. RIGHT: An important part of the renovation was updating the kitchen to American standards. Ample cabinetry was created and painted in a blue by Farrow & Ball, and a beadboard ceiling was added overhead.

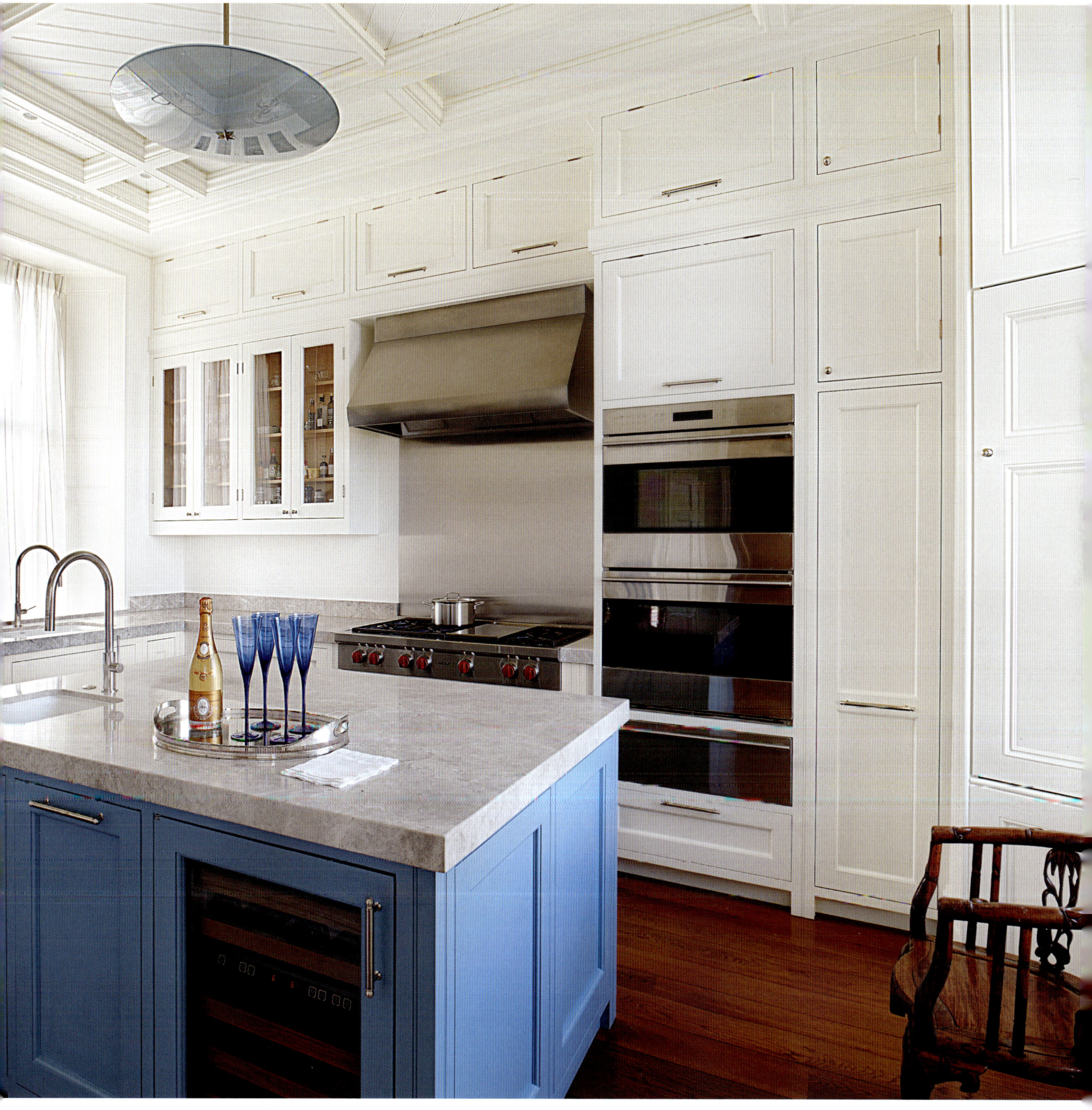

RIGHT: A scenic wallpaper by de Gournay acts as the focal point of the primary bedroom. Lyre-based side tables and an early nineteenth-century mahogany bench continue the commitment to brown furniture in this house.

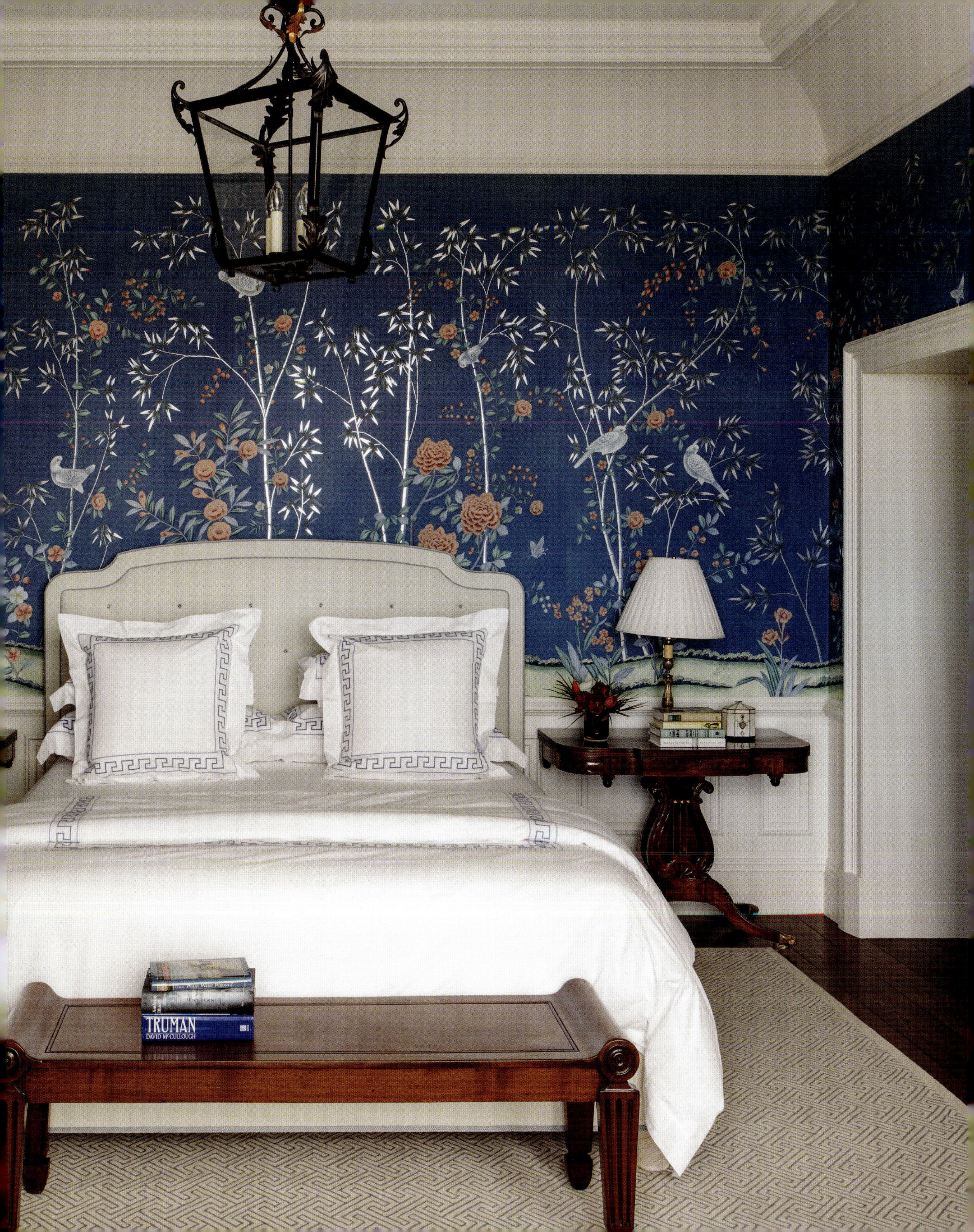
TRUMAN
DAVID McCULLOUGH

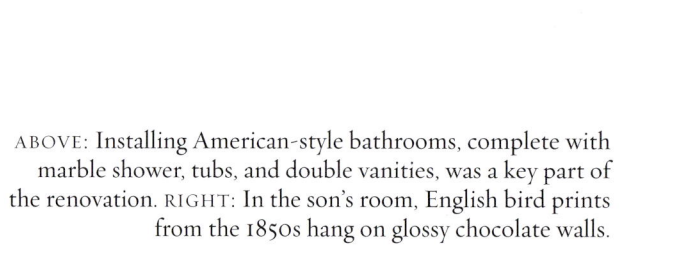

ABOVE: Installing American-style bathrooms, complete with marble shower, tubs, and double vanities, was a key part of the renovation. RIGHT: In the son's room, English bird prints from the 1850s hang on glossy chocolate walls.

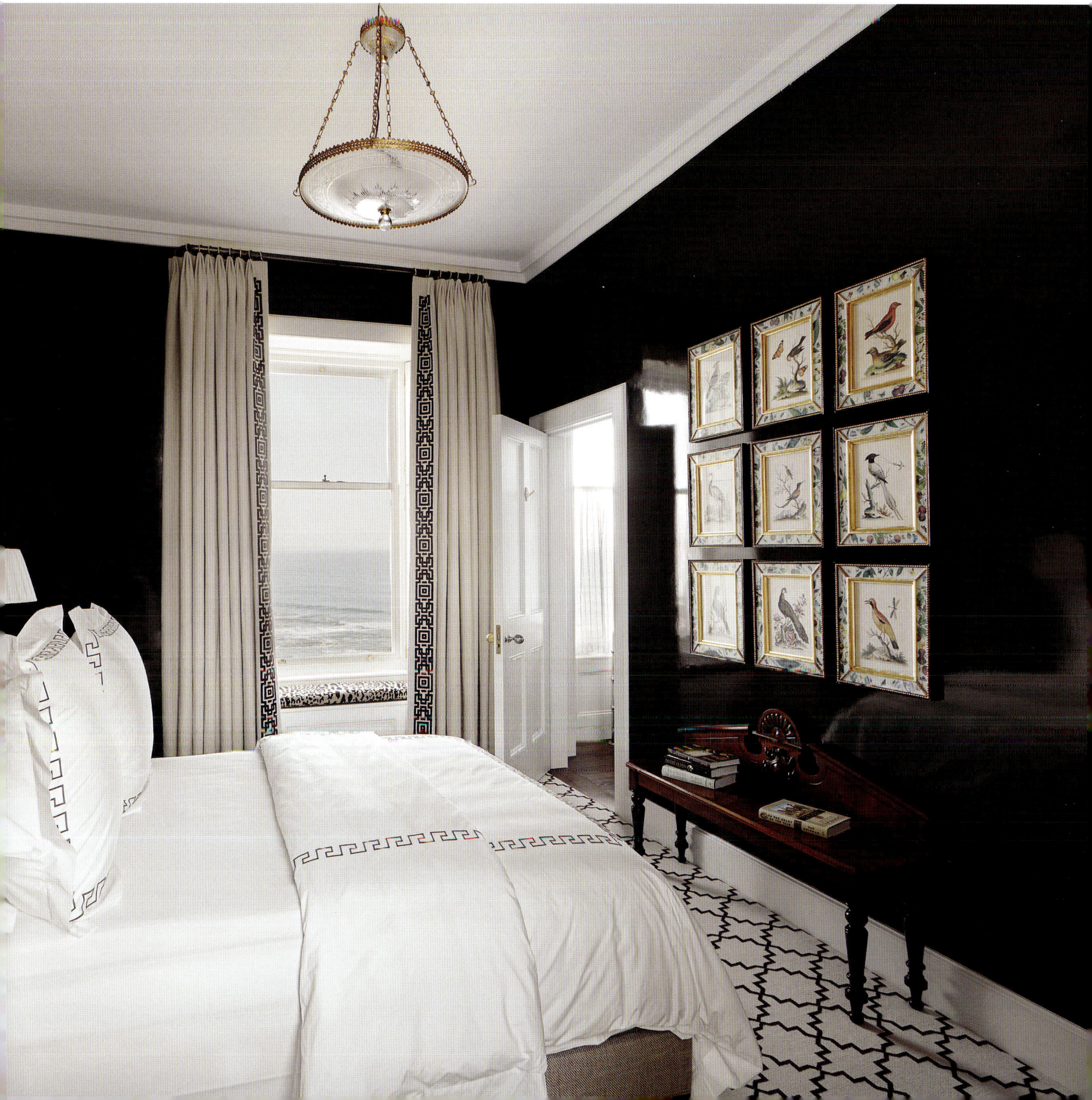

RIGHT: In the former basement, the stained-oak billiard room, featuring all new wood paneling designed to match the house's existing architecture, is a popular place to gather after dinner. An assortment of Robert Kime pillows brings the charm of an English country house.

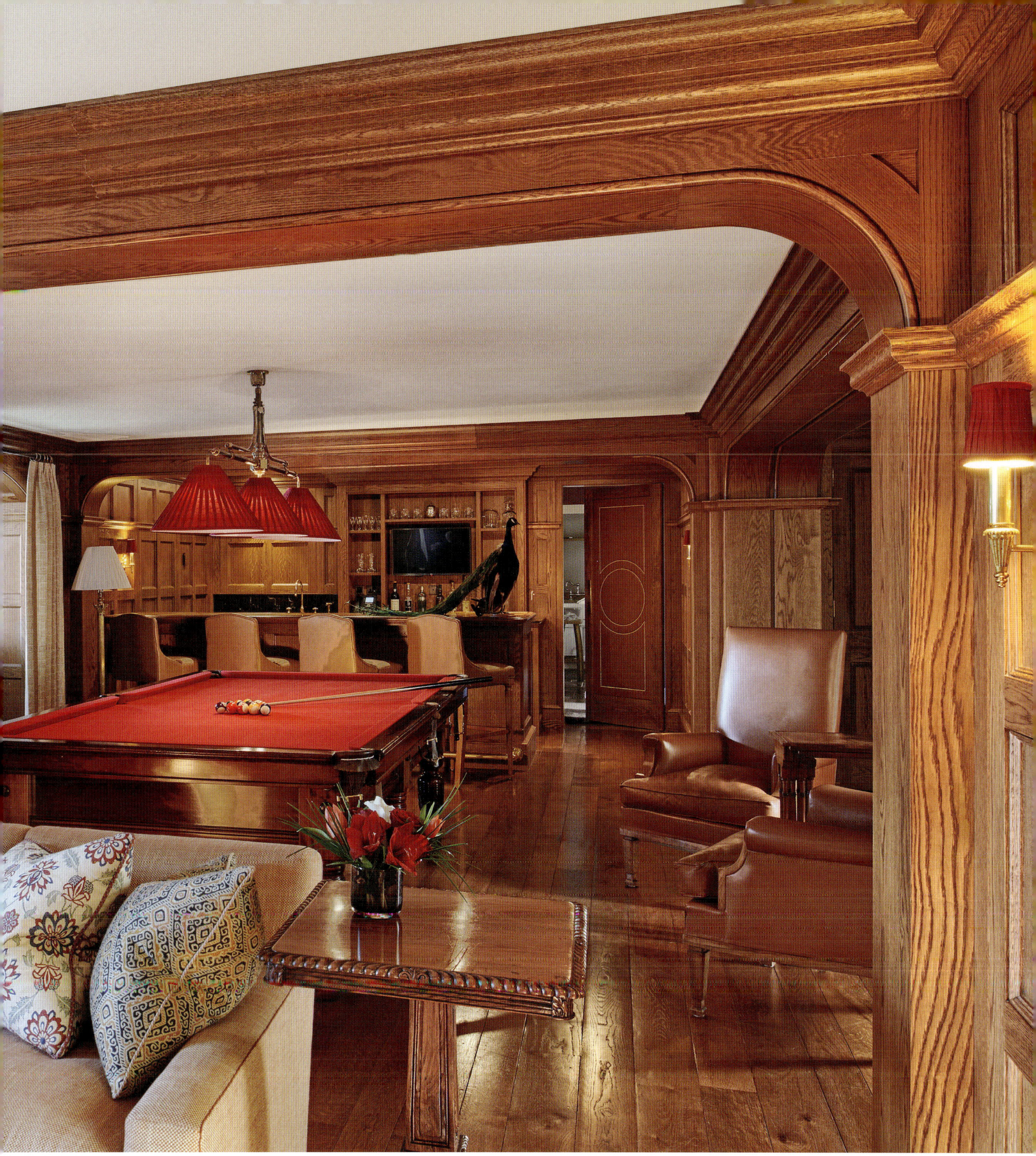

RIGHT: After four years of restoration, the house sits proudly along the Scottish coastline and presides over lush green gardens that pop in contrast with the slate gray sea.

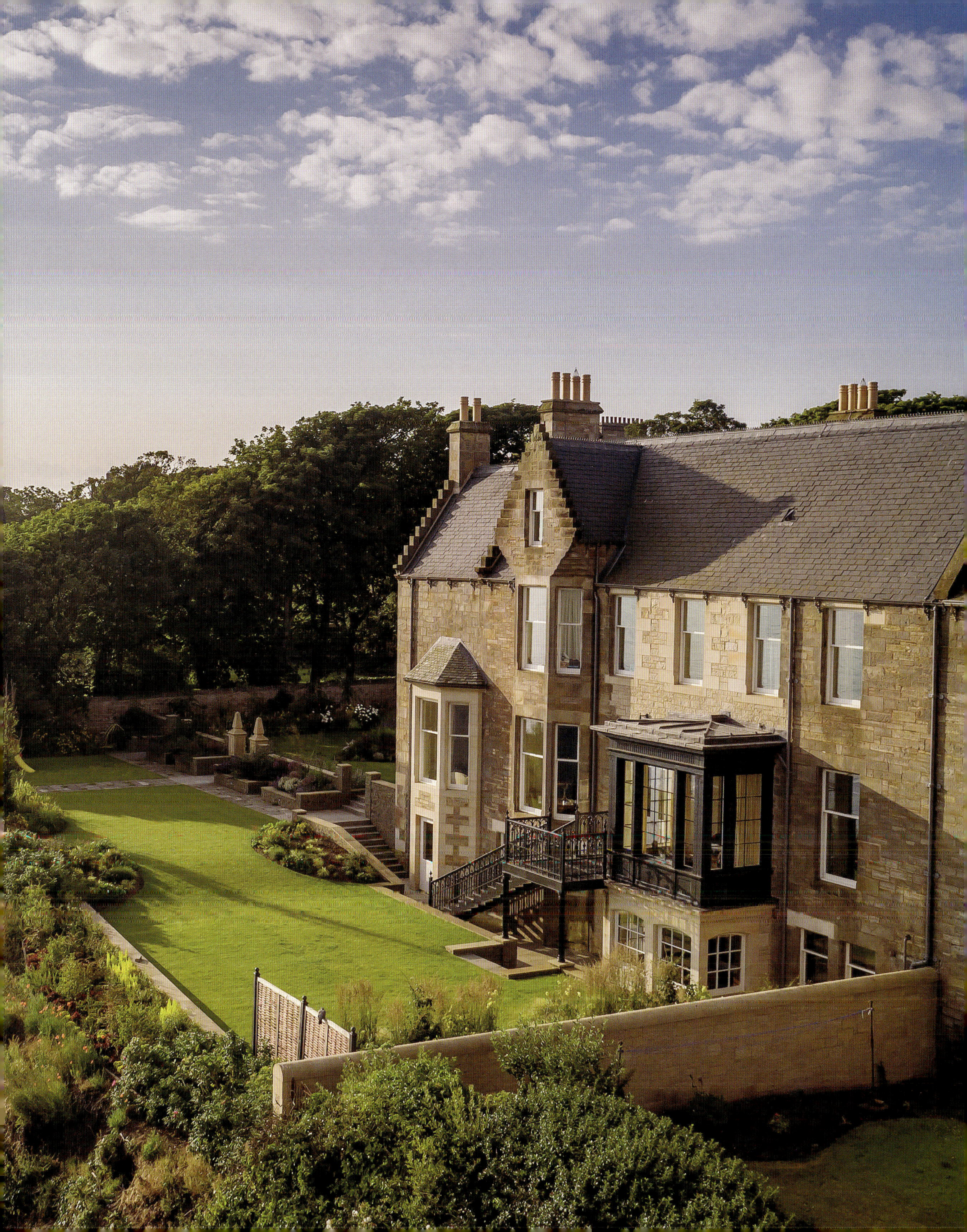

RESTORING A SHINGLE-STYLE COTTAGE

Steeped in tradition, Southampton, New York, is a place known for being mindful of the beauty and elegance of the past. Stately trees shade streets stretching from the beach, while tall hornbeam hedges surround shingle-style houses, many of which have been there for a century. When clients purchased one such house from 1910, I was immediately drawn to the prospect of undoing several questionable interventions that had transpired over the years and restoring the residence to its former glory.

One of the most distinguishing characteristics of this house is its deep porch. At some point in the 1970s, this wondrous space had unfortunately been enclosed with sheet glass. By ripping away these additions, the family could now enjoy the outdoor room in all its splendor. Surrounded by rhododendron, the wide space allowed me to create the dream plein air room. By painting the ceiling an old-fashioned porch blue and mixing wicker furniture, patterned pillows, cozy throws, and contemporary lighting, the area now feels just as layered and rich as the interiors.

Inside, the rooms reflect the homeowners' love of color. We kept the entry hall quite spare but warmed it up with a red console table and graphic stencil work on the floor. Splashier tones enliven the living room. Building off the colors in a flat-weave rug inspired by a Swedish geometric pattern, I had chairs upholstered in an eye-catching fabric from John Rosselli & Associates while keeping a floating sofa in ivory and the opposing one in a blue that picks up on the pool beyond. A subtle wavy texture in the plaster finish gives a shimmering depth to the walls, while not competing with the strong hues.

OPPOSITE: In the entry hall of the shingle-style home, a hand-painted checkerboard floor in soft grays complements Venetian plaster walls, a John Rosselli & Associates bell light lantern, and a vintage console.

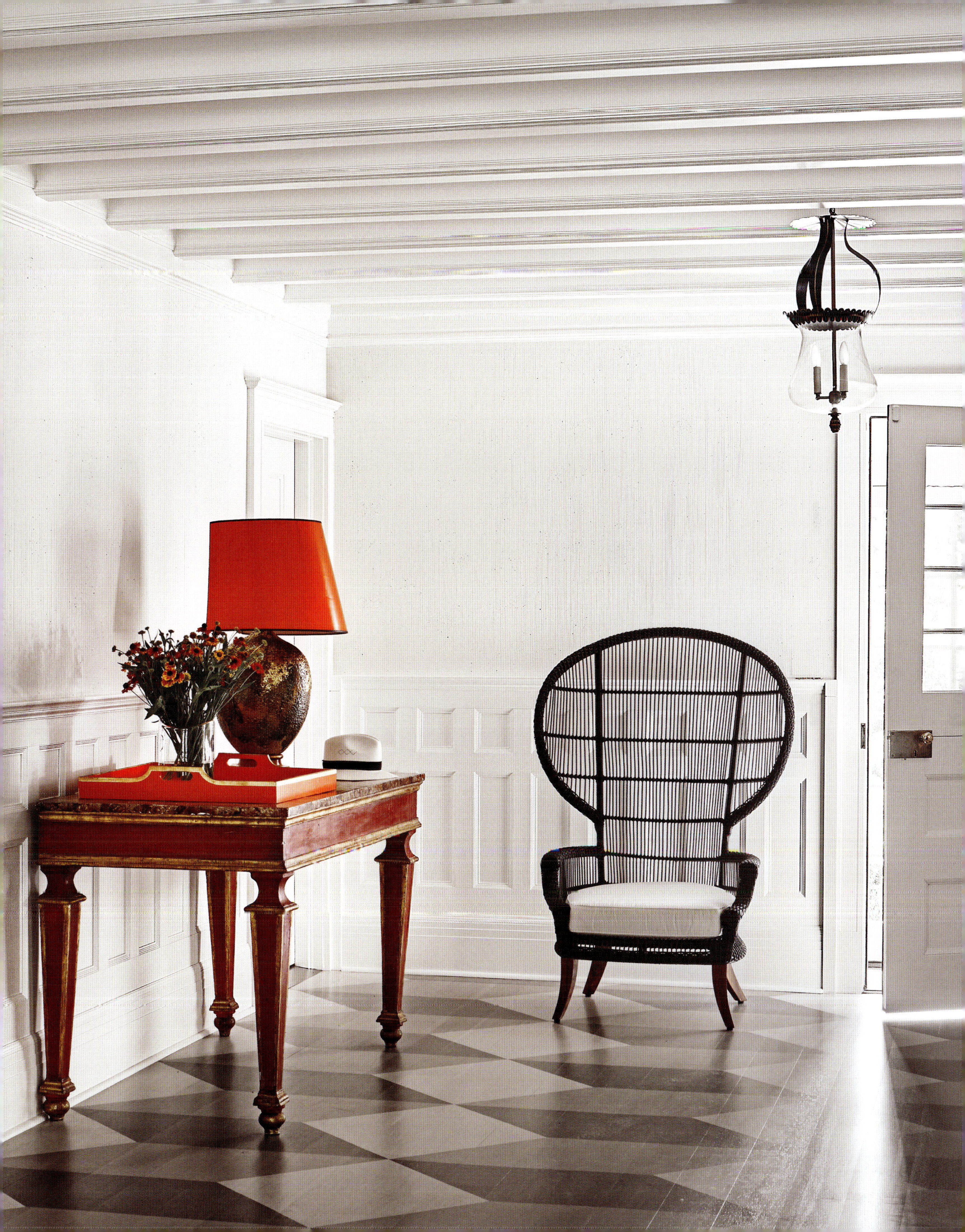

Upstairs, each bedroom has a unique look while fitting into the overall concept of the home. As my dear friend and once boss Bunny Williams would say, "You have to broaden the vocabulary." So, in the master sitting room, I added a watery mirror to reflect the light into the interior room, then paired it with a sculptural wicker console. There's a Tiffany-blue guest bedroom and another that has a sea-foam-green bed with the insides of the bookcases painted a similar hue. In the daughter's room, I had a stencil created to match the fabric of the curtains. Every room has its own sensibility.

In the end, we not only returned the home to its original beauty, but we also infused every space with elements that nod to the past while enlivening them with a feeling of happiness. Best of all, the family that lives there matches each of these gestures with energy, joy, and spirit.

ABOVE: The porch of the house, dating to 1910, was restored to its former glory. OPPOSITE: The expansive living room is carved into multiple seating areas, including a floating, curved Schneller sofa, adorned with pillows with Penn & Fletcher embroidery.

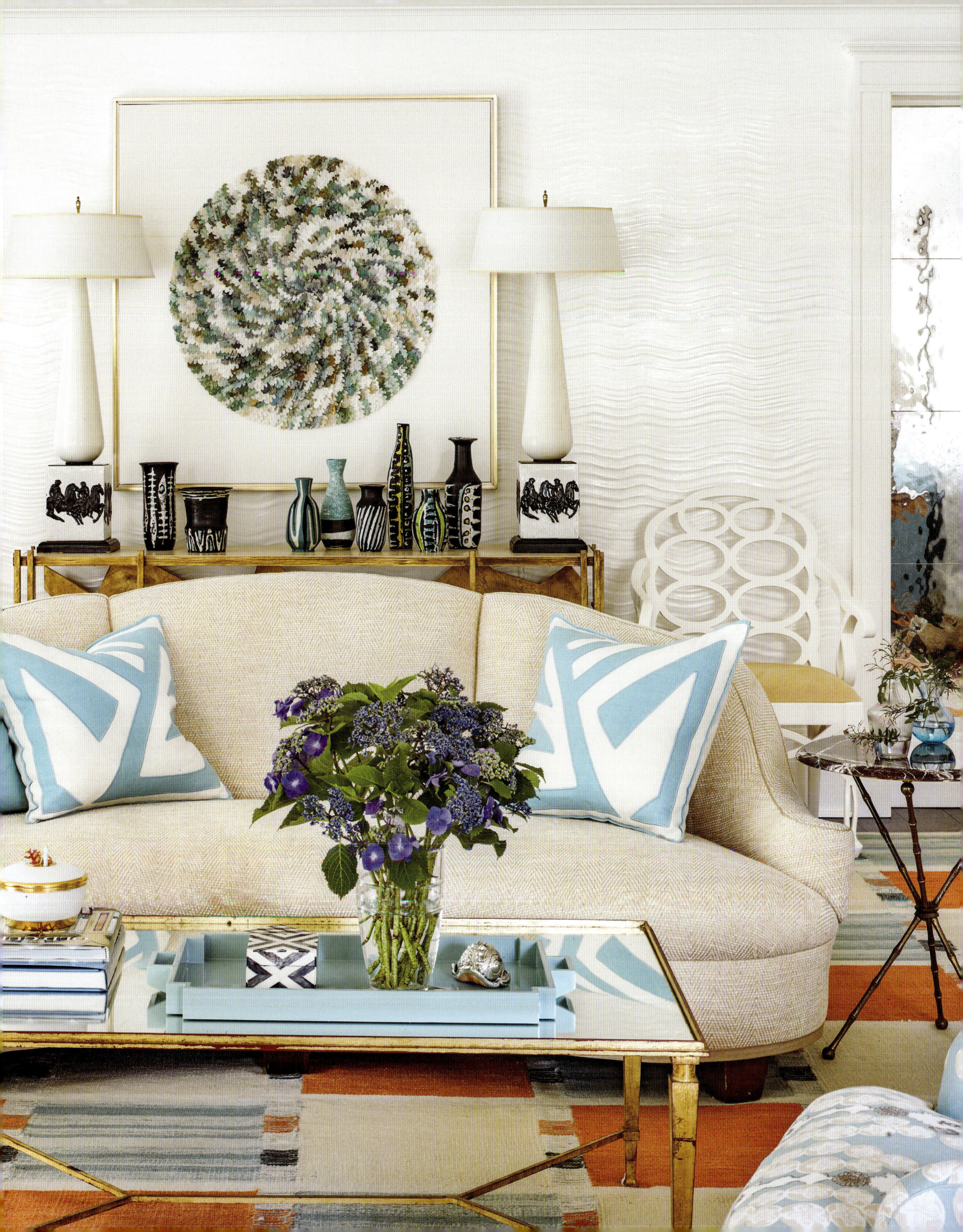

RIGHT: Based on a Swedish pattern, the custom Beauvais rug unifies the room while adding color. A pair of vintage mirrors, placed between the French doors, and a lacquered ceiling contribute to the light-filled atmosphere.

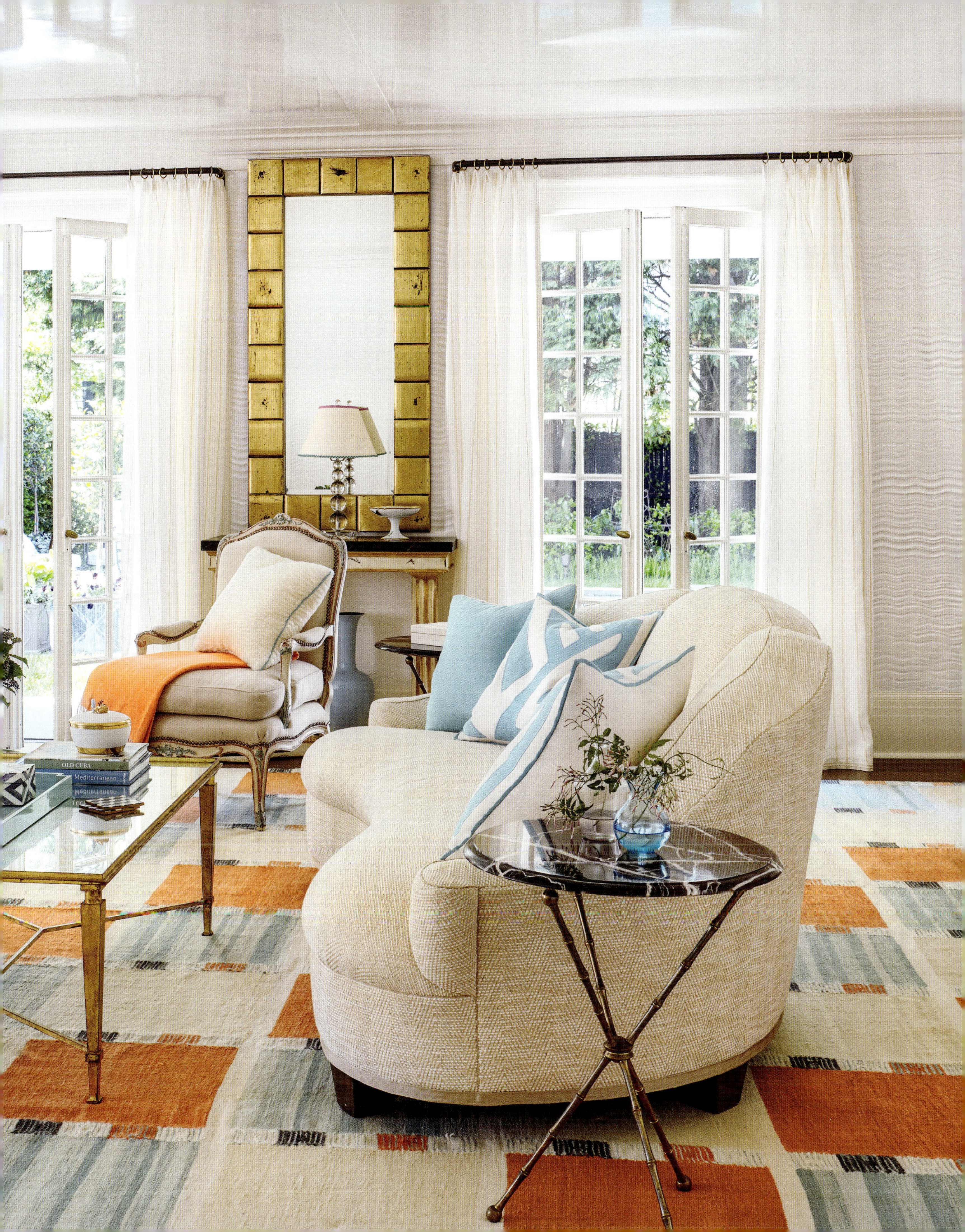
OLD CUBA
Mediterranean

RIGHT: Frances Elkins loop chairs flank a sculptural Patrice Dangel console, which is set against an undulating motif in the Venetian plaster wall.

FLORENCE
TREASURES OF THE SMITHSONIAN
HAMPTONS GARDENS
THE WORLD'S BEST SAILBOATS
YACHT CLUBS of the WORLD
Leonardo da Vinci

ABOVE: An all-white palette keeps the kitchen fresh and cheerful. OPPOSITE: In the dining room, a custom-painted tree motif is accented with mother-of-pearl above the original wood paneling. Lanterns by Paul Ferrante hang over a pair of circular tables, which provide more options for entertaining than one larger traditional rectangular one.

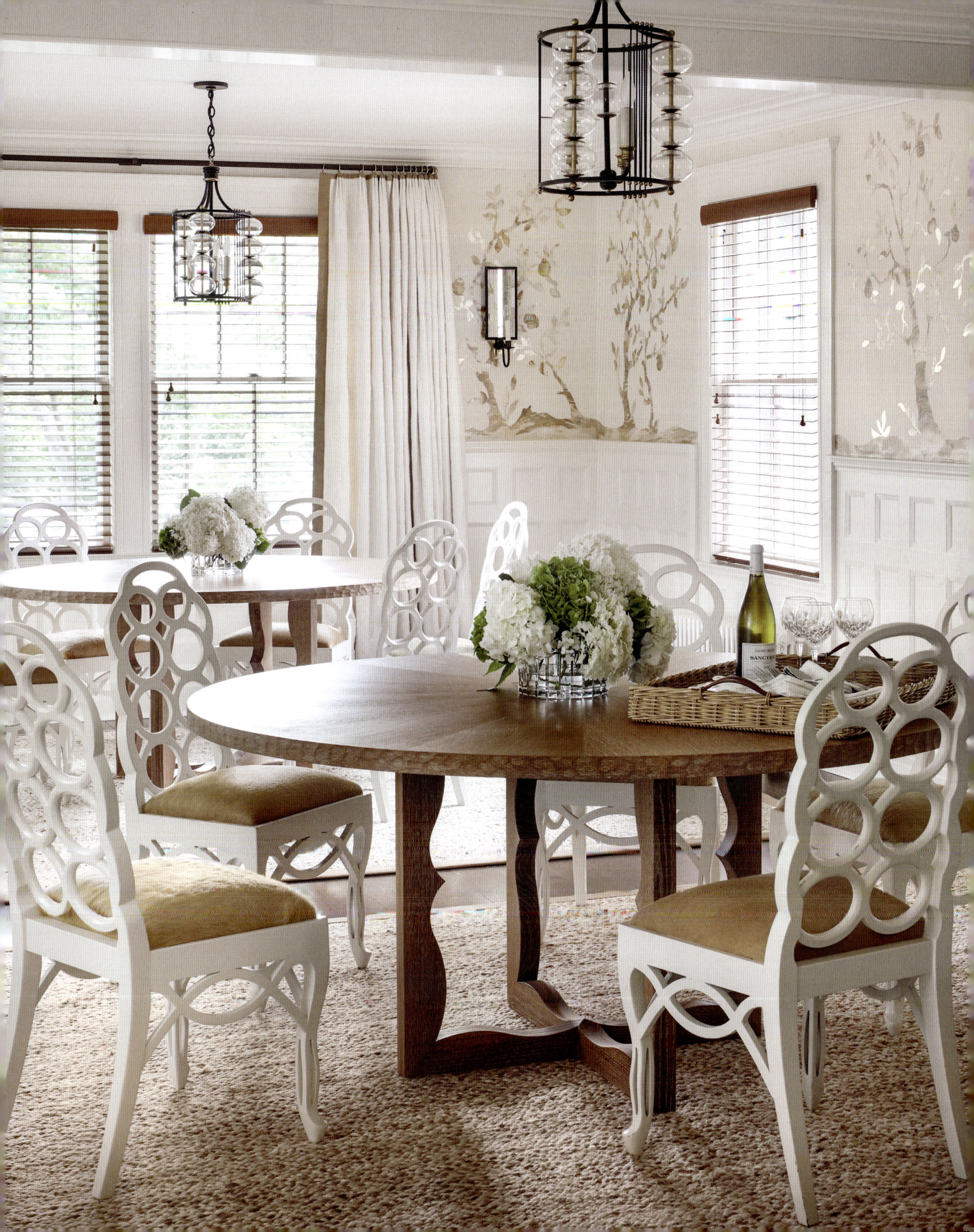

Inspiration *de* Matisse

While this home has punches of color throughout, none is more unique than the concept for the library. The client and I fell in love with a fabric from Madeline Weinrib that reminded us of Matisse's spirited cutouts, and the wall treatment flowed from there. I've always loved the works Matisse created with simple paper and scissors in the 1940s, and the idea of how he surrounded himself with them in mural, room-size works, such as *The Swimming Pool*, which he created for his dining room in Nice, France.

Collaborating with a decorative painter, we devised an adaption of the pattern that suited the scale of the room. The technique involves executing the design in plaster in the studio and then applying it to the wall like wallpaper. We tweaked the colors from the original to reflect the palette of the room by opting for colors with more depth. I often gravitate to these shades that are little off, finding they bring more interest to a space than standard ones.

The concept acts as the artwork for the room. It's a wonderful solution when there isn't a budget for art, or even when every other room is filled with art and things need to be mixed up. Most of all, it proves that inspiration can be found anywhere, but it doesn't hurt when it starts with one of the most beloved artists.

OPPOSITE: In the library, colorful patterned plasterwork was inspired by a vintage textile from Madeline Weinrib and executed in the spirit of Henri Matisse.

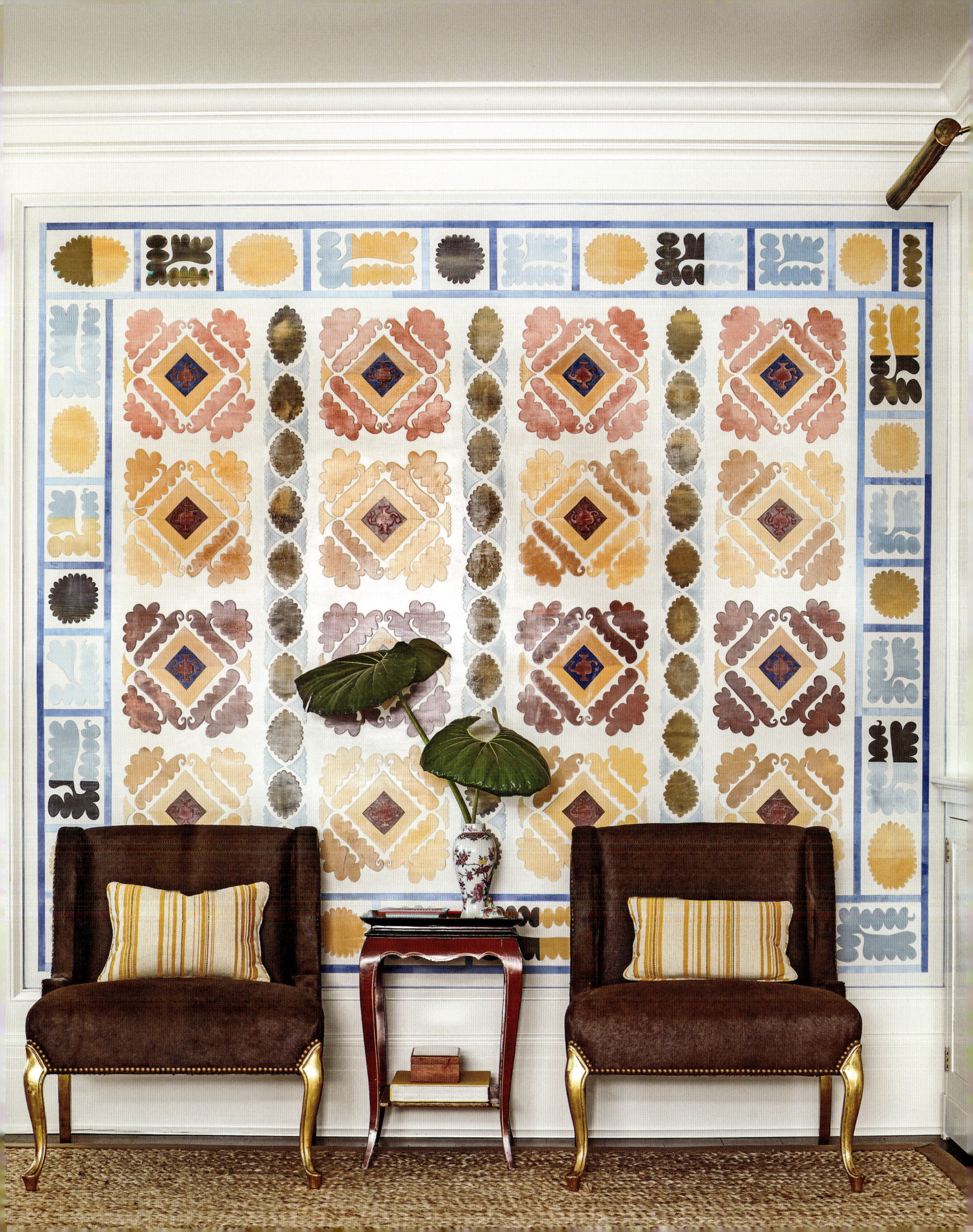

ABOVE: The entry vestibule is accessorized with beach hats and totes. OPPOSITE: The Dutch door beyond the breakfast area gives a bit of a country feel. A pendant from Soane hangs above the parchment-topped table from Vosges and is surrounded by vintage chairs from Lobel Modern.

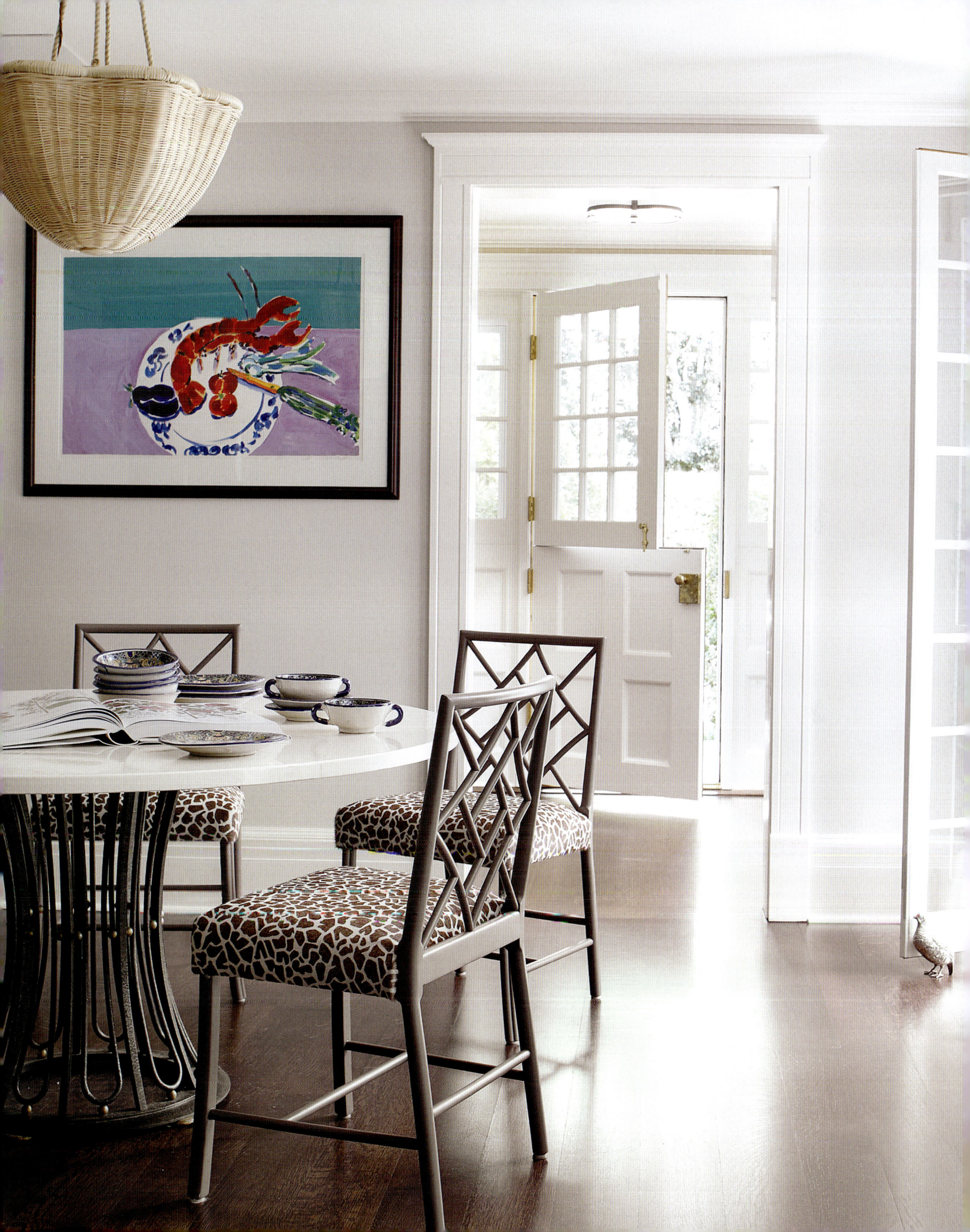

RIGHT: In the primary suite's sitting room, mirrored panels bring light into a windowless space, while a woven console from Soane feels both sculptural and beachy.

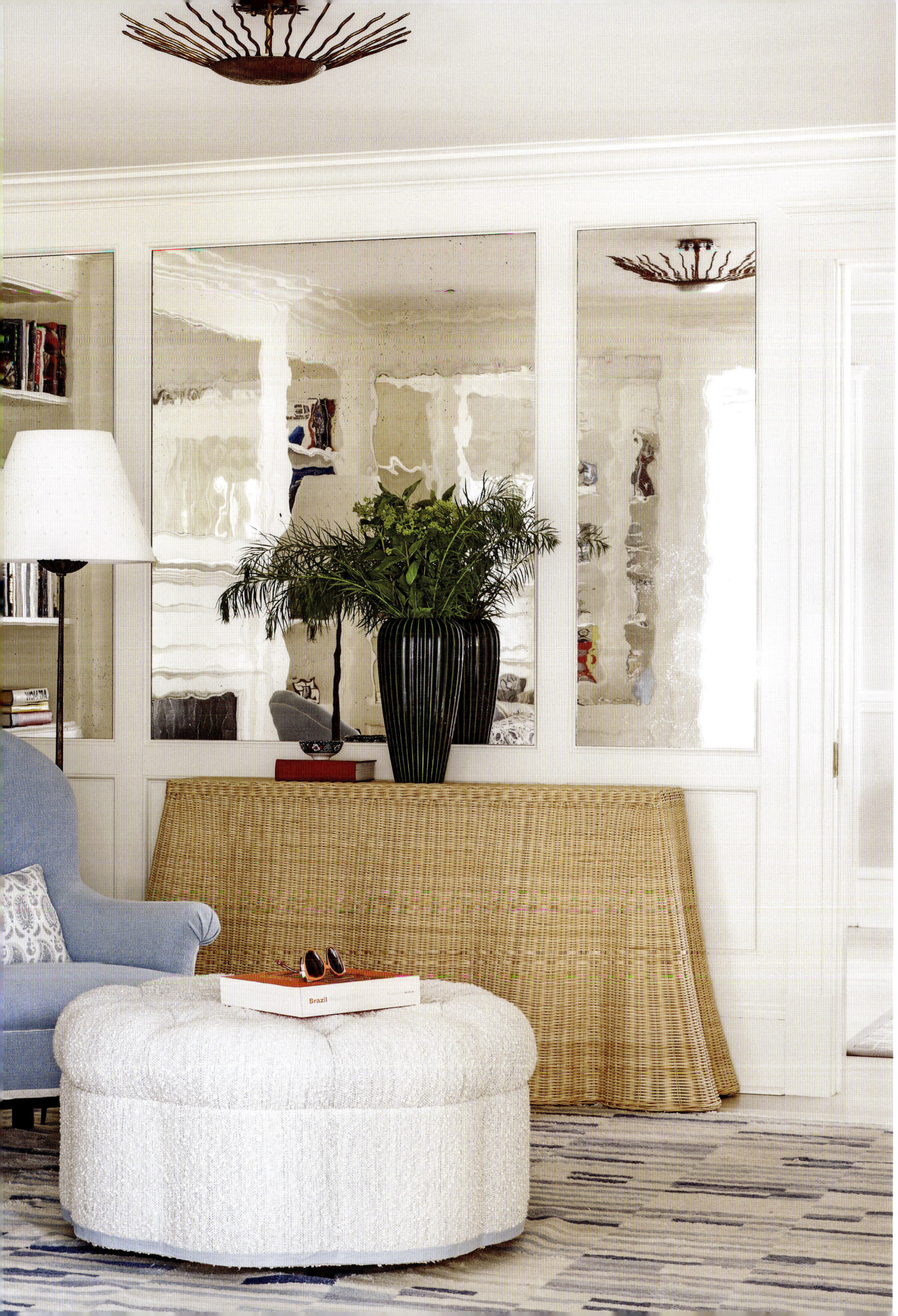
Brazil

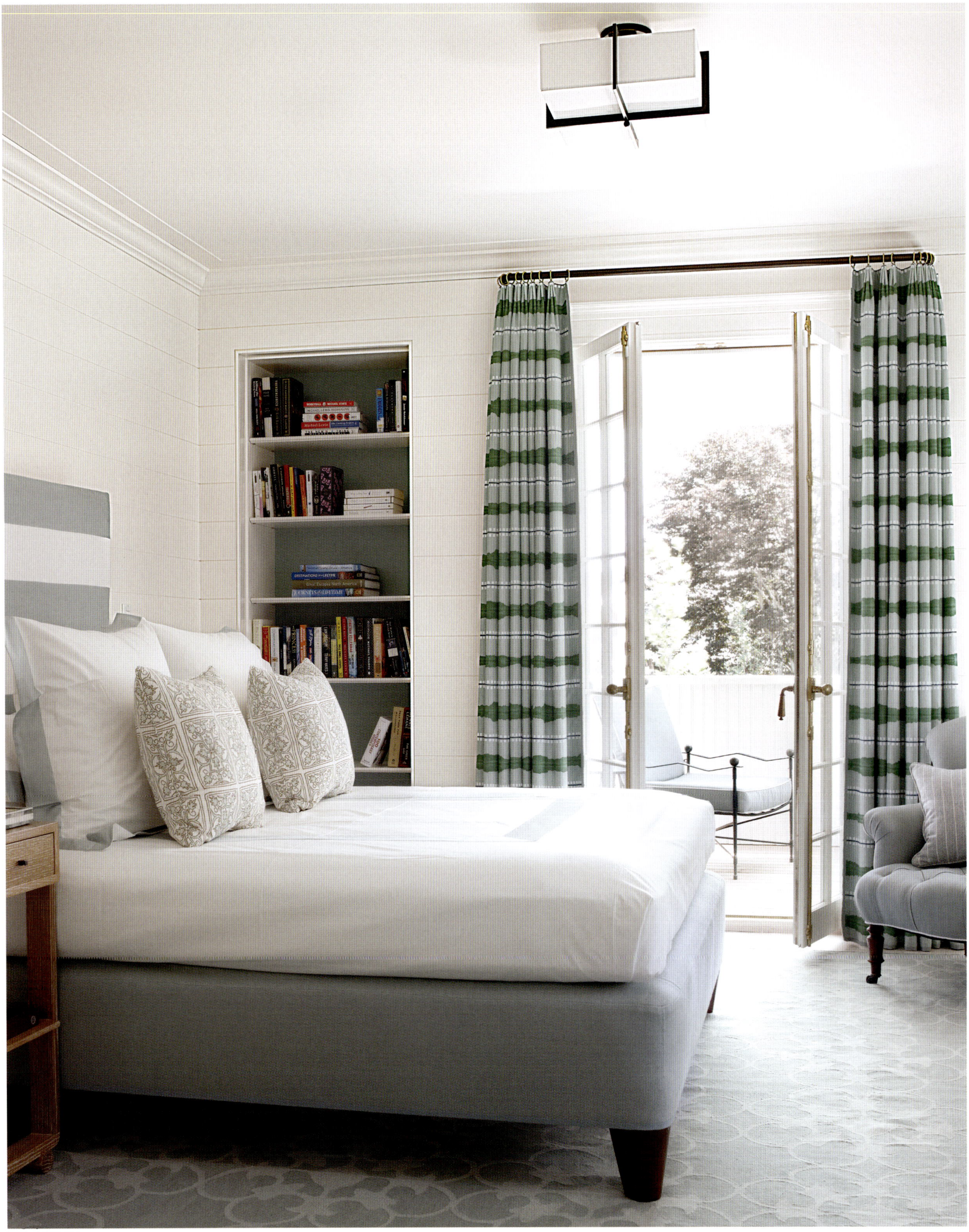

OPPOSITE AND ABOVE: Guest bedrooms should have distinct personalities and never be carbon copies of each other. OPPOSITE: Notes of blue are picked up from the curtains, made of fabric from John Rosselli & Associates, and then applied to the back of the bookshelves, the custom bed, and the Madeline Weinrib rug. ABOVE: A custom-stenciled pattern drawn from the curtain fabric provides an unexpected backdrop for a vintage Coca-Cola poster.

RIGHT: The existing porch was restored to its former glory, and the wide space has a mix of Sutherland outdoor furniture and vintage wicker pieces, upholstered in fabric by Quadrille, creating the ideal outdoor room.

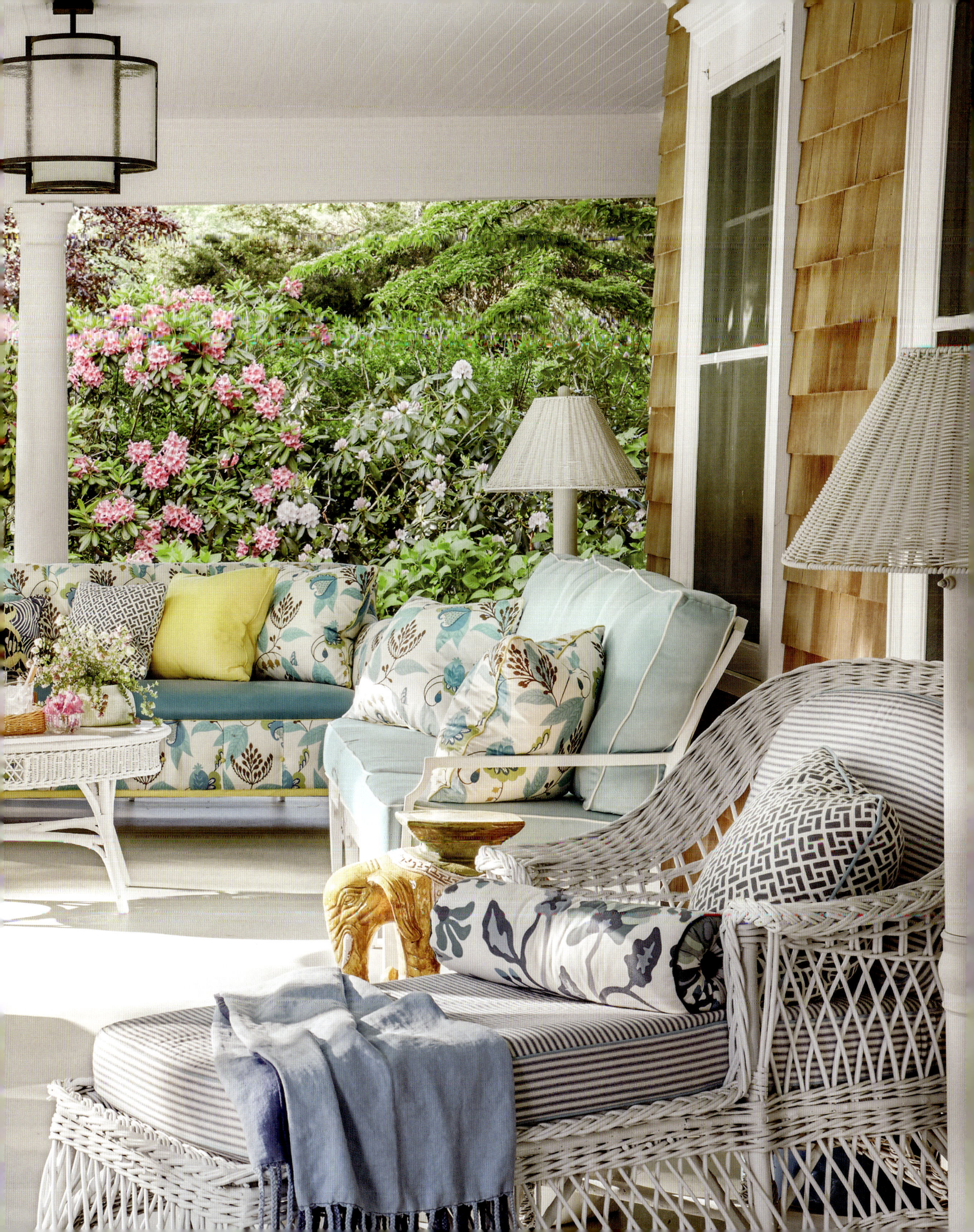

MALLORCA MODERN

When revealing a completed project to longtime clients, they told me they had something important to share with me. At first, I feared it was the worst news a decorator can hear after finishing an arduous installation: "We sold the house." But that wasn't it at all—quite the opposite. They had bought a beach home in Mallorca, Spain, and wanted me to work with them on the design. This time, they were interested in shaking things up and going with a much more contemporary look—even going so far as to say that they didn't want to have a single antique in the house, not even vintage pieces. Of course, I was excited by the prospect of creating something so far outside my usual tastes for classically shaped upholstery and a mix of antiques and vintage pieces. But the real dilemma remained how to work with all-new furnishings without having the space come across looking like a showroom.

When I arrived for my first site visit, I instantly understood their direction. Cantilevered off a seaside cliff and jutting into the Bay of Palma, the house was so incredibly modern, with lots of glass, hard edges, and an infinity pool. I decided that the decor could match this spirit but had to still feel unique. Quality Italian brands, like Minotti and B&B Italia, felt right in the contemporary space. Their angular lines complemented the architecture, and the low backs on the sofas made way for the views. Yet it was essential to mix in unexpected elements. Select pieces were covered in custom-woven fabrics, and some original designs such as the quirky pair of chairs with teardrop arms in the living room went a long way toward making things feel fresh.

The overall feeling of the home is established in the entry hall. Artisan Hubert Le Gall conceived the showstopper console that animates the space, and everything else fell into place around its wonderfully textured wood grain and contrasting parchment top. Its curves create rhythm and movement in the otherwise angular space. The white plaster Stephen Antonson mirror works beautifully with the white-and-cream palette, while the circles of its frame echo that of the cutouts in the pair of table lamps. Not everything needs to be beigey white, though.

OPPOSITE: In the entry hall of a home in Mallorca, Spain, a plaster mirror by Stephen Antonson presides over a wood and goatskin cabinet by Hubert Le Gall, who also created the open back chairs. A pair of lamps from Bernd Goeckler continues the circular theme. Wood floors were replaced with creamy slabs of local stone, which is ideal for the beachside location.

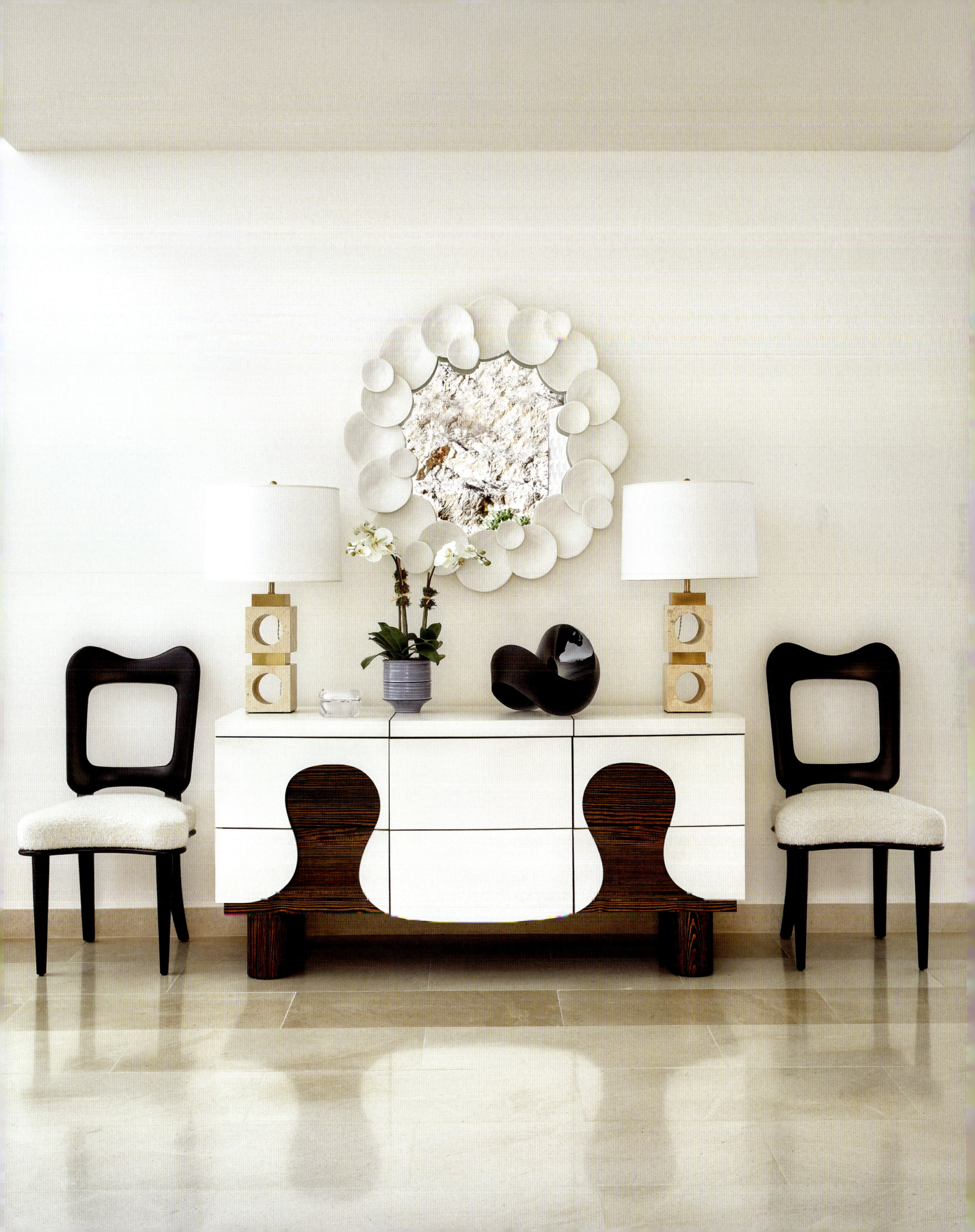

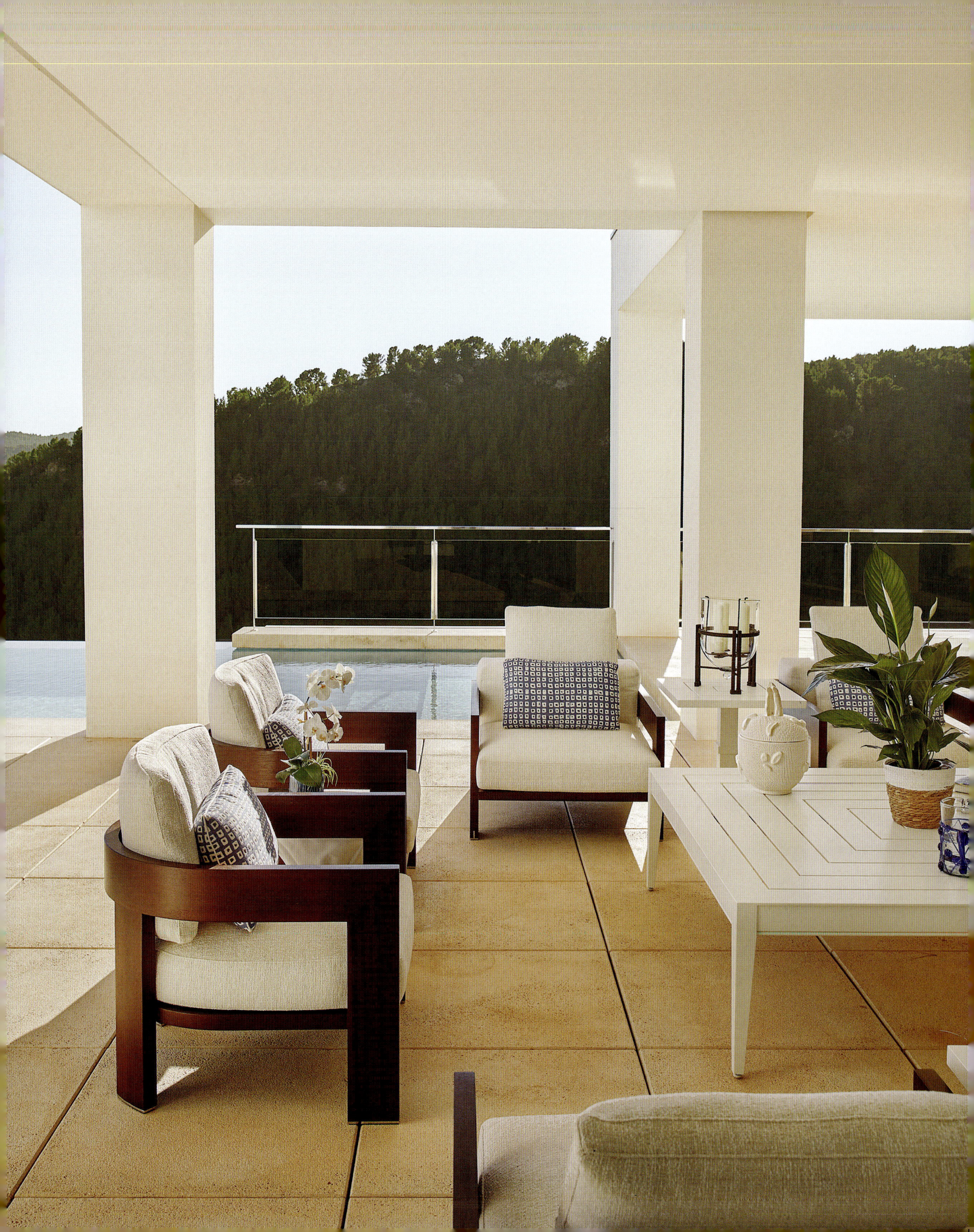

The black-framed, open-back chairs, also by Le Gall, provide just the right amount of contrast. Sometimes people think black comes across as too severe or too urban, but that contrast creates such a wonderful tension—a strong silhouette against the wall is all the proof one needs.

The expansive terrace plays an important role in how the homeowners spend time here, so it was essential that the area function as an outdoor room with comfortable seating for the family plus guests as well as dining tables. Again, I worked with a dark wood stain to provide a modern contrast with all the white upholstery. Patrice Dangel made the metal hurricane lamps, which provide such beautiful candlelight at night. A variety of blue-and-white accessories bring in shades from the sky and water. Those hues extend into the adjoining living room, which has a pale periwinkle tone on the ceiling, an array of center-button pillows, and a ceramic work by Kate Malone, who created three commissions for the home based on local indigenous plants. Small details like these bring a personality and uniqueness that make modernist homes welcoming and warm.

OPPOSITE: An outdoor living room on the sweeping terrace overlooking the Bay of Palma is furnished with seating by Minotti and a sand-blasted coffee table and side tables by McKinnon and Harris. The hurricane lanterns are by Patrice Dangel. ABOVE: The modern house's angular lines dictated the fresh, contemporary furniture direction.

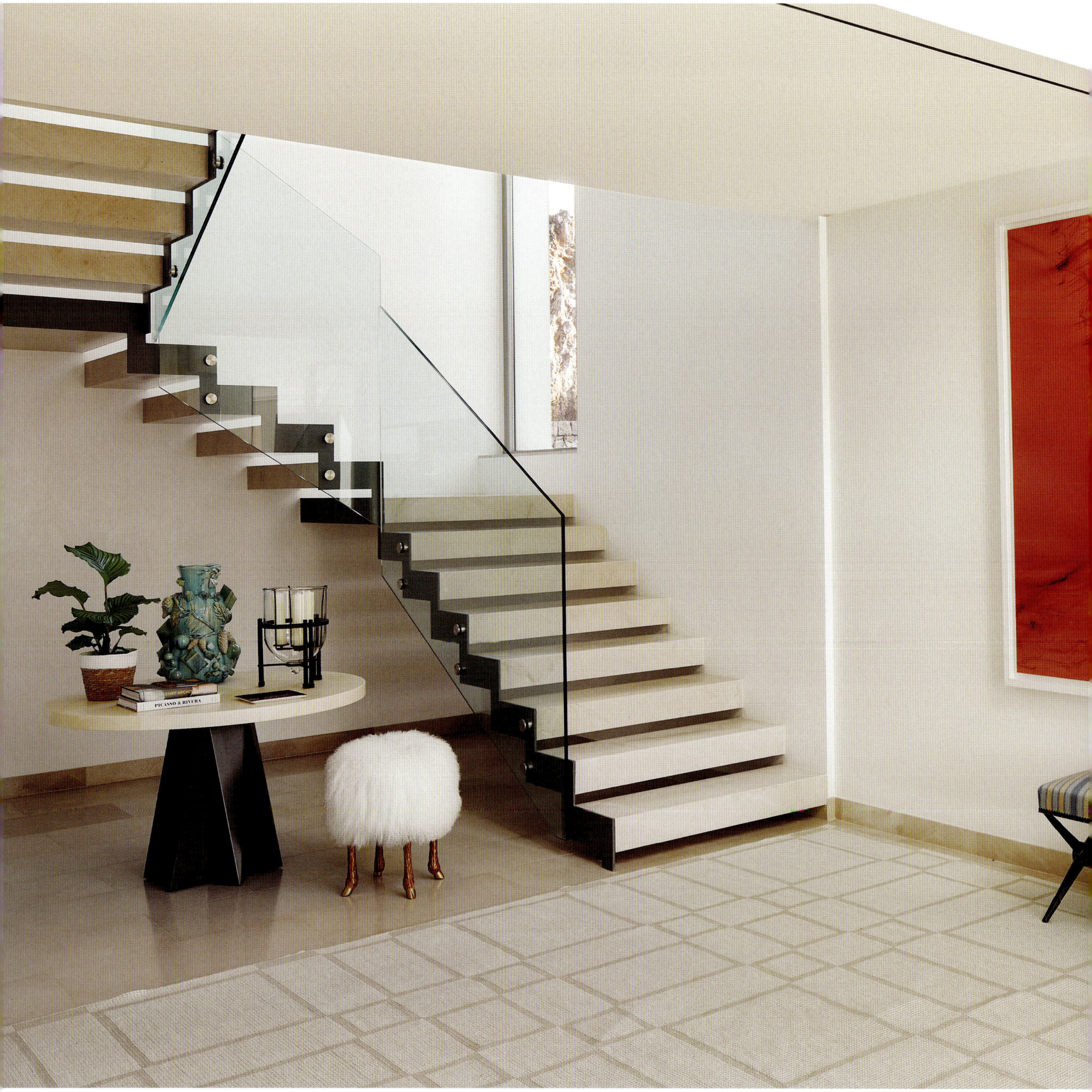
PICASSO & RIVERA

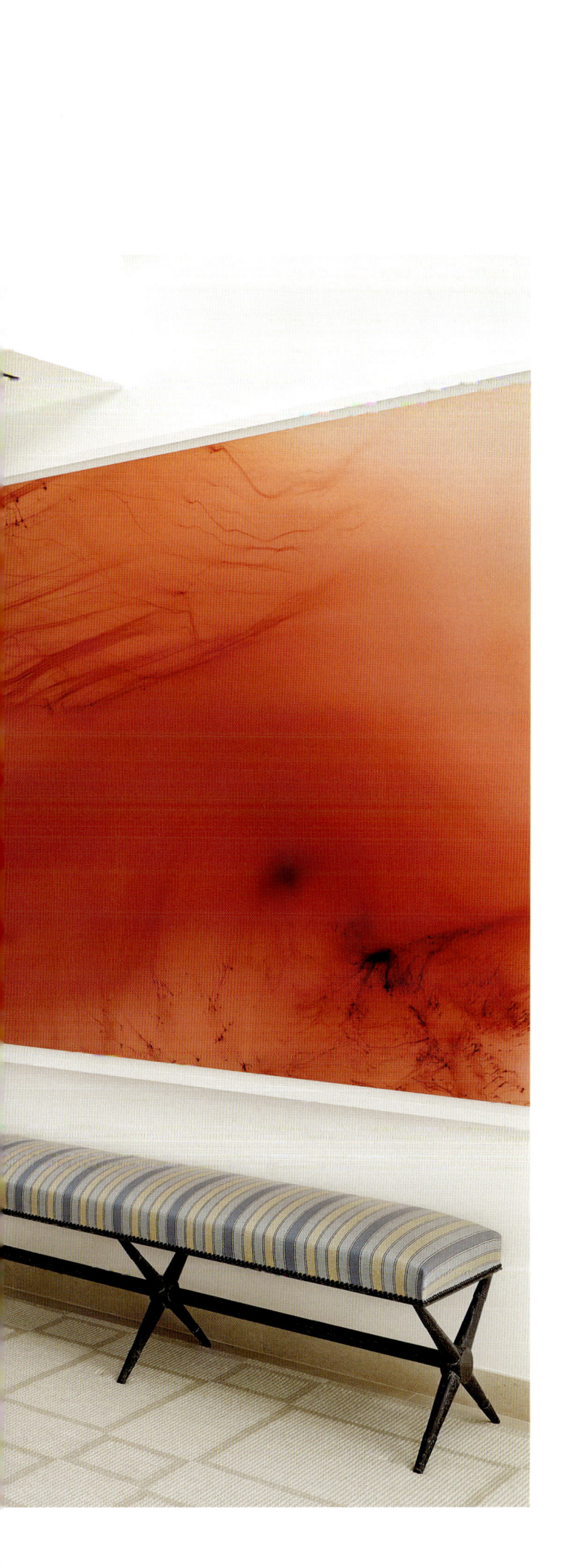

LEFT: The entry of the stair hall is enlivened by a Wolfgang Tillmans photo from the estate of George Michael purchased at auction. The entryway scheme of black and white is picked up again in the center table in the stair hall and complemented by the geometric rug. The striped-fabric-covered bench as well as the Marc Bankowsky lambskin stool bring some softness to the otherwise hard space. ABOVE: On the second floor of the entry, a Philippe Anthonioz chandelier is suspended above a Hubert Le Gall table with a black metal base. That insertion of black is picked up again in the frame around the canvas by Georg Baselitz.

RIGHT: Low-backed sofas and chairs by Minotti make way for the incredible views of the Bay of Palma from the living room. A pair of custom chairs is covered in a Tara Chapas fabric, and a Liaigre coffee table is adorned with a blue ceramic vase by Kate Malone.

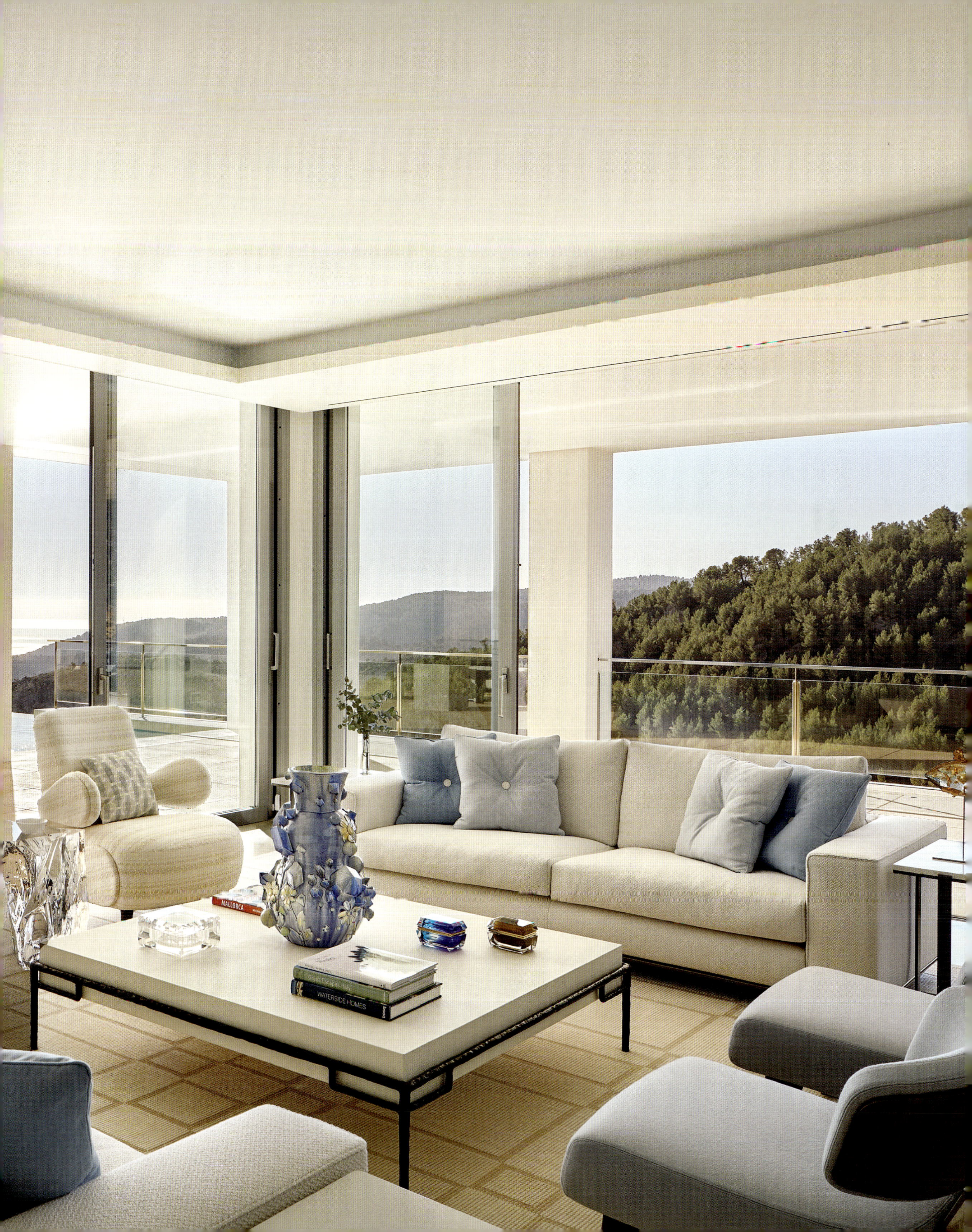

Adding Special Touches

Accessories and layering are essential to any project. But when it comes to rooms compiled of more widely available furniture, these details must work even harder. Whether it's art, objects, or a special accent piece, these additions elevate the design and bring it out of the dreaded straight-off-the-showroom look. In Mallorca, we had to balance all the contemporary Italian furniture with its clean lines with unexpected moments. For example, the teardrop chair with its unusual arms lends a personality that the other seating options in the room lack. When paired with the Fredrikson Stallard sculptural acrylic table, the conversation gets very interesting. The arm shape also echoes the wood grain shape in the Hubert Le Gall chest. In addition, we commissioned Kate Malone to create site-specific ceramics, for which she referenced indigenous plants and covered the works in aqua, amber, and sea-foam glazes reminiscent of the ocean. Bringing in unique pieces like these lends such personality to the space. Another detail that takes the design to the next level is great artwork such as a graphic Leon Polk Smith, which is paired with a bench covered in hide to accentuate the blue-and-black palette. Interesting furniture shapes, bold artwork, and unexpected accessories make the house truly feel like a home.

OPPOSITE, CLOCKWISE FROM TOP LEFT: Details complete the look throughout the home: a custom teardrop chair in a Tara Chapas fabric with a Fredrikson Stallard table, a ceramic vase by Kate Malone, a Leon Polk Smith artwork with a bench covered in hide, and the wood inset of a cabinet by Hubert Le Gall.

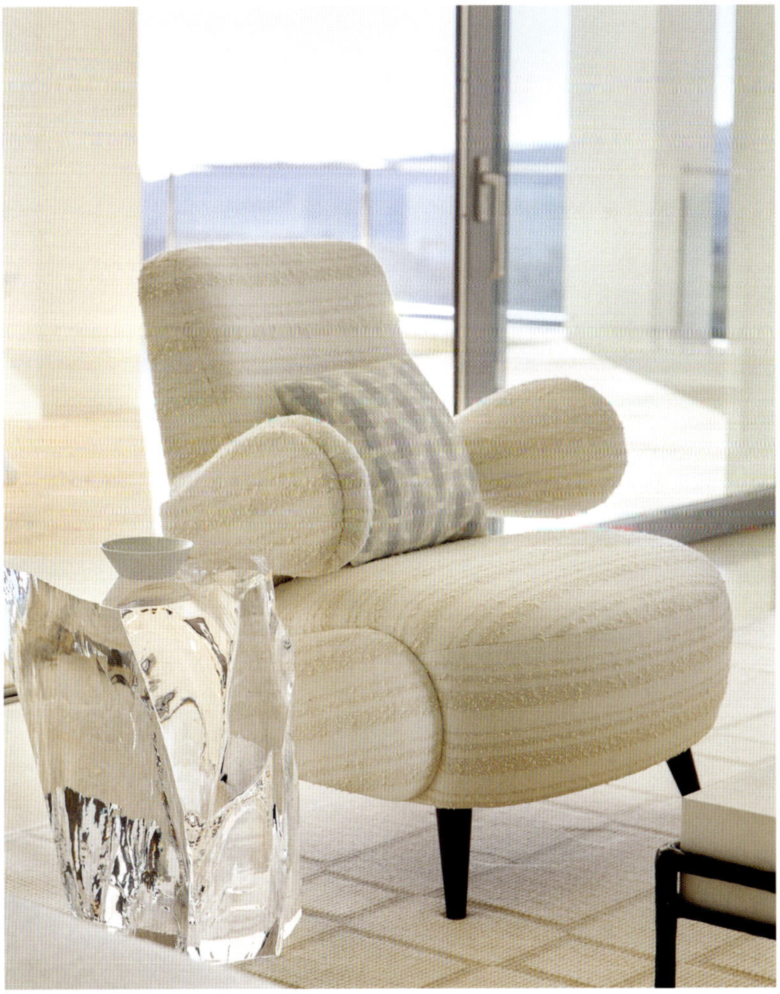
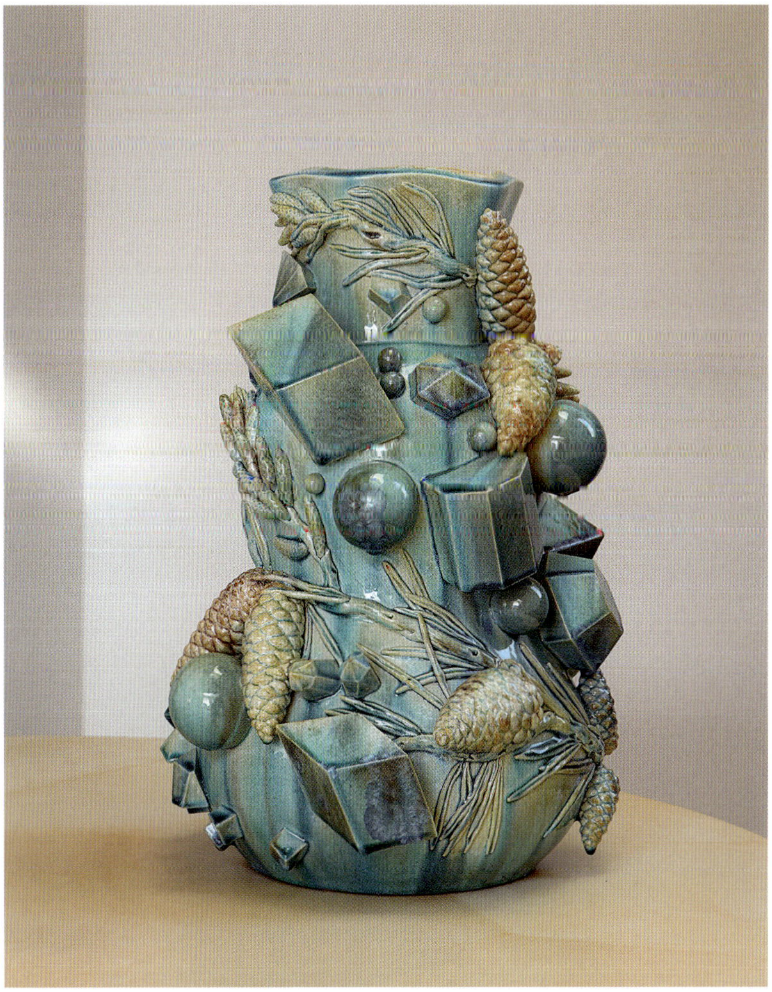
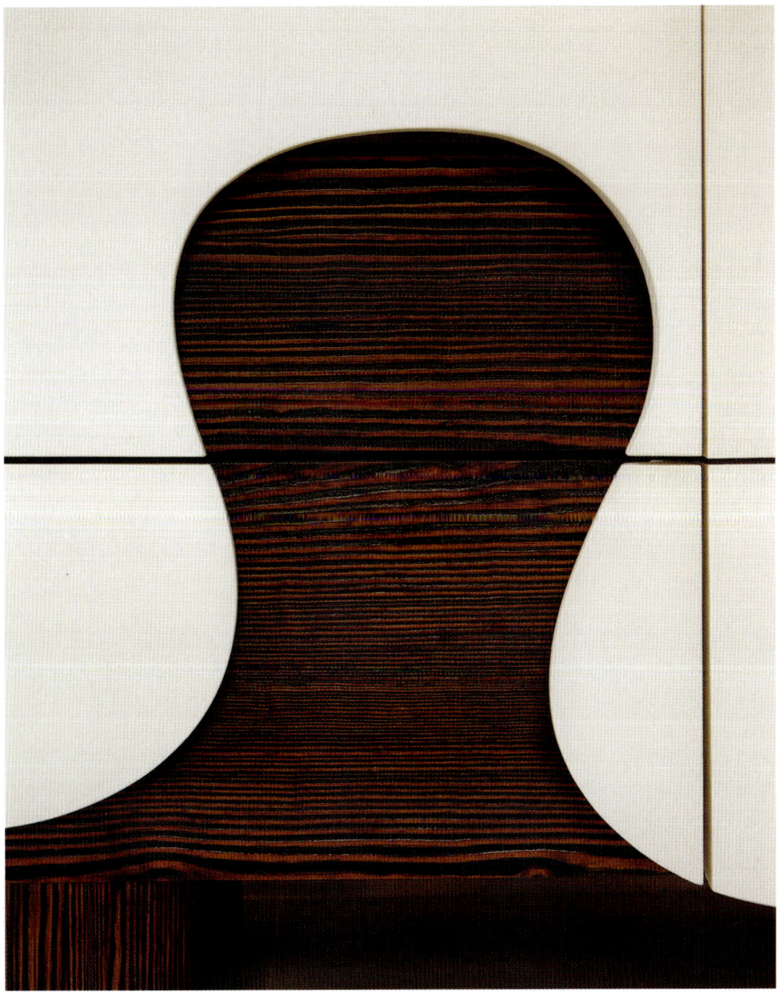
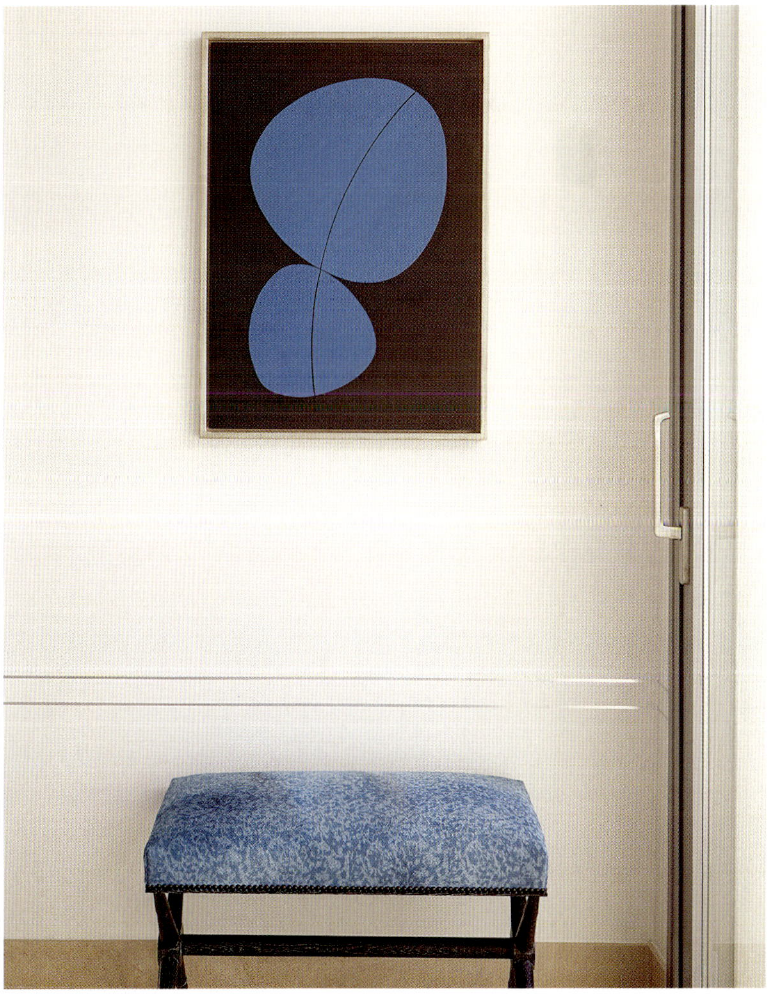

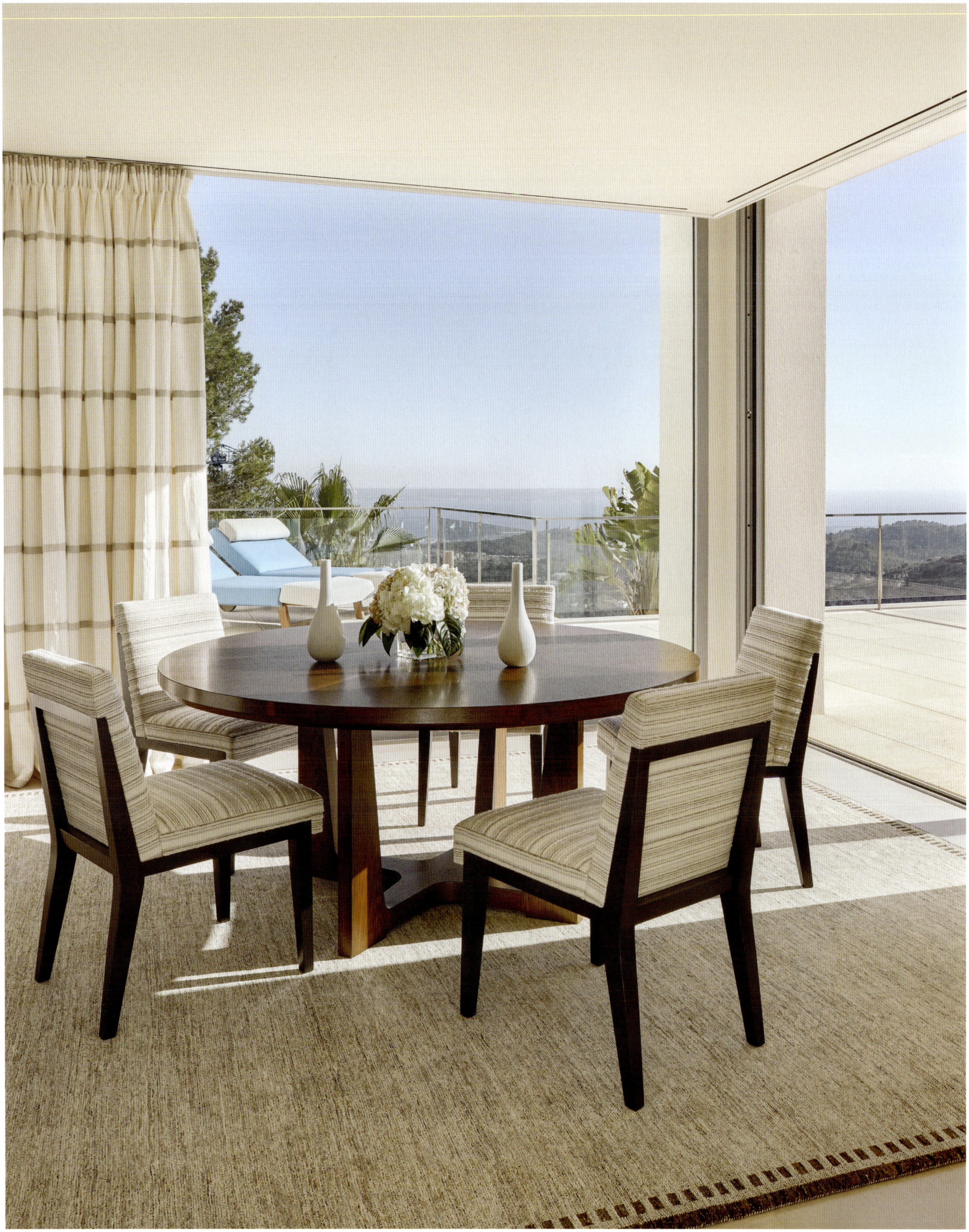

OPPOSITE: The dining room is composed of a serene mix of tactile neutrals, including a hand-tufted Beauvais rug, Holly Hunt table with chairs covered in a Tara Chapas fabric, and curtains made of a de Le Cuona linen with a modern banding. ABOVE: The sleek, white-lacquer kitchen is accented by stainless-steel appliances. A four-inch edge on the gray and white veined stone countertop brings a healthy dose of strength and modernity, while custom Jouffre stools in a Tara Chapas fabric soften the island.

RIGHT: Shimmering details, including a mirrored-glass wall sculpture by Rob Wynne, an Yves Klein coffee table, and silver banding in the Venetian plaster walls, bring life to the family room. Lighting acts as sculpture with an overhead chandelier by Minotti and a floor lamp by Mauro Fabbro. Pillows by Ankasa add new dimension to a sectional from Minotti.

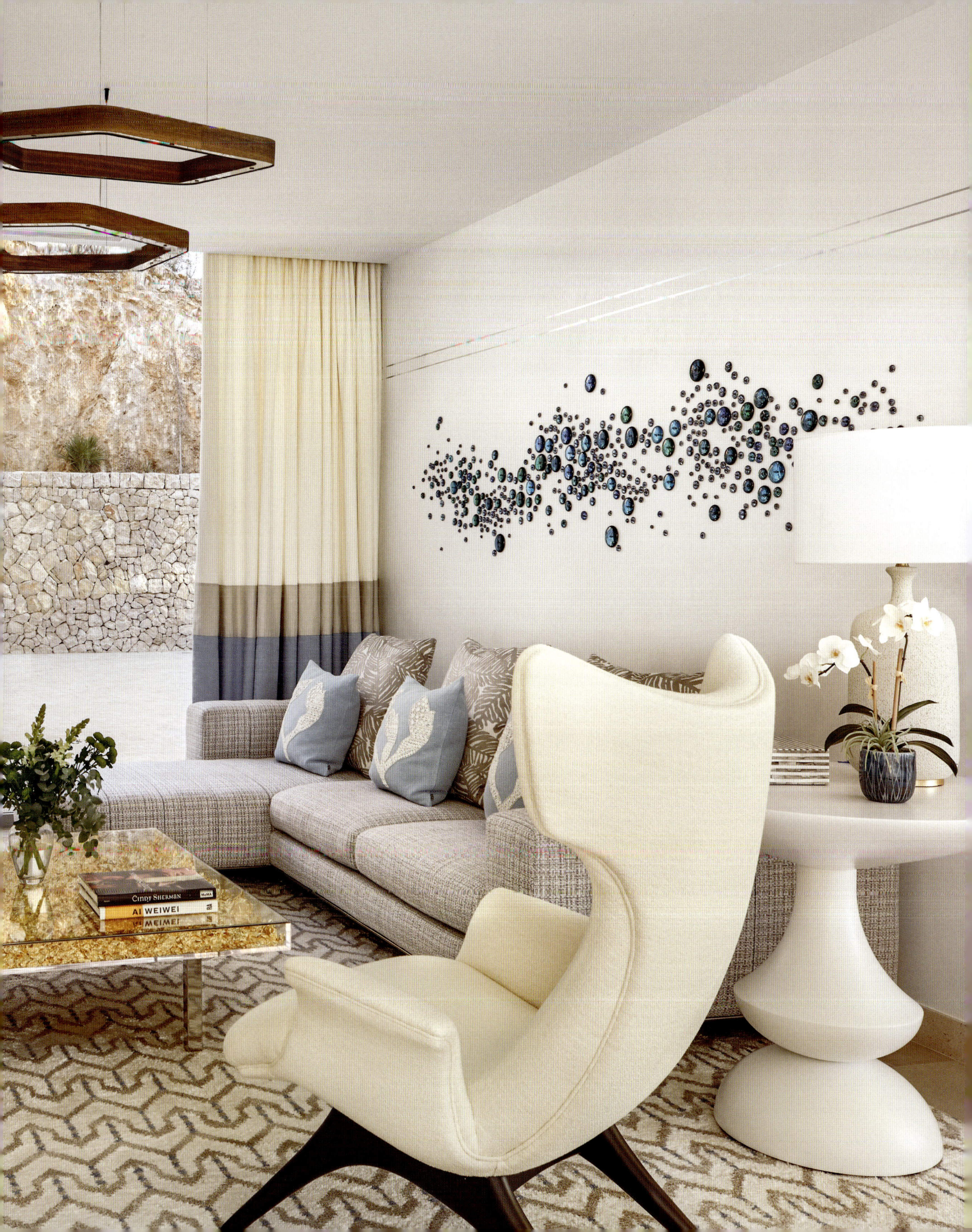
CINDY SHERMAN
MoMA
AI WEIWEI

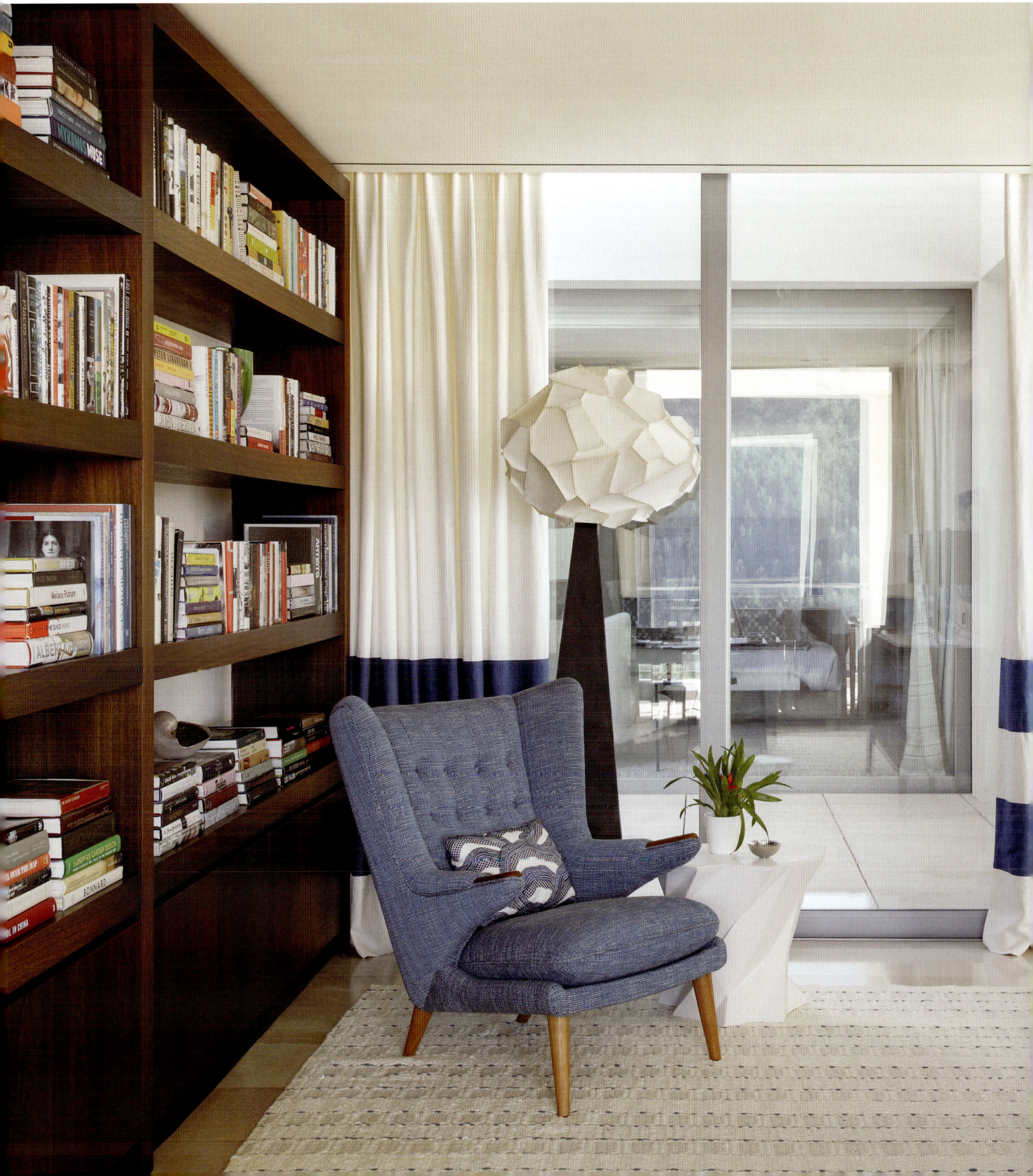

LEFT AND ABOVE: In the library, warm wood tones complement intense shades of deep blue in the Lucio Fontana artwork, the fabric on the Hans Wegner chair, and double banding on the curtains. The shape of the ceramics by Andrew Wick on the rich wood shelving reiterates the shade of the sculptural floor lamp by Mauro Fabbro.

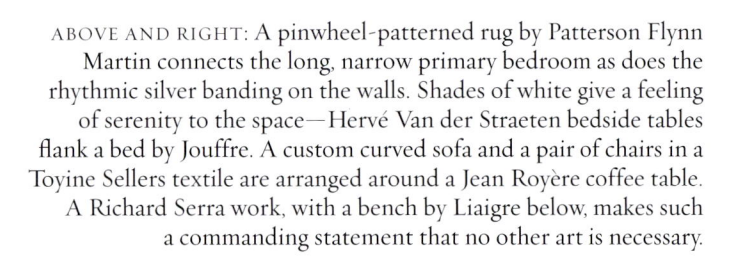

ABOVE AND RIGHT: A pinwheel-patterned rug by Patterson Flynn Martin connects the long, narrow primary bedroom as does the rhythmic silver banding on the walls. Shades of white give a feeling of serenity to the space—Hervé Van der Straeten bedside tables flank a bed by Jouffre. A custom curved sofa and a pair of chairs in a Toyine Sellers textile are arranged around a Jean Royère coffee table. A Richard Serra work, with a bench by Liaigre below, makes such a commanding statement that no other art is necessary.

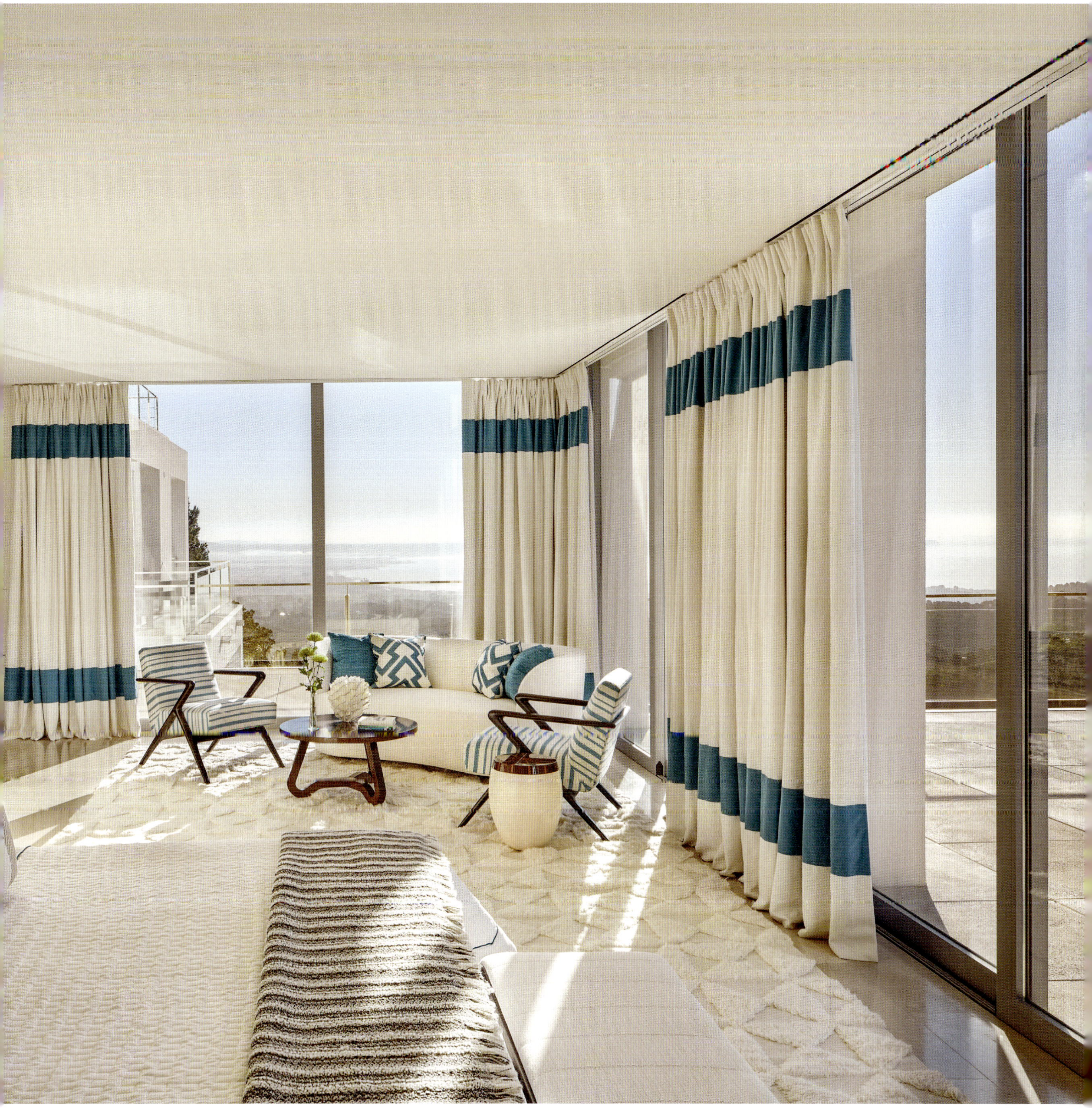

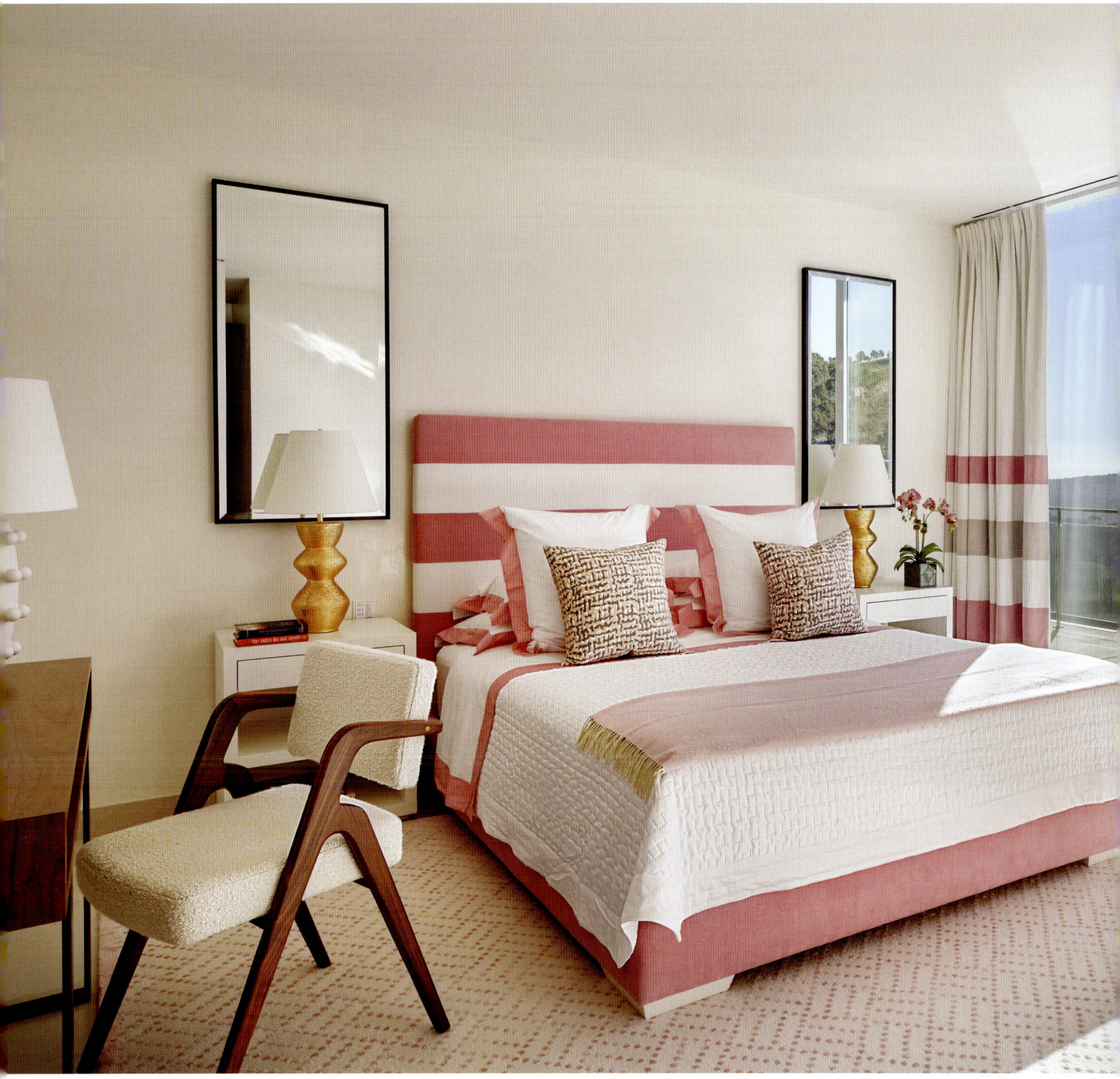

LEFT AND ABOVE: In the daughter's room, pink makes an appearance. The custom bed features horizontal pink-and-white stripes that emphasize the banding on the curtains. A pair of mirrors hung over the bedside tables adds something geometric while bringing in the light. The very modern bathroom gets a delicate contrast with pink-piped towels by D. Porthault.

ABOVE: In the guest bath, modern angular lines are warmed up with plush white towels and an array of accessories. RIGHT: Pattern comes into play in the guest bedroom. A graphic Patterson Flynn rug complements a Jim Thompson fabric for the curtains. The modern bed by Jouffre is dressed up with a stamped-hide bench from Vosges and flanked by Holly Hunt bedside tables. FOLLOWING SPREAD: A generous overhang providing ample shade allows the outdoor living room to be enjoyed all day—from reading the paper in the morning to enjoying cocktails in the early evening.

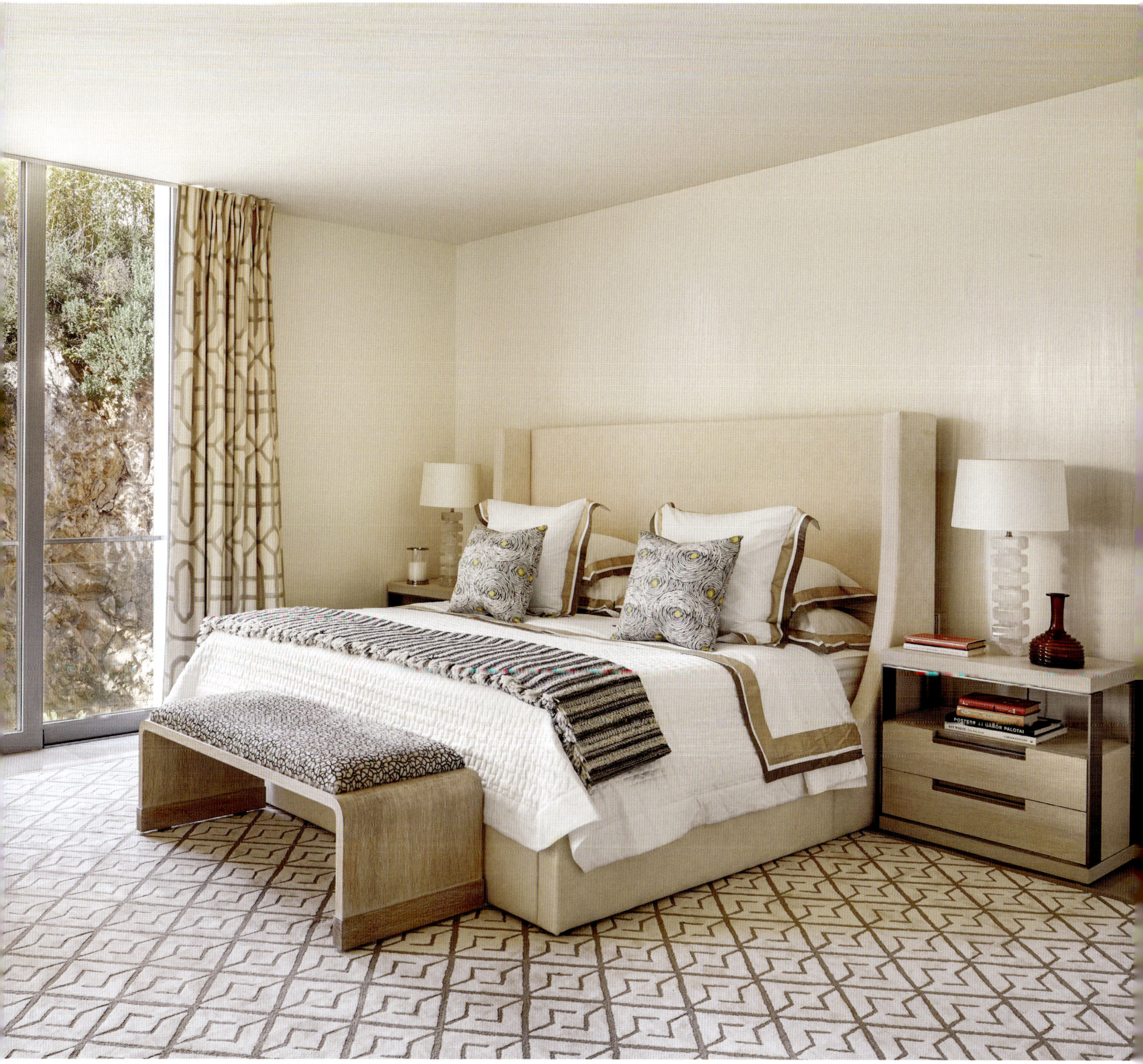

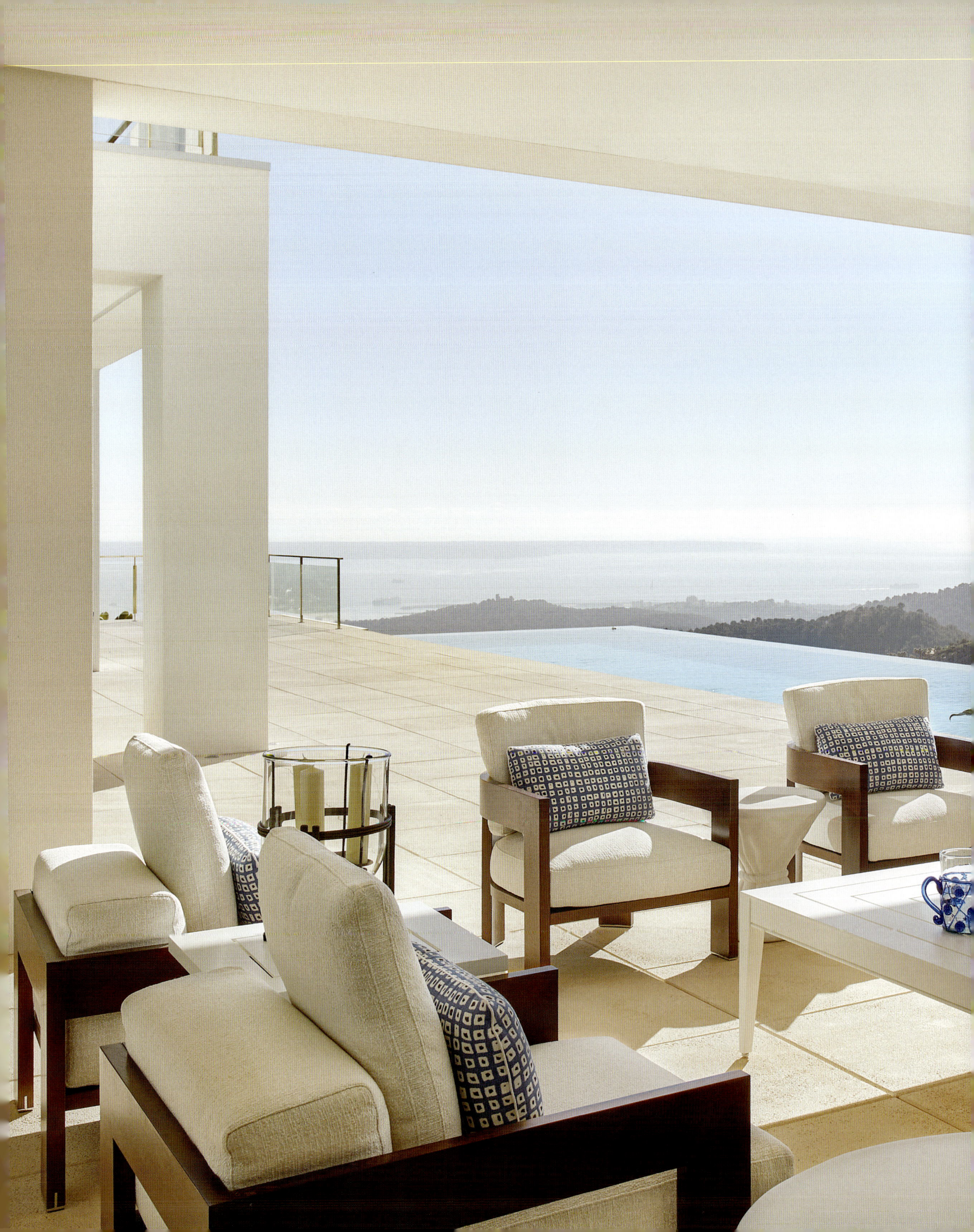

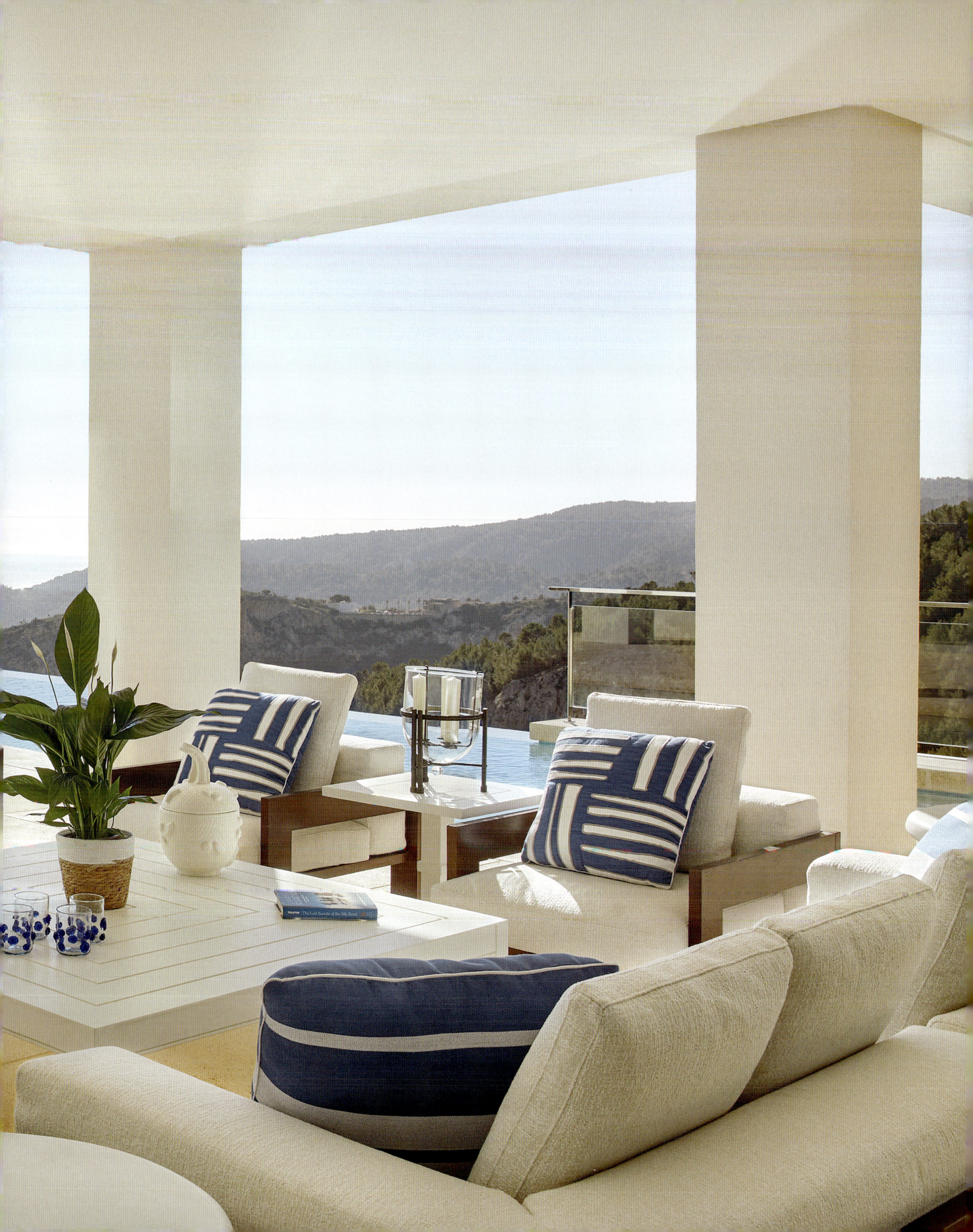

A POSH SOUTHAMPTON COUNTY HOUSE

When a young couple with two children reached out for help with their first home in the Hamptons, I knew that budget and comfort would be top priorities. Working with an impersonal spec house, I still found ways to make the space functional, friendly, and stylish. The entryway sets the beachy tone. A chandelier by artisan W. P. Sullivan takes advantage of the soaring ceiling height and was worth the splurge for the impact the handsome fixture creates.

From room to room, elements of blue make an appearance: chairs around the games table in the family room, the striped sofa in the library, and a cigar chair in the living room. The homeowners love the color, and I agree that the hue fits so well at the beach. But when any client gravitates toward a choice, as a decorator you must use it sparingly. When given options, clients will go with what makes them comfortable time and again, and you can't let them make the rookie mistake of choosing the same thing. There's no quicker way to dull any existing charm and style.

Throughout the house, the furniture reflects a tendency toward the traditional. Classic pieces can evolve with the family and their tastes over time. To make the most of the view in the great room, the sofa faces out toward the pool and the garden. This plan also allows for a console behind the seating area that divides the large space into living and dining areas as well as serving as a buffet. Flanking the sofa with a pair

OPPOSITE: In a home in the Hamptons, the double-height entry hall takes on a welcoming personality with a W. P. Sullivan light fixture, a graphic rug from Todd Alexander Romano, and a vintage center table from Balsamo. Each piece has a strong point of view because they must stand up to the thirty-foot ceiling height.

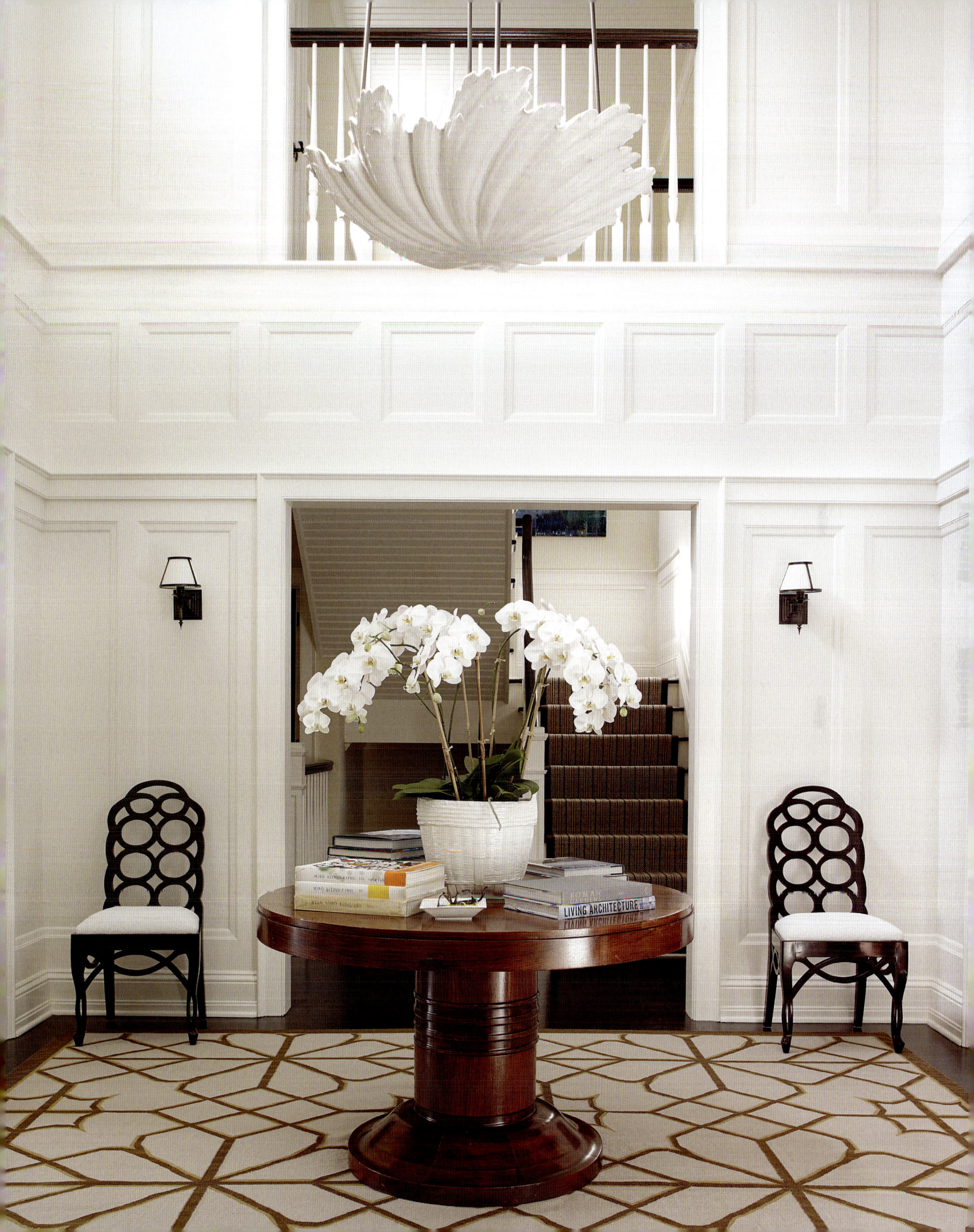
LIVING ARCHITECTURE

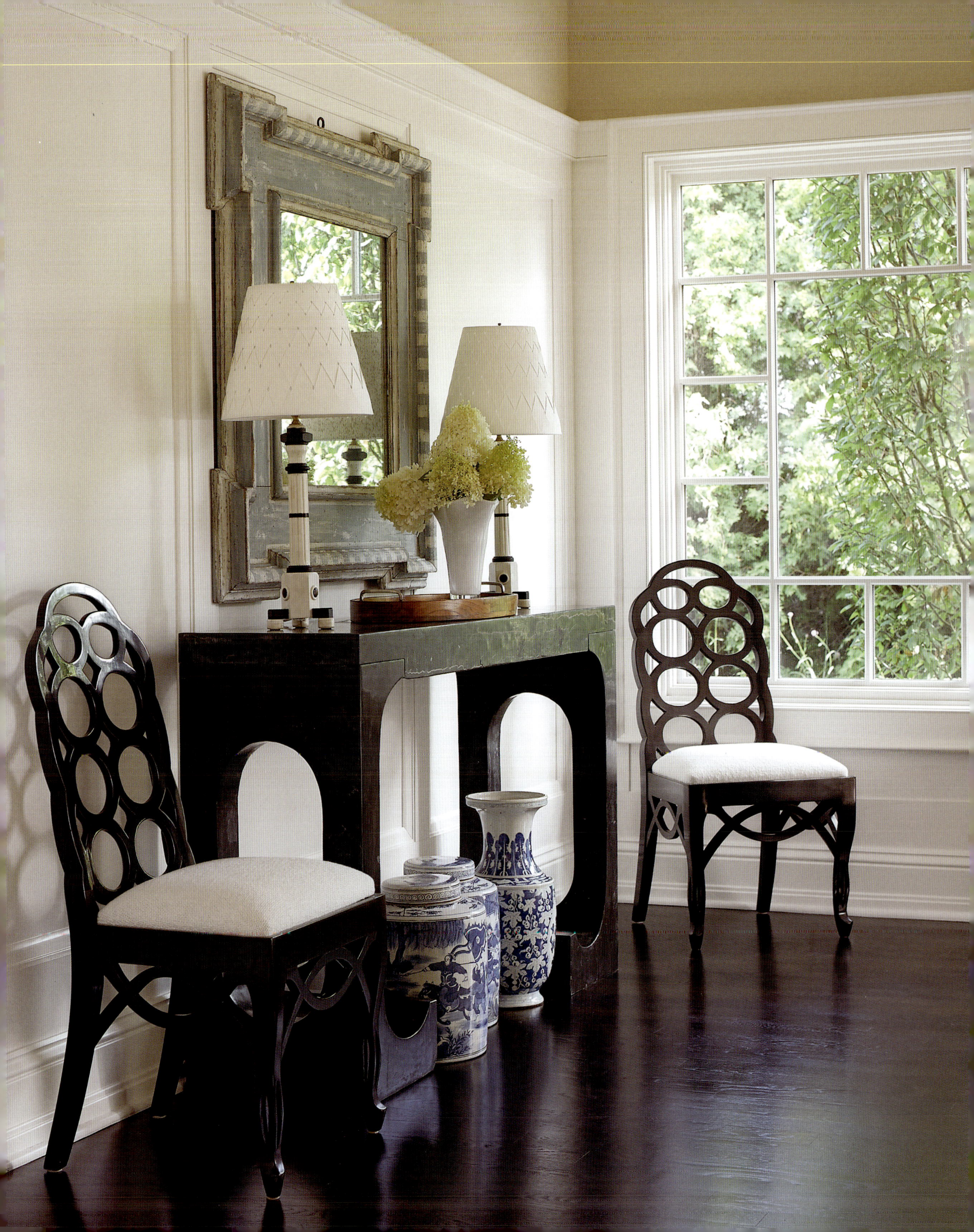

of spiral plaster floor lamps helps to define areas in the large space. I had seen this done long ago in a Mark Hampton project and always marveled at the genius of how they brought light into the center of the room as well. Recognizing the expanse of the wall, we commissioned a pair of paintings by Susan Vecsey, a friend of the client. An artist with studios in both East Hampton and New York City, her modern landscapes lend a sense of place and evoke the local scenery as well as the works of Mark Rothko and Helen Frankenthaler. That breezy, out East feel is furthered by the unlined linen curtains that soften the long run of windows that leads out to the pool.

I turned up the drama, albeit quietly, by allowing bright artworks to dominate an otherwise creamy palette. A set of four loop-back chairs provide a graphic element upon arrival. Another playful element is the set of trestle chairs covered in a bold blue South China Seas fabric. All these seemingly small additions make the room standout and lend a certain sensibility without requiring a hefty budget. But more than that, they strike the perfect balance between young and sophisticated, comfortable and attractive—exactly the point of this home.

OPPOSITE: A sunny corner of the entry is outfitted with a mirror from John Rosselli & Associates and a pair of Frances Elkins loop chairs. A display of blue-and-white porcelain animates the area under the stone console.
ABOVE: The exterior of the family-friendly, shingle-style house offers a porch and a pool area for gathering.

RIGHT: In the family room, two paintings by Susan Vecsey surmount a pair of chairs upholstered in a Carleton Varney print. A generously sized coffee table from Lars Bolander invites relaxation and conversation. The positioning of the sofa takes advantage of the view out to the pool.

Riefenstahl Africa
BOB RICHARDSON
CHANGING NEW YORK
KANDINSKY
From Folly to Follies

Commitment to Local Artists

Art finishes a room like no other accessory. As prices for many well-known artists continue to soar at auction and in galleries, I find that filling a home with local talents, even if they aren't yet bold-faced names, brings an unparalleled level of personality. Just a stroll through neighborhood galleries can reveal a wealth of possibilities that enliven any room with their connection to place. With time, there's the opportunity to establish a real collection devoted to a locale that shows the eye of the collector.

In the Hamptons, there's the added benefit of so many fantastic artists choosing to find their inspiration there. For this home, the couple had a personal relationship with Susan Vecsey, so her paintings can be found throughout. There's an ethereal magic to how she takes a landscape and strips it down to abstraction. Her works truly capture the mood of the beach—without being beach paintings at all. In the guest room, a jockey painted by Southampton artist Henry Koehler, beloved for his equestrian and sailing scenes, adds dimension and a bit of history. His 1960 *Sports Illustrated* cover of a regatta led Jacqueline Kennedy to have him paint a portrait of her husband, John F. Kennedy. These types of stories bring so much to an interior.

RIGHT: The traditional arrangement of the living room is warmed by a Jane Wilson painting above a chair upholstered in a jolly Robert Kime print, vintage silk ikat pillows, and a pair of Christopher Spitzmiller lamps.

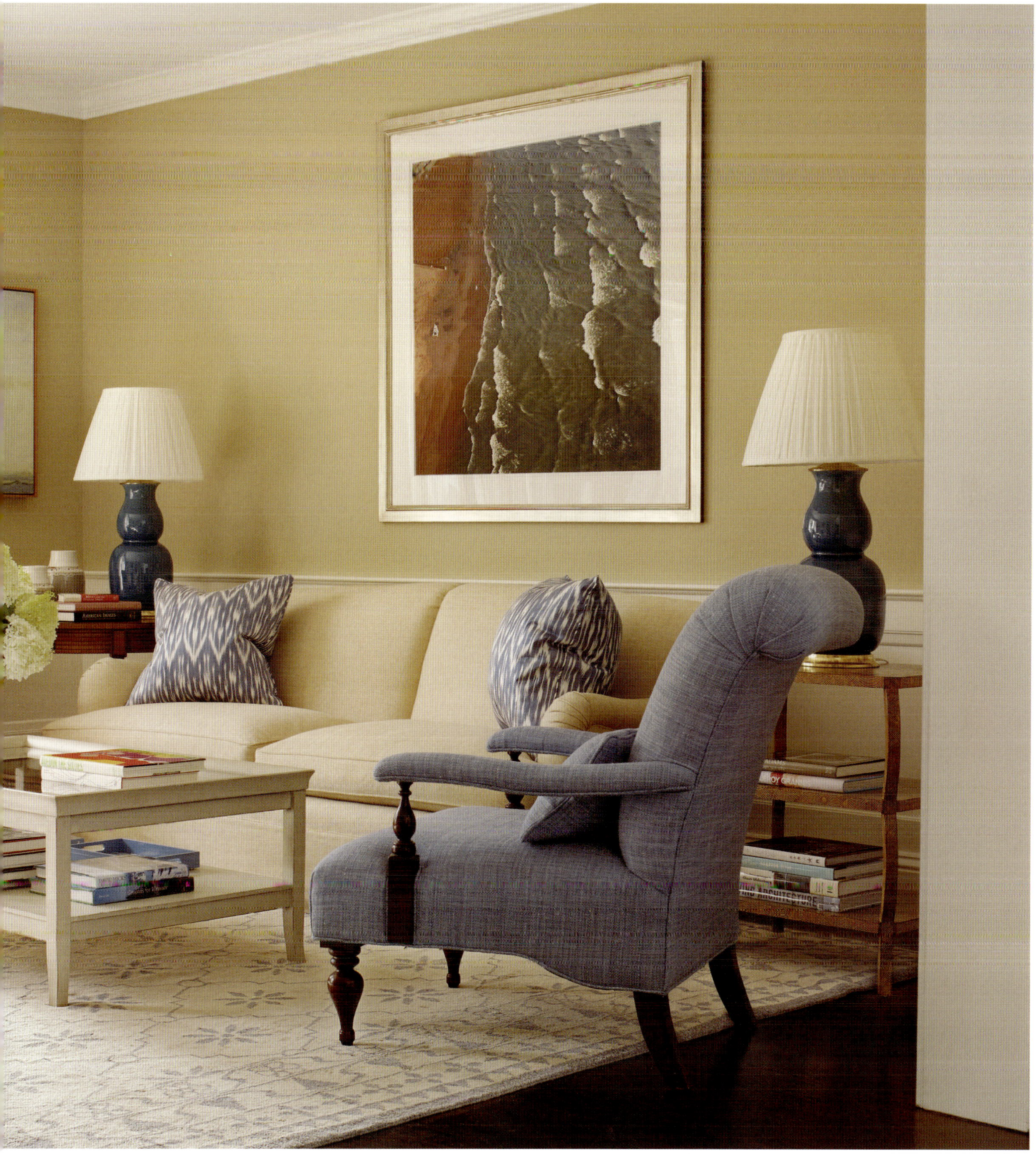

ABOVE: A clean, white kitchen with glass-front cabinets is accented with woven bistro chairs. OPPOSITE: A painting by Günther Förg and a blue-and-white Quadrille fabric add zip to the family room. A vintage spiral floor lamp is the perfect solution for bringing light into the center of the room.

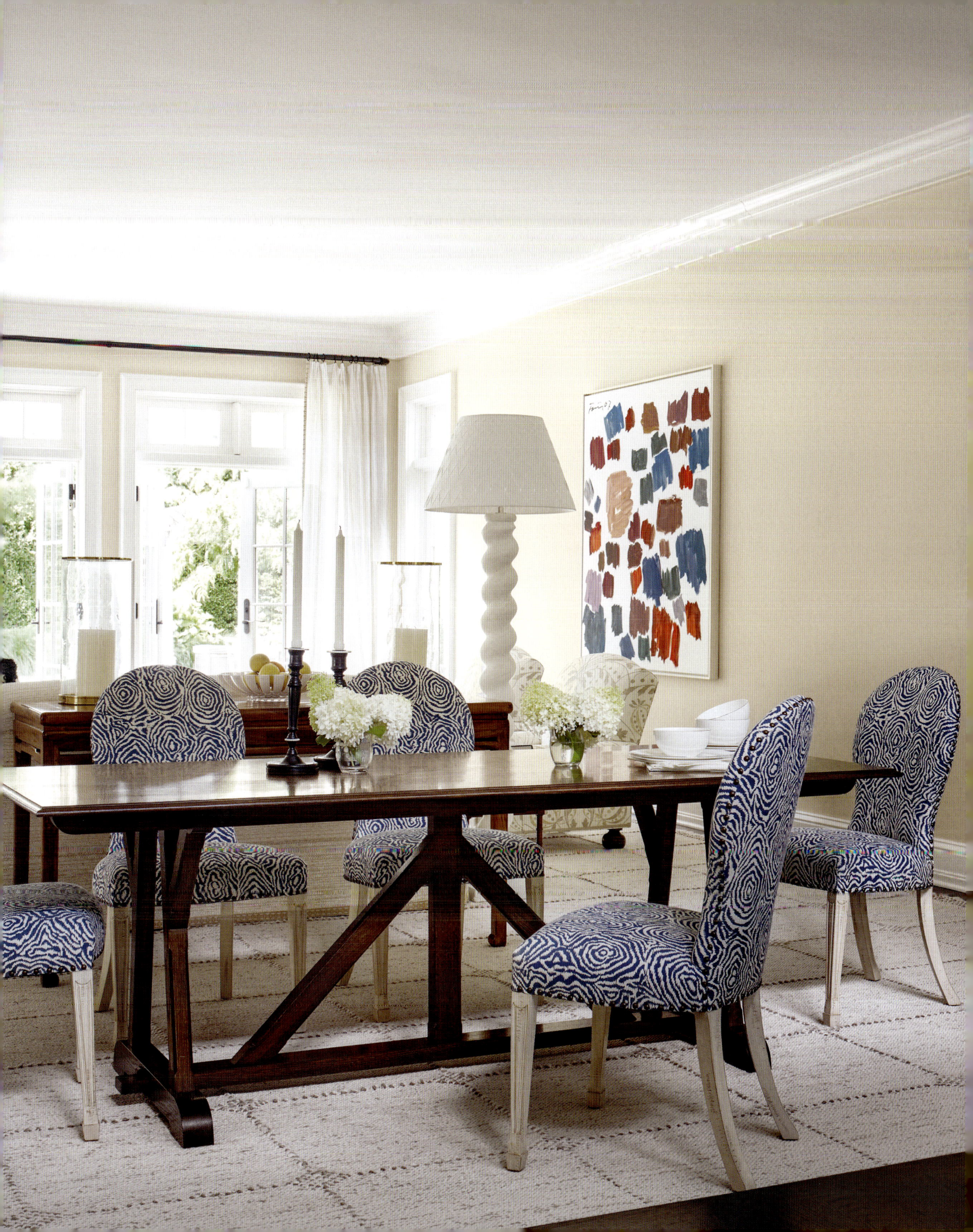

ABOVE: A well-made bed is the heart of any guest room. As long as the sheets are crisp and the pillows are plentiful, visitors are happy.
RIGHT: A Susan Vecsey painting hangs atop striped wallpaper by Farrow & Ball. A Schneller chair covered in Quadrille fabric along with a custom bamboo bed and bench make for a cozy bedroom arrangement.

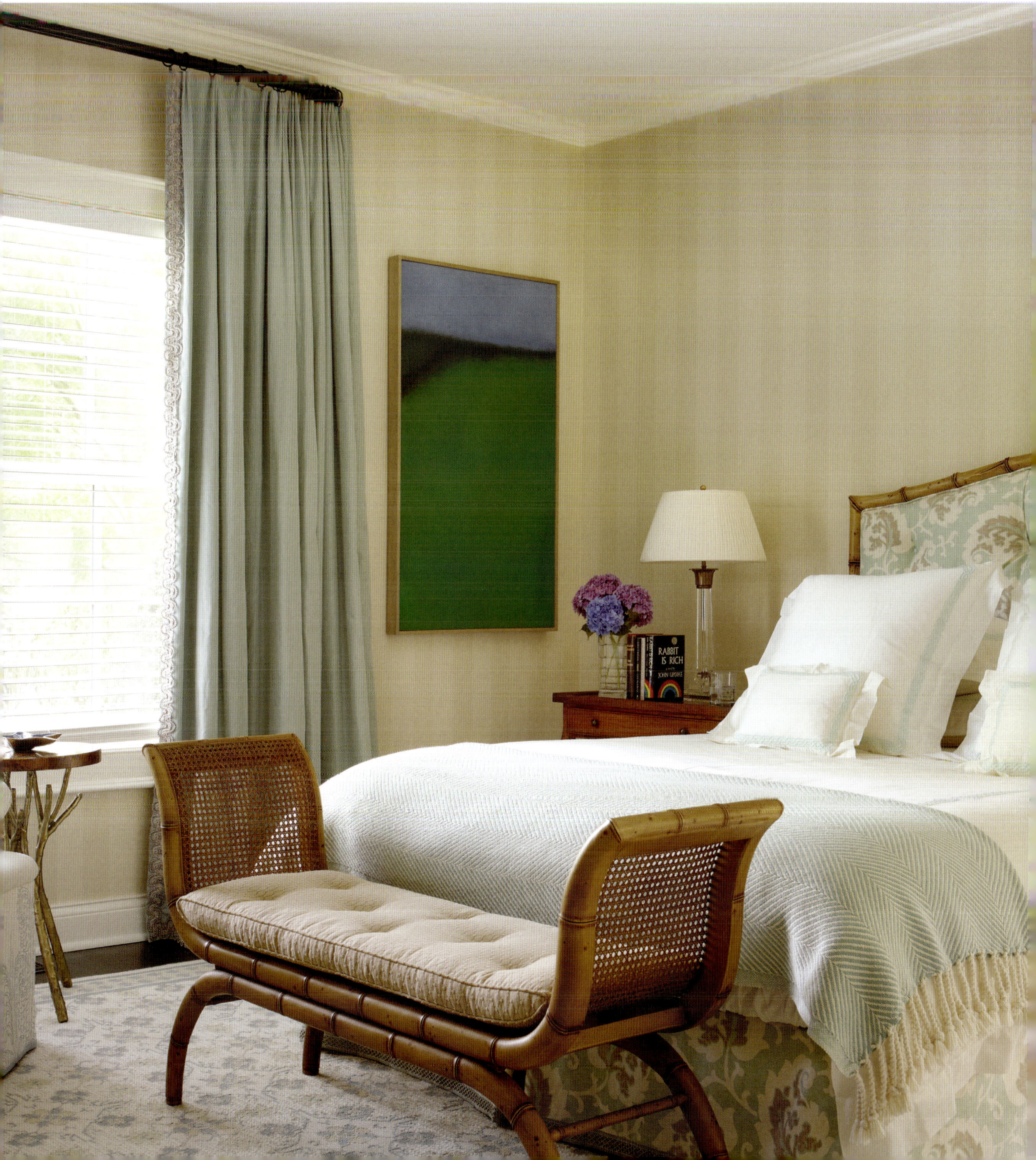
RABBIT IS RICH
JOHN UPDIKE

TOP O'DUNE

For me, the Hamptons mean spending time with family. Every summer, I head East to our home in Southampton, known as Top O'Dune. Built in 1889, this shingle-style cottage certainly stands out among the others that line the beach. With a distinctive octagonal tower that resembles a windmill and recalls the agricultural spirit of the community's past, the home is one of the original cottages built along Gin Lane when New Yorkers started to venture to the farthest reaches of Long Island with the extension of railway service. Over the decades, there have been a series of renovations, but for us, it's always been crucial that they preserve the original character of this place, especially its unique asymmetry and facade of windows that face this way and that.

The most recent updates were made to the breakfast room. To freshen things up, I added shiplap walls and had the floor stenciled in a pattern inspired by the designer Albert Hadley. Since the room was once a porch that had been enclosed, the ceiling is painted a traditional pale blue. There's even a ship's bell to call everyone down when the eggs or pancakes are ready—such a perfect reminder that this is a place where many generations gather and come together throughout the course of a day.

With its flattering peach walls and octagonal shape, the dining room also plays host to many meals. In an effort to avoid the crush at local restaurants during peak months, we prefer to eat in—and the number around the table can easily be ten and, with guests, swell to fourteen or more. I'm always coming up with new tabletop setting combinations—mixing family linens with new finds from a trip to Vietnam, changing up the florals, and incorporating colorful glassware.

OPPOSITE: Shiplap walls, beadboard ceiling, and a stenciled floor feel as fresh as the ocean air.

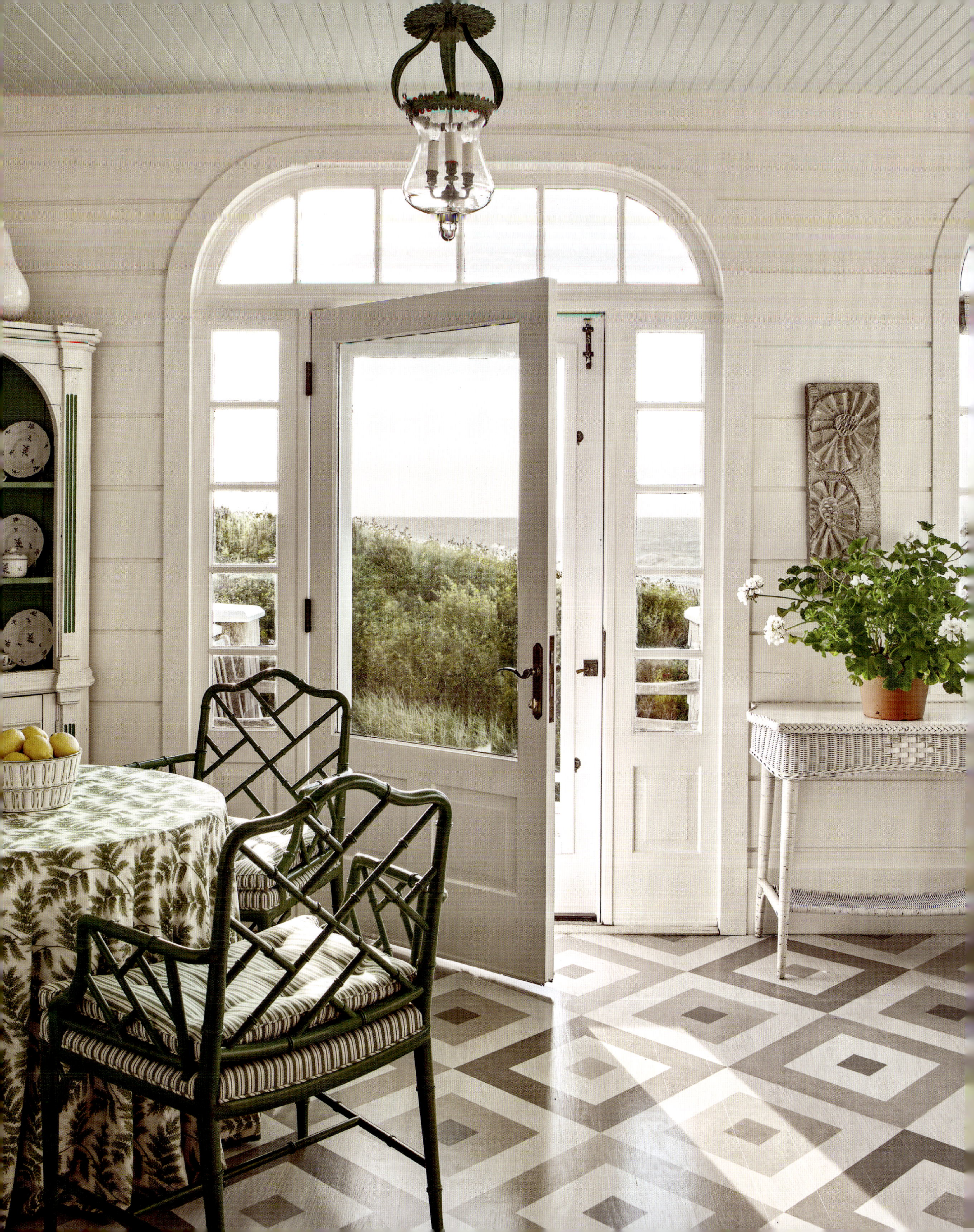

Since the house remains so multigenerational, there's a certain formality and tradition that goes into the decoration. The furniture plans for sitting areas follow classic guidelines. The living room is the picture of prettiness with a glowing mahogany library table and overscale prints by Pierre-Joseph Redouté. In the family room, another octagonal space, the warm beige wall color springs from the original yellow tiles around the fireplace. Things do get slightly looser on the top floor of the tower with floors painted white, plenty of wood-framed furniture, and breezy matchstick blinds.

But the true heartbeat of the house is the stair hall. Everybody loves to hang out there, so we keep it fully furnished with a sofa, a backgammon table, and a set of comfortable armchairs. The woodwork is left unpainted with a traditional oak stain. That detail adds warmth and gives it a special identity within the house, which is filled with so many memories—cemented in its enduring look.

ABOVE: The house's uniquely charming architecture makes a grand statement along the beach.
OPPOSITE: Arriving at Top O'Dune, with its distinctive octagonal tower, always feels inviting.

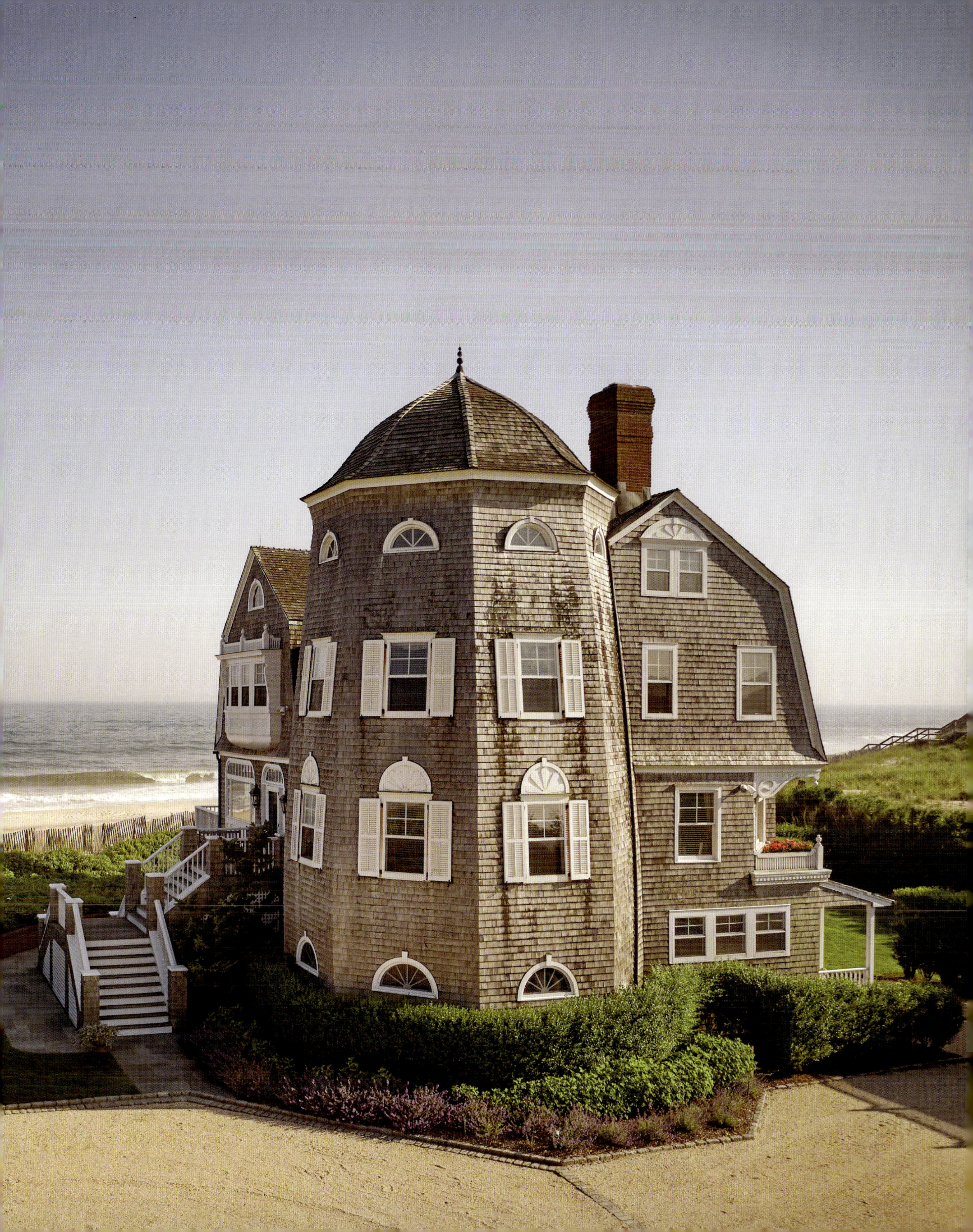

RIGHT: The stair hall becomes a place to gather—not just pass through—with the addition of a backgammon table and other furnishings. Unlike the paneling in other parts of the house, the wood is left unpainted in a warm brown here. FOLLOWING SPREAD: With its pistachio walls, the living room captures a garden-fresh sentiment with a pair of overblown Pierre-Joseph Redouté silk screens, a chair covered in a Scalamandré chintz, and chinoiserie lamps. The Regency rosewood center table is always outfitted with a fresh bouquet.

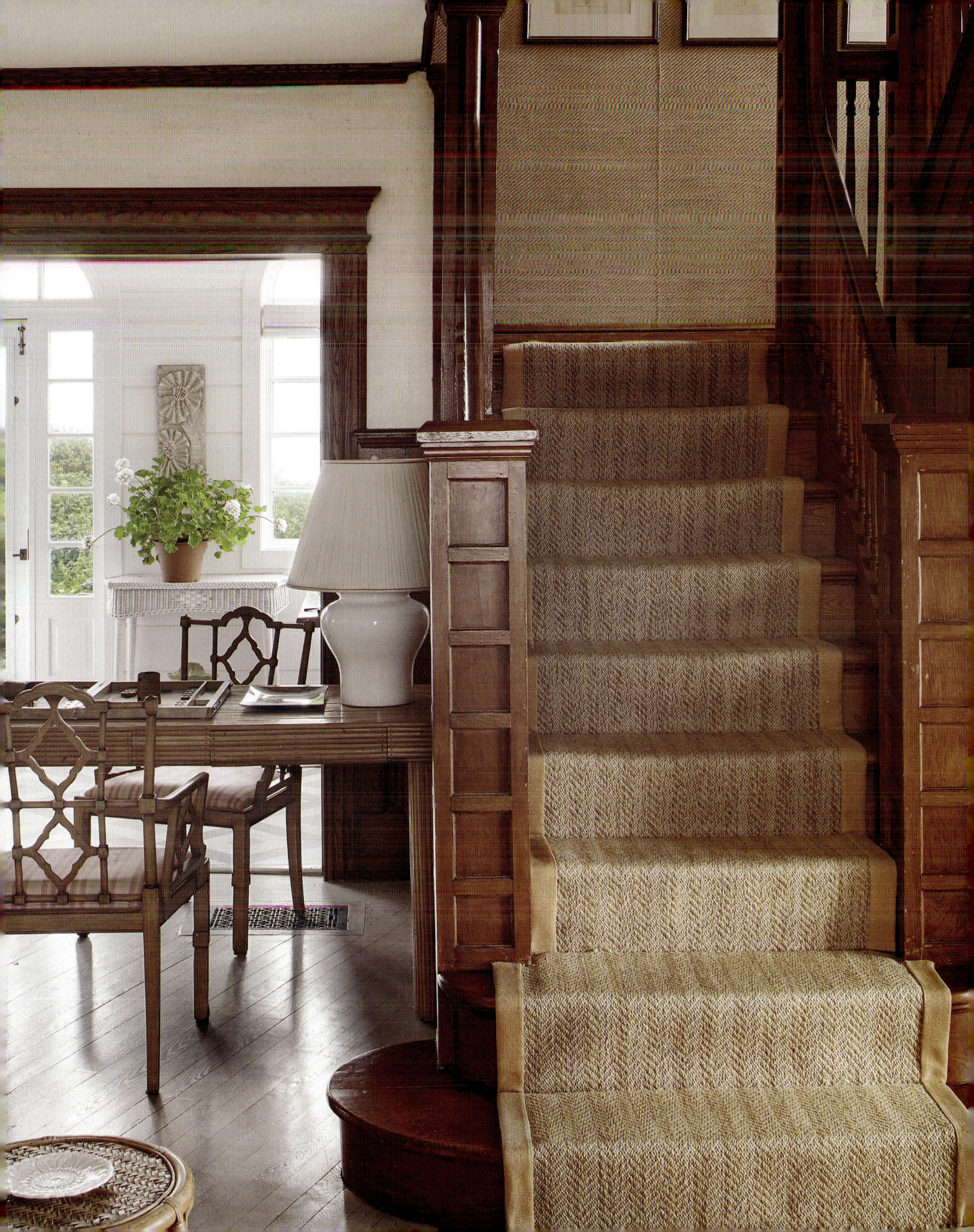

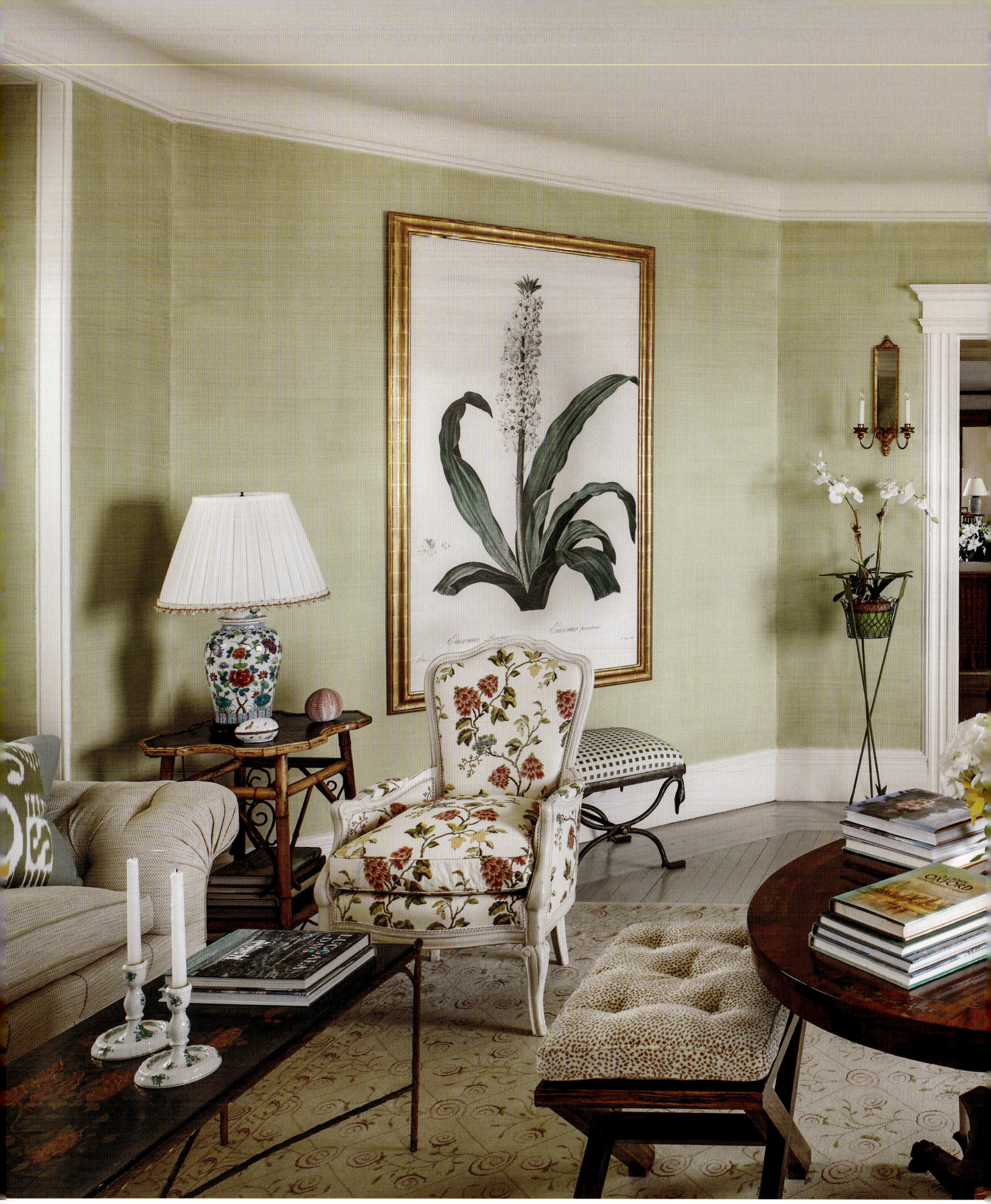

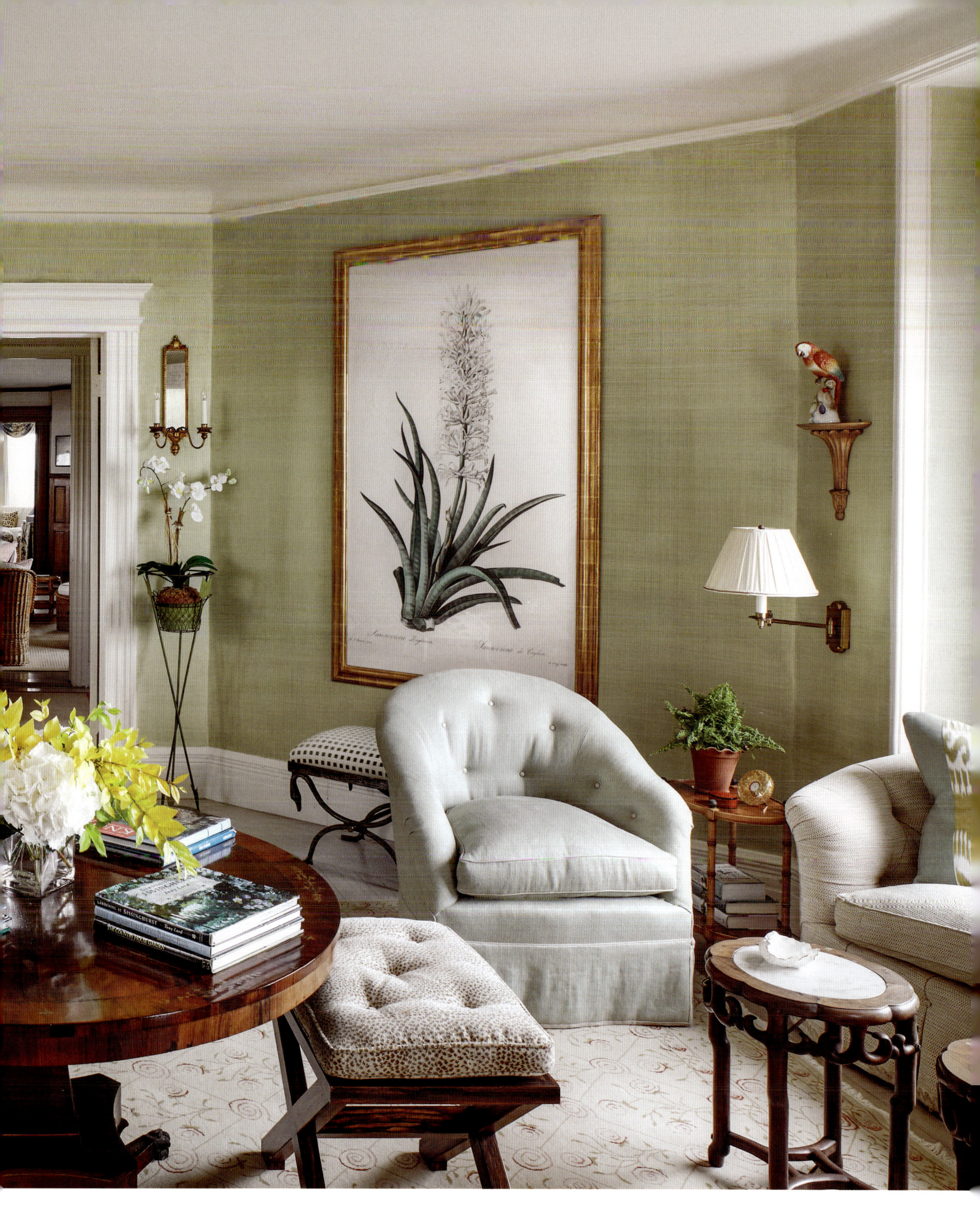

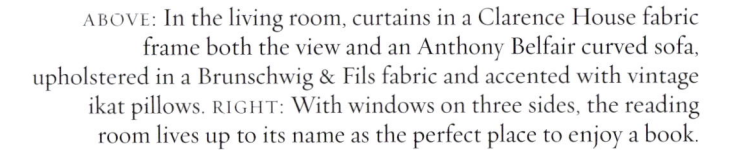

ABOVE: In the living room, curtains in a Clarence House fabric frame both the view and an Anthony Belfair curved sofa, upholstered in a Brunschwig & Fils fabric and accented with vintage ikat pillows. RIGHT: With windows on three sides, the reading room lives up to its name as the perfect place to enjoy a book.

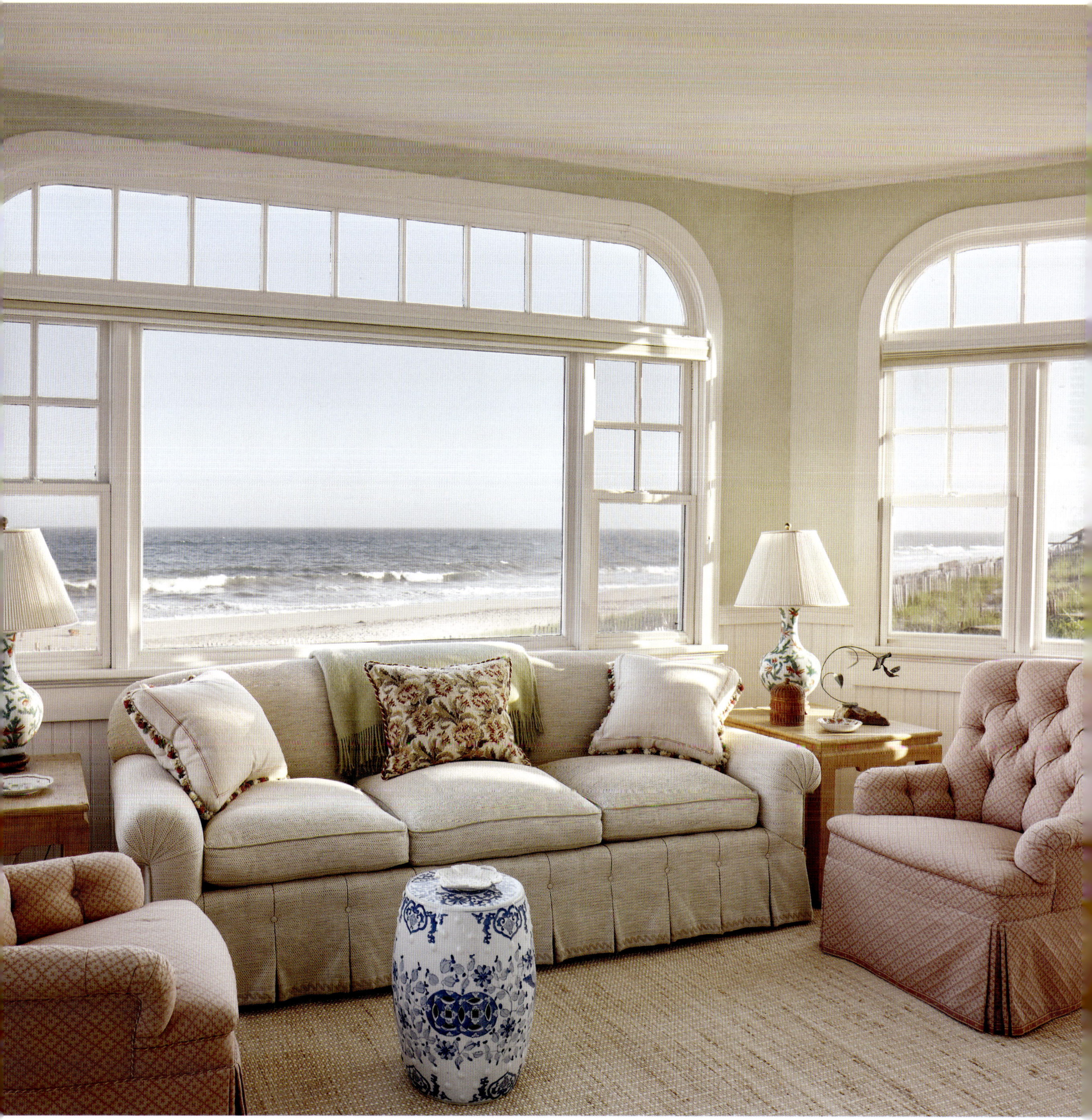

ABOVE: The bell in the breakfast room isn't just for show. It's still used to call the family to dine at the table, which has a John Rosselli & Associates bell jar lantern overhead. OPPOSITE: Hand-painted grass cloth casts a golden glow in the dining room, where the table setting is elevated to an art form multiple times each weekend.

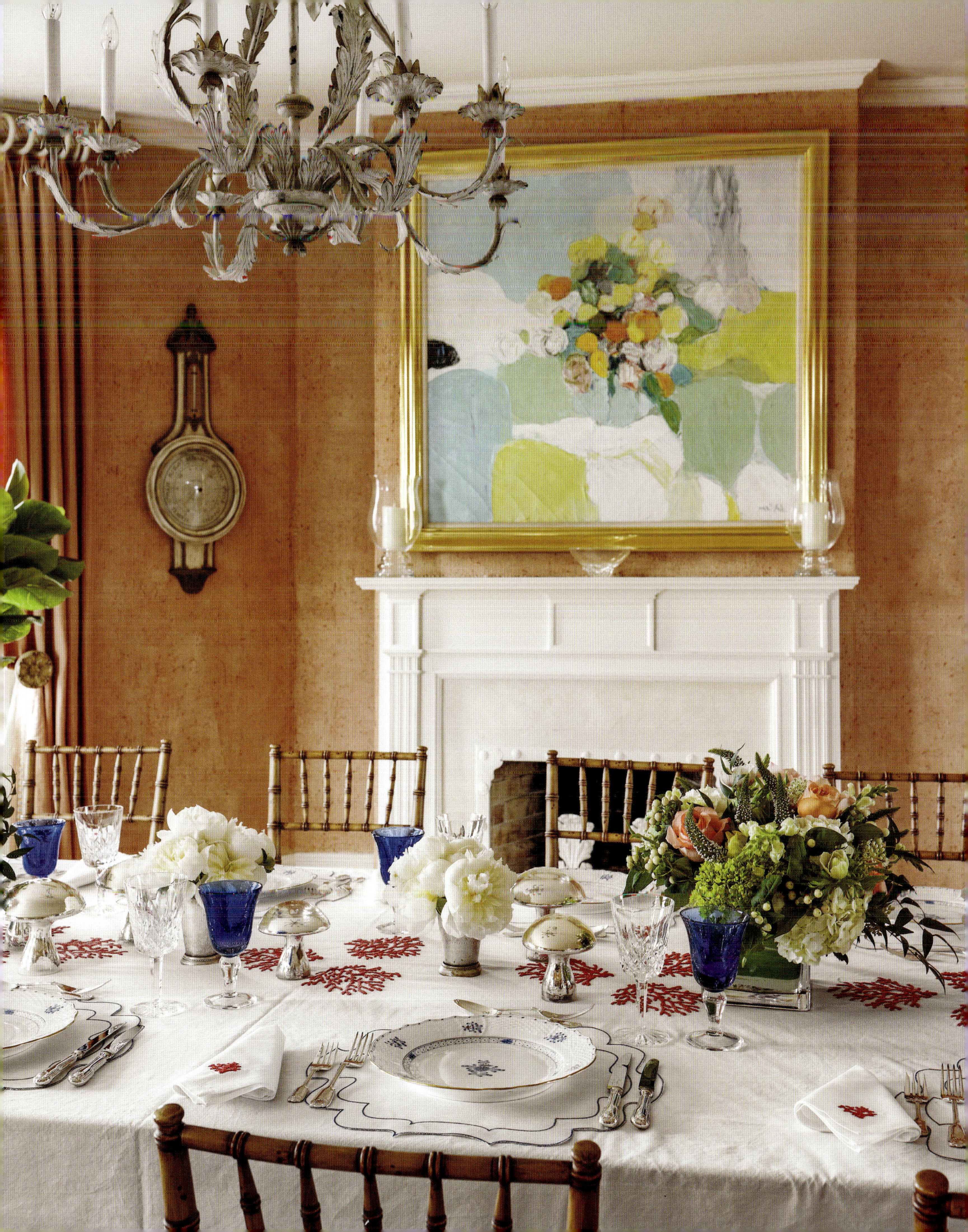

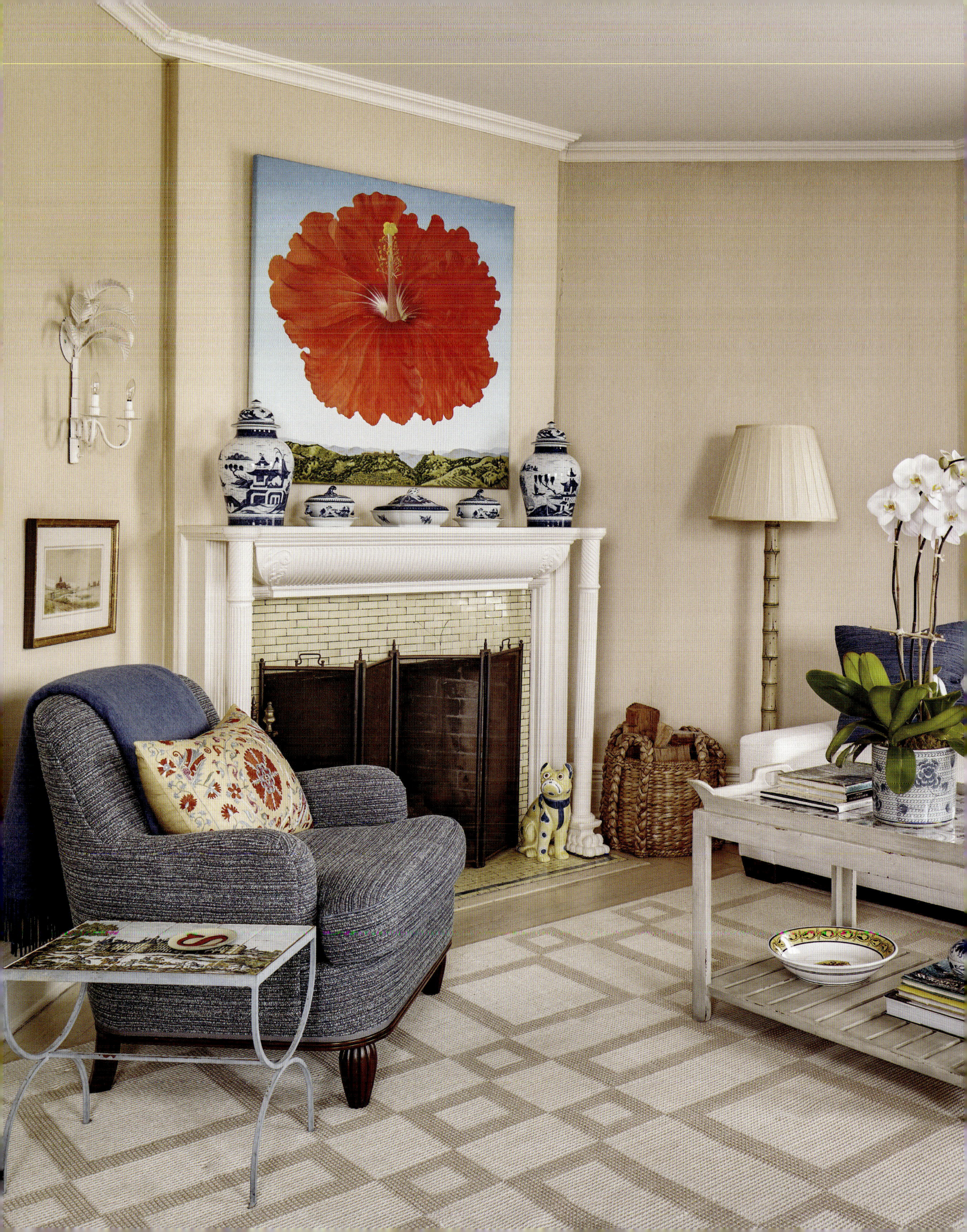

LEFT: In an octagonal-shaped sitting room, the Patterson Flynn Martin geometric rug embraces the graphic spirit of the original 1890s fireplace surround tiles, while a sense of whimsy comes from vintage ceramic-topped tables and an array of blue-and-white porcelain. FOLLOWING SPREAD: The opposite side of the room is defined by a favorite Pierre Frey fabric the family just loves. It would not be the same without it.

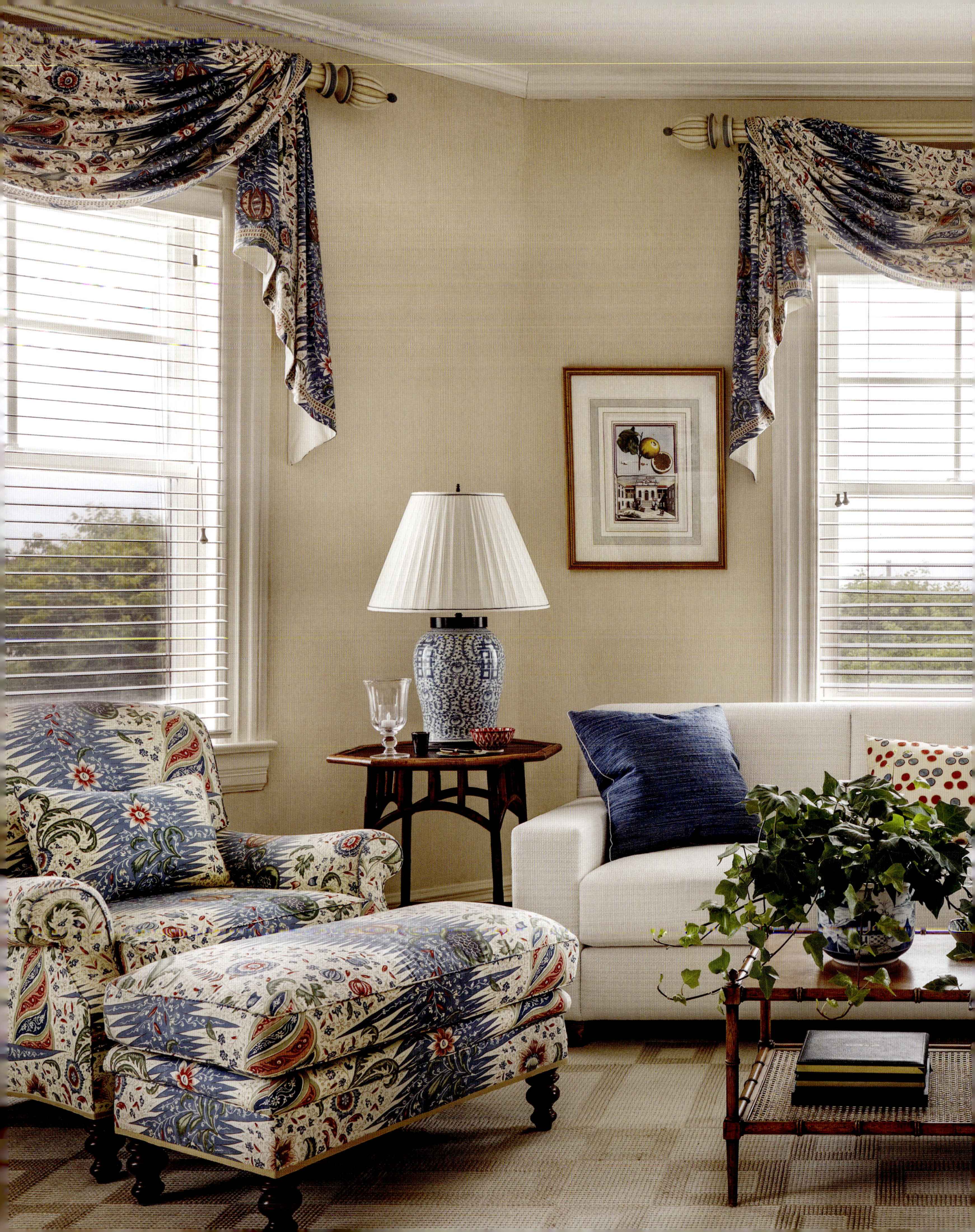

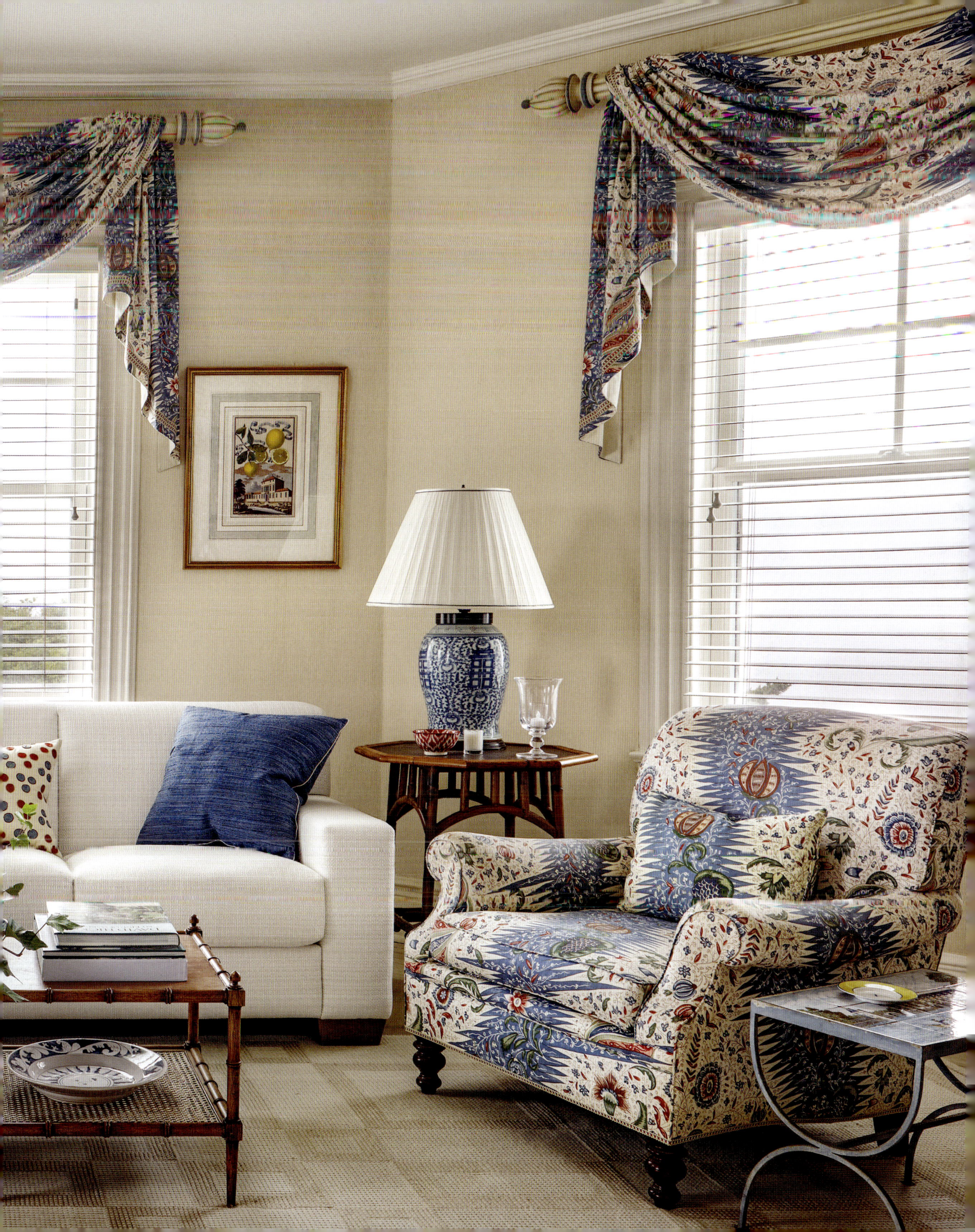

ABOVE: In a guest bathroom, a work by Sugimoto hangs above an oval tub. RIGHT: Sheathed in grass cloth, a guest room is the definition of crisp and clean. A custom bed is flanked by nightstands at just the right height, with an actual alarm clock on top of one.

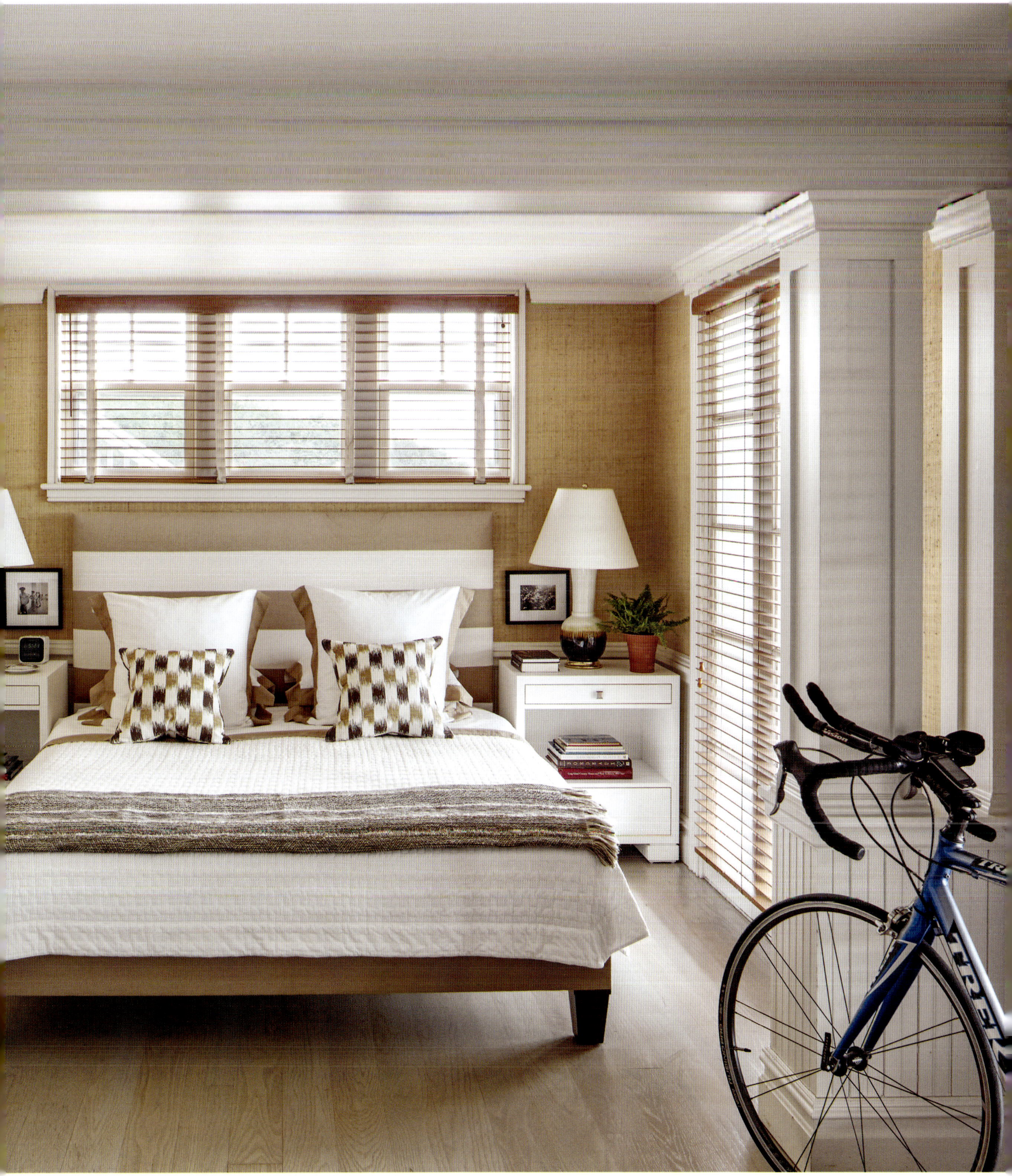

ABOVE: The primary bedroom features a classic seating area across from the bed. The traditional curtains are made of a Quadrille fabric. RIGHT: The tower guest bedroom is a favorite, especially for its quirky eyebrow windows decorated with a green-and-white Scalamandré toile.

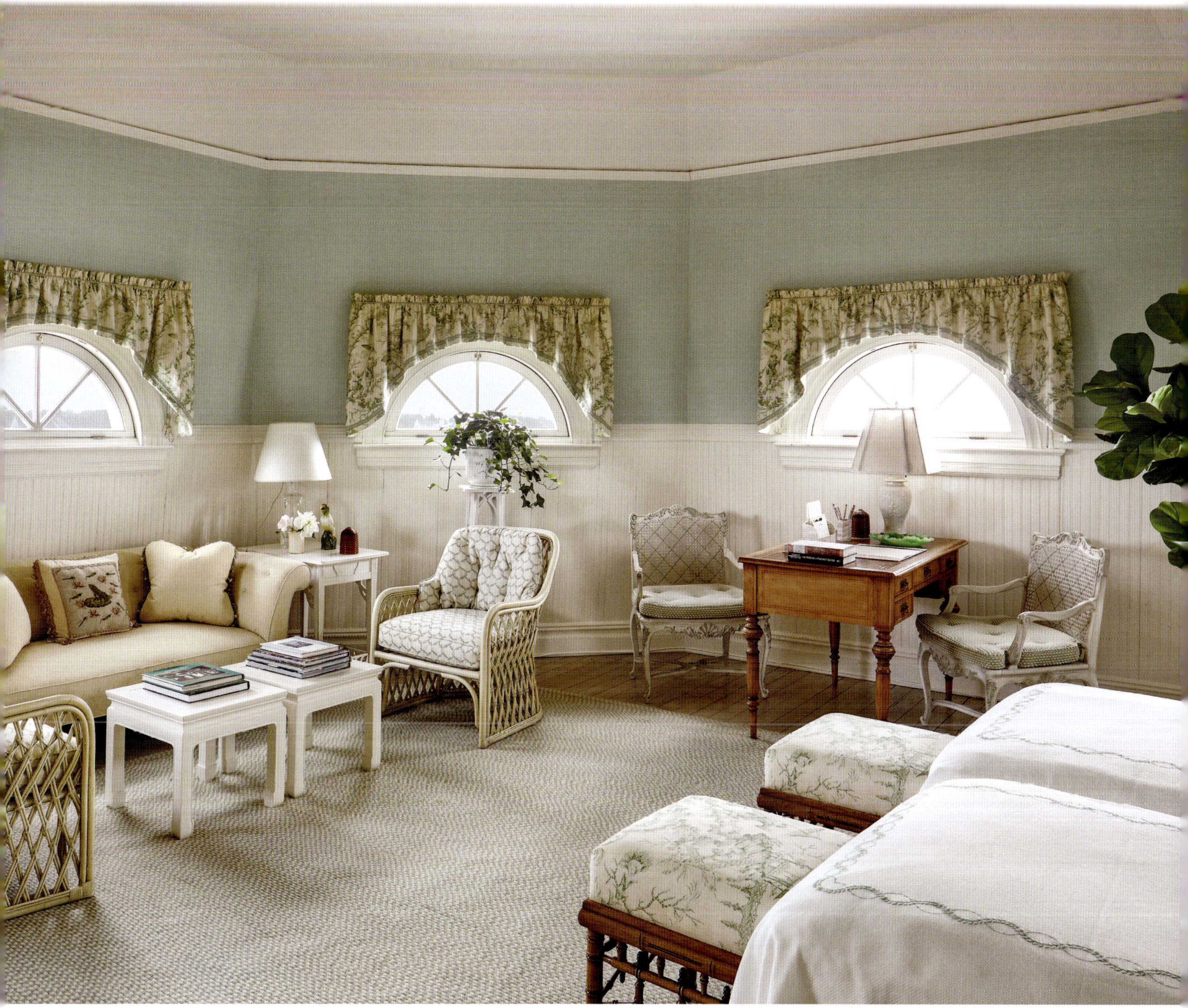

Timeless Fabrics

Re-covering furniture is always a good way to keep things current. Patterns do so much to set the mood for a space, but not every one of them should be a showstopper. In my family's multigenerational home, many pieces have been re-covered time and again, but I always prefer to keep things quiet. The sun and salty air would wreak havoc on fine fabrics this close to the beach, so it's important to opt for materials that can stand up to this kind of ruthless treatment. The classic Scalamandré used on the wood-framed furniture in the room at the top of the tower reminds me of the ripples on the ocean. Used as the lone print in the room, it feels both classic and fresh. In the family room, the blue and red Pierre Frey is used more sparingly, just on the armchairs and valances, and toned down when paired with a Jean-Michel Frank sofa in white, solid blue pillows, and a neutral handwoven rug. This print is a family favorite, and we've returned to it time and again, choosing to use the same fabric when the chairs and valances are in need of re-covering. Even in the recent redecoration of the breakfast room, the fabric choices stick to the tried-and-true—a green ticking stripe to complement the ferns on the tablecloth. These decisions are as much of what gives the house's interiors character as the tower makes its exterior unique, and I relish the tradition of good taste they represent.

OPPOSITE: The sunroom with its Bernard Thorp blue-and-white fabric makes a strong case for covering all the furniture in a room in one strong print.

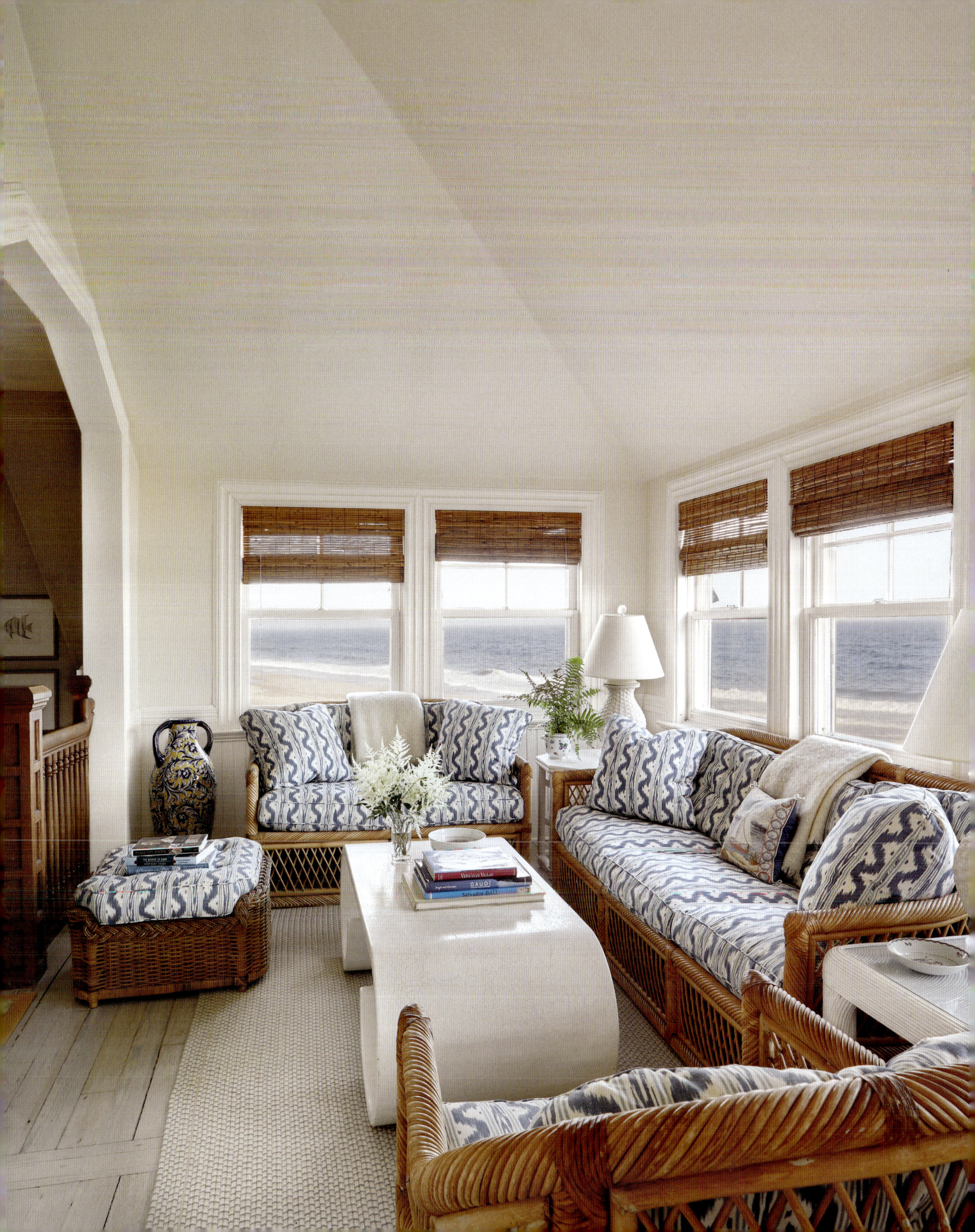

ABOVE: The porch overlooking the ocean is equipped with a set of Country Casual deck chairs in a fabric by Sutherland. RIGHT: The poolside pergola provides just the right amount of shade.

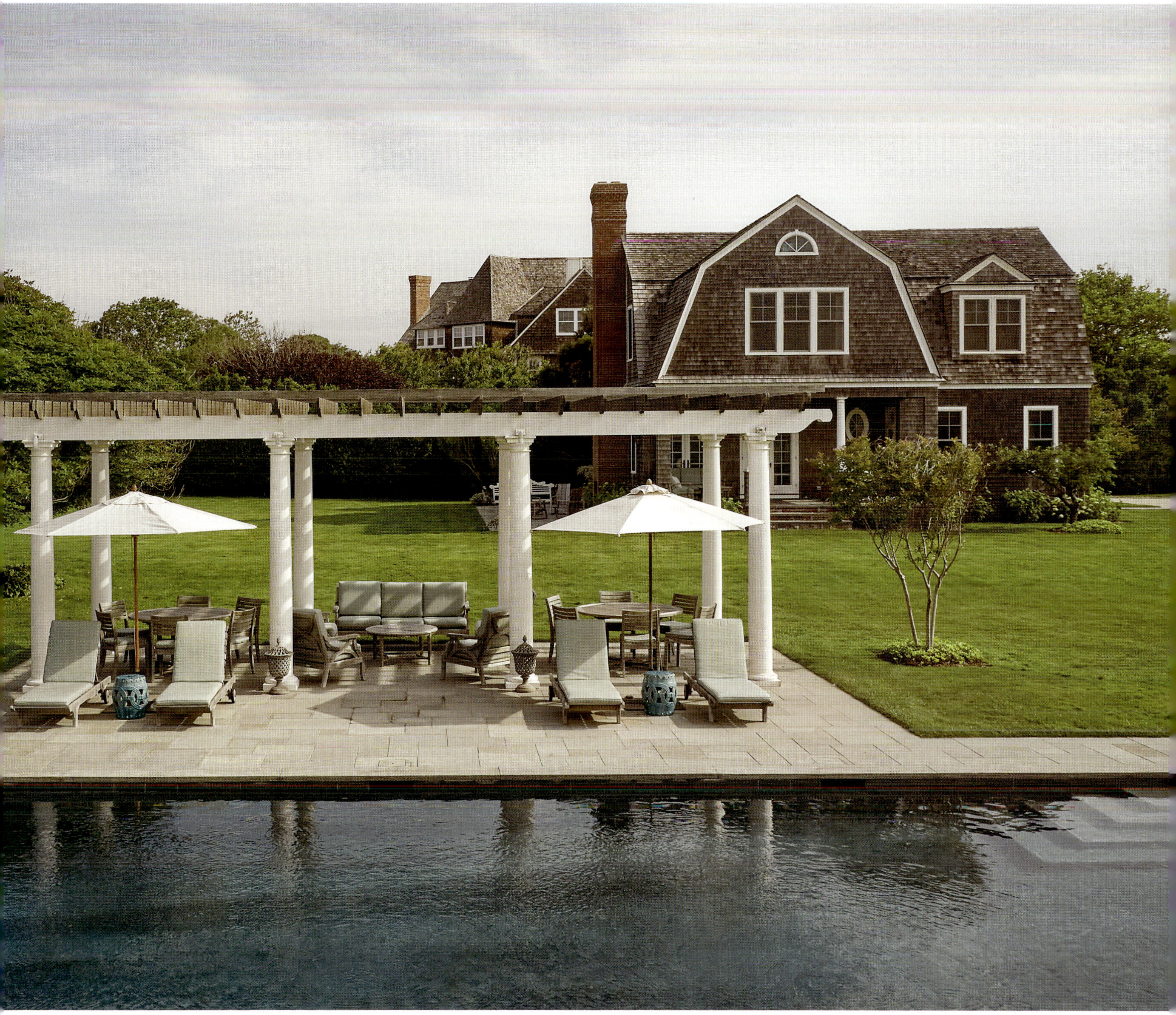

PLAZA DE TOROS de SEVILLA
DOMINGO DE RESURRECCION
Y
FERIA DE ABRIL 1.961
CHICAGO
LUXURY HOTELS

YOUNG AND BOLD IN THE HAMPTONS

Most homes in the Hamptons can hardly be called starter homes, but for these young clients, that's exactly what this was. They wanted a place to escape to on the weekends that was stylish, but they didn't have an unlimited budget. To get them the most bang for their buck, as they say, I devised a plan to keep things bold and graphic, thereby relying on pattern to carry the spaces and make a statement. Since the clients made a specific request not to go the typical blue and white beach route, I opted for a brown and white palette instead. Although seldom known as a chic color combination, it proved to be both fresh and impactful.

When you're faced with budgets not everything can be custom, but a few trusted sources can net fantastic finds within your range. A Noguchi coffee table and a Saarinen dining table from Design Within Reach are classic picks, while you can't go wrong with a headboard from a catalog when dressed up with the right linens or outdoor furniture from RH Outdoor Furniture done up with decorative pillows. With layers of bold striped rugs and bright ikats, these pieces merely become backdrops with great lines upon which layers of personality are then added.

With a common thread running throughout, the house felt polished and finished. By repurposing furniture the clients already had in bold patterns and mixing in some new, more contemporary ones, we achieved their goal while staying cost conscious. Not every project comes with unlimited funds, but that doesn't mean it can't still be fun.

OPPOSITE: Making a statement by layering strong graphic patterns can be delightfully refreshing, especially with a Madeline Weinrib graphic rug, a sofa covered in a China Seas Quadrille fabric, and a chair sheathed in a graphic pattern.
FOLLOWING SPREAD: Textures play well with graphics. A custom sofa rests on a bold rug from Madeline Weinrib and is paired with woven chairs from John Rosselli & Associates in a Lee Jofa fabric and a Bunny Williams Home oak side table.

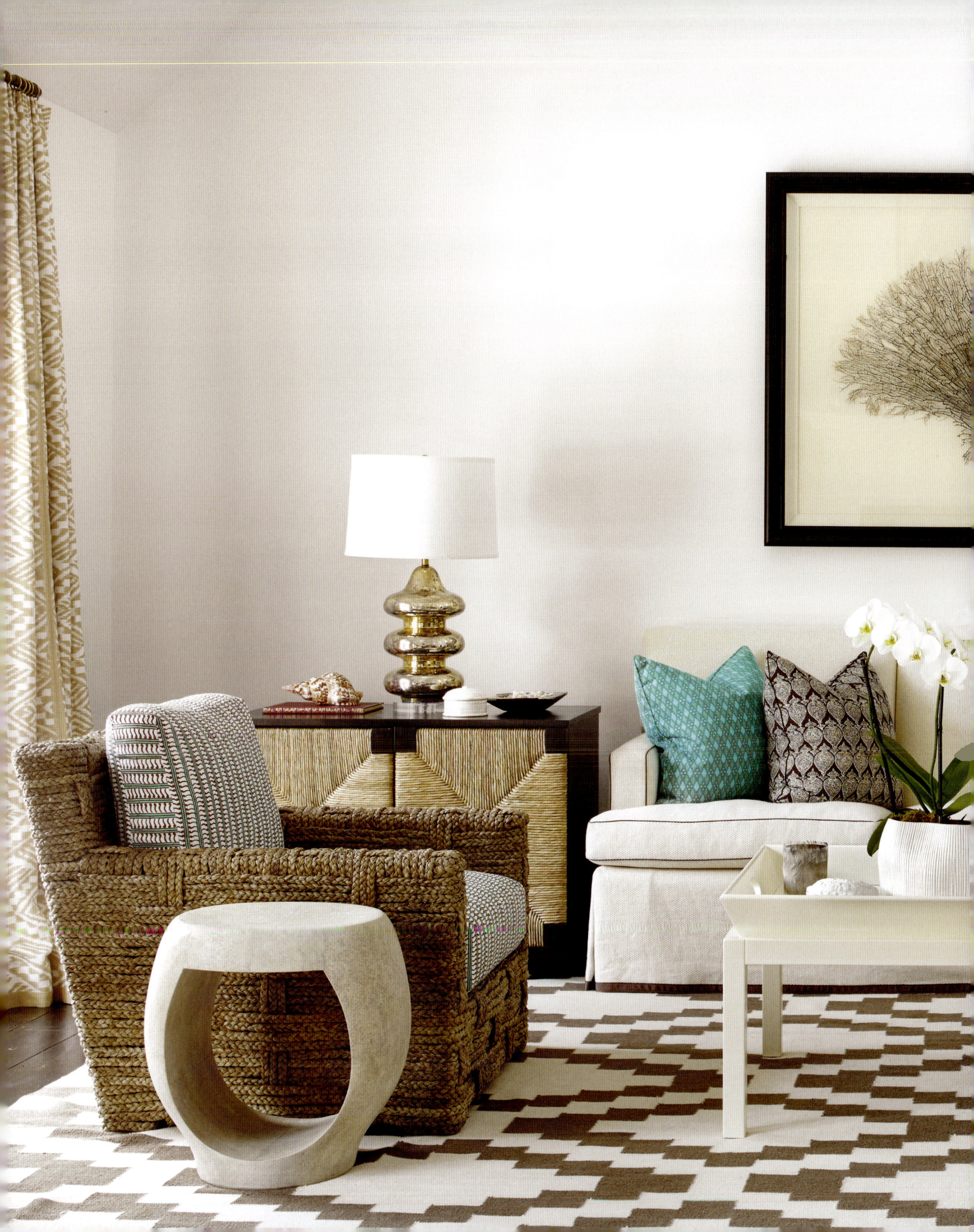

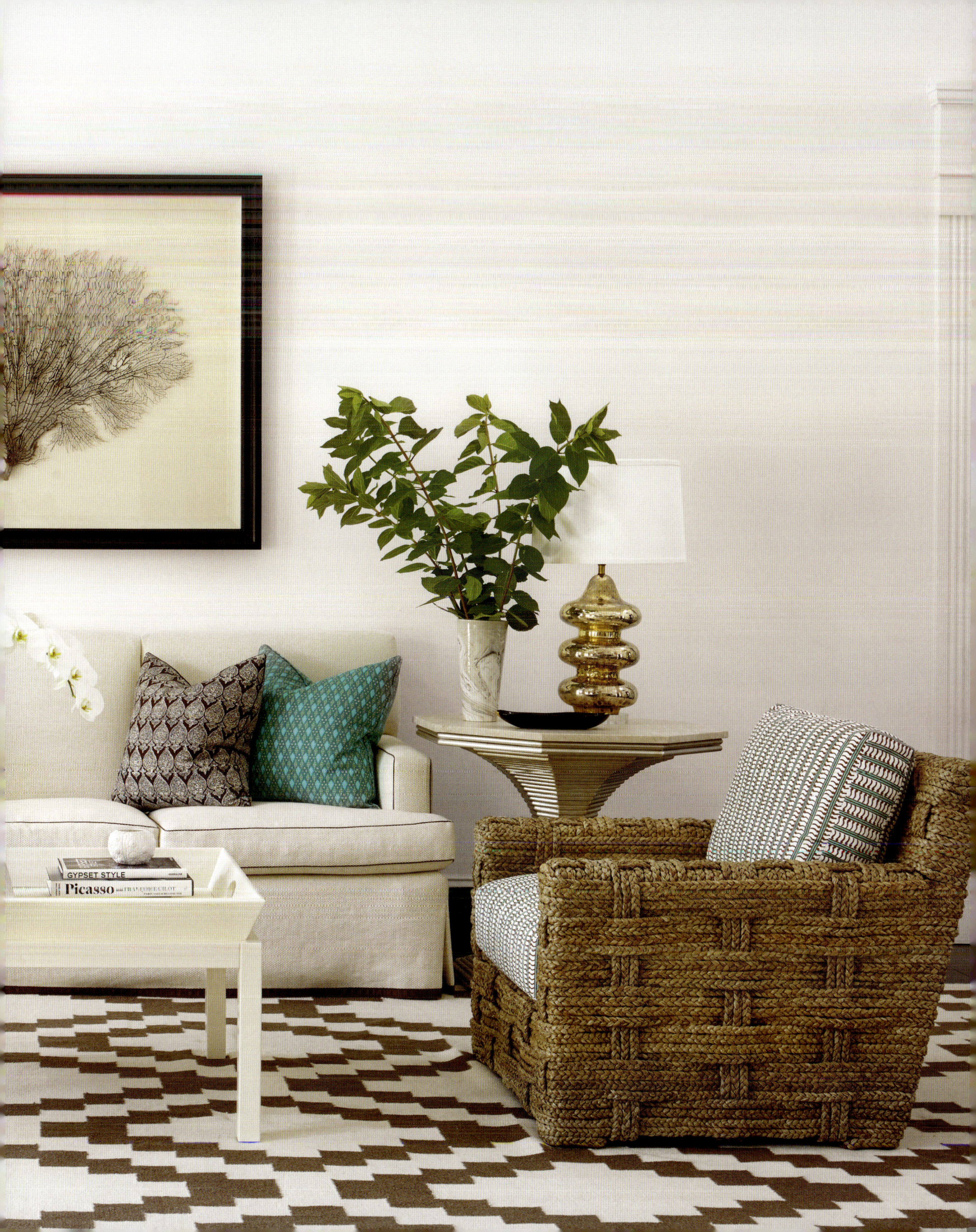
GYPSET STYLE
Picasso

A Play on Graphic Patterns

Those of us who believe in the power of a punchy graphic statement owe a world of thanks to the inimitable David Hicks and his mastery for putting strong pattern just about anywhere—whether it was on the floor in one of his revolutionary 1960s rugs or even in Windsor Castle. These types of adventurous decorating decisions can go a long way when you need to bring a room together and there isn't the budget for a more bespoke approach.

Starting with the rug, I build a room from there. The eye-catching floor coverings in this Hamptons home living room, with taupe diamonds on the white ground, make you look first. Only after that initial glance does the rest of the room take shape. More graphic elements, such as the pattern on the wingback chair as well as on the sofa, permeate the space, although not quite as boldly. The red-and-white striped rug in the library plays a similar role. I also frequently take the opportunity to add a classic pattern, whether paisley, ikat, or animal print, in an unexpected color. We're so accustomed to seeing these patterns that they read almost as neutrals while enhancing the room with visual interest.

RIGHT: In the library, red makes for an unexpected accent color at the beach, with roman shades in a fabric by Lee Jofa, a chair covered in a Madeline Weinrib print, vintage ikat pillows, and a striped rug, also designed by Madeline Weinrib.

249

RIGHT: Patterns are still at play in a guest bedroom but in a toned-down manner. The Lee Jofa fabric on the roman shades and the patterned Zimmer + Rohde European shams are calming as is the beige-and-white ikat on the bench.

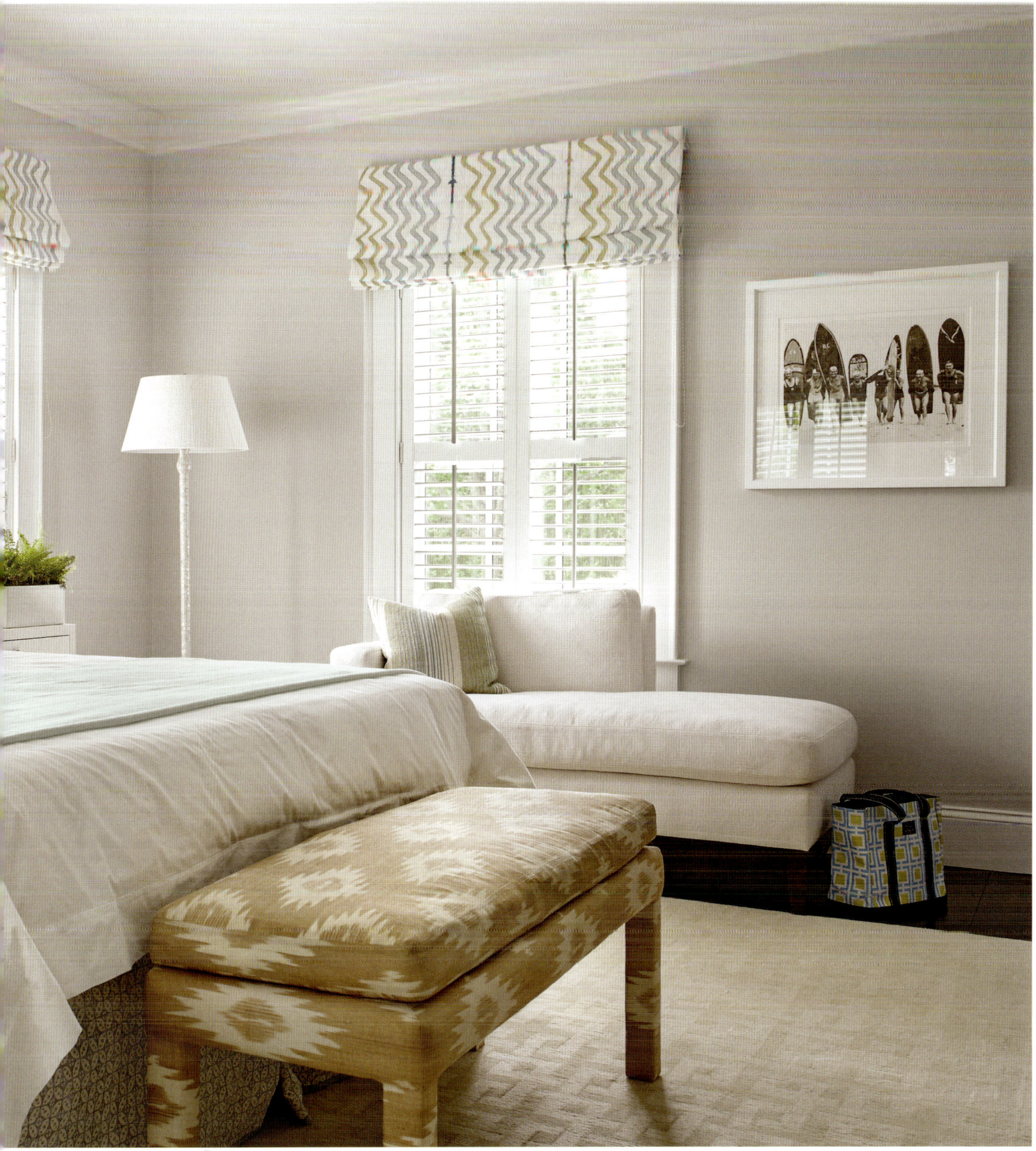

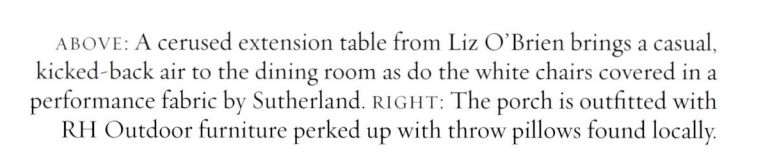

ABOVE: A cerused extension table from Liz O'Brien brings a casual, kicked-back air to the dining room as do the white chairs covered in a performance fabric by Sutherland. RIGHT: The porch is outfitted with RH Outdoor furniture perked up with throw pillows found locally.

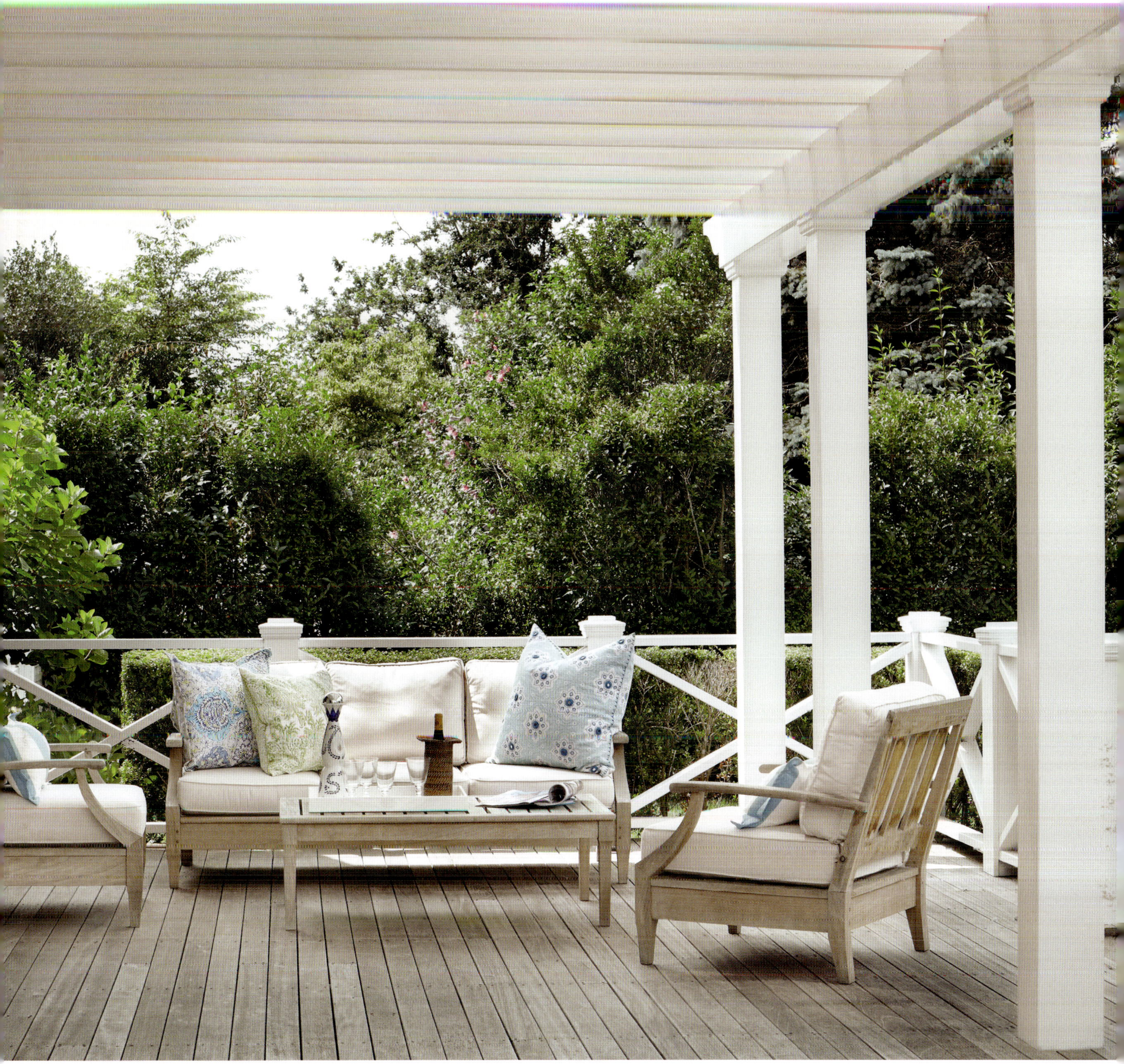

ACKNOWLEDGMENTS

I would like to acknowledge all those who have inspired and helped me in my career: first, I am indebted to my immediate family, who taught me the value of teamwork and that the good of the whole is more important than that of your own good. I am also grateful to all of my childhood teachers and coach, Skip Grant, who taught me that discipline and hard work pay off. Thank you also to those who inspired me to sail offshore and dig deeper, including Rev. Mark Anschutz, Dr. Maurice Boyd, and Canon Mark Mullin.

I could not have become the designer I am today without the friends who took a risk on me and gave me a chance in the early years: Marion Bevan Gay and Marion McEvoy. Also, the three most important people who shaped my design sensibility and taught me how to run a business: David Easton, David Kleinberg, and Bunny Williams, who contributed such a thoughtful foreword.

For all the homes I've designed, the end results would not be the same without the talented workrooms that have supported me for decades: Schneller, Jouffre, Albert Menin, Patterson Flynn Martin, P.E. Guerin, Nicolas Monjardino, Stefano & Co., Tara Chapas, Sylvie Johnson, Ruka Mustapha-Widmer, Toyine Sellers, Lauren Hwang, Patrice Dangel, Philippe Anthonioz, Louis Cane, Vosges, Penn & Fletcher, W. P. Sullivan, Stephen Antonson, Kate Malone, and Hubert Le Gall. I also thank the dealers whose patience and kindness have taught me so much about decorative arts: David Amini, Liz O'Brien, Bernd Goeckler, and Benoist Drut.

I'm so grateful to the team who made this book come together beyond my expectations: the photographers Fritz von der Schulenberg, William Waldron, and Francesco Lagnese for so beautifully capturing the homes; stylist Howard Christian for adding his brilliant touch; Jacqueline Terrebonne for her patience and creative expertise; my office, which supports me day in and out; my editor, Sandy Gilbert Freidus; and the team at Niven Breen. I would also like to acknowledge Doug Turshen and David Huang, who have created such a wonderful book design.

Most of all I want to thank the friends who have trusted my creativity and without whom this book would not be possible: George and Wendy David; Donald and Melinda Quintin; Kristen and Michael Swenson; Pamela and Gabriel Rabinovici; Noelle and John Pierce; and Kitty and Tom Kempner.

OPPOSITE: In a Park Avenue apartment, shimmering mica-flecked walls add glamour to the dining room.

PHOTOGRAPHY CREDITS

Francesco Lagnese: pages 2–3, 5, 19–31, 33–47, 74, 76–89, 185–191, 193–207, 221–239, 241–243, 252

Annie Schlecter: pages 167, 168–169, 176

Fritz von der Shulenberg: pages 49–57, 59–73, 113–123, 125–131, 145–150, 152–163

William Waldron: pages 6, 9, 10, 12, 14–15, 16, 17, 90, 92–93, 95–106, 108–111, 132, 134–138, 139–143, 165, 166, 170–173, 175, 177–183, 209–219, 244, 246–251, 253, 255

First published in the United States of America in 2022 by
Rizzoli International Publications, Inc.
300 Park Avenue South
New York, NY 10010
www.rizzoliusa.com

Text and photography © 2022 Stewart Manger

Publisher: Charles Miers
Editor: Sandra Gilbert Freidus
Editorial Assistance: Hilary Ney, Kelli Rae Patton, Rachel Selekman
Design: Doug Turshen with David Huang
Design Assistance: Olivia Russin
Production Manager: Maria Pia Gramaglia
Managing Editor: Lynn Scrabis

All rights reserved. No part of this publication may be reproduced, stored in a retrieval system, or transmitted in any form or by any means, electronic, mechanical, photocopying, recording, or otherwise, without prior consent of the publishers.

2022 2023 2024 2025 / 10 9 8 7 6 5 4 3 2 1

ISBN: 978-0-8478-7255-8
Library of Congress Control Number: 2022935641

Visit us online:
Facebook.com/RizzoliNewYork
instagram.com/rizzolibooks
twitter.com/Rizzoli_Books
pinterest.com/rizzolibooks
youtube.com/user/RizzoliNY
issuu.com/Rizzoli

PRINTED IN CHINA

PAGES 2–3: Vibrant works on paper by Günther Förg hung as a group make a traditional room feel more contemporary in a family home in Southampton. PAGE 5: In the library of a beach house in Mallorca, Spain, a chair by Hans Wegner casts a striking silhouette against a wall of custom shelving. PAGE 6: In Southampton, a hand-painted geometric floor updates the classical architecture of a historic 1910 house. CASE WRAP: A hand-painted faux-wood-grain finish envelopes the library of a seaside home. ENDPAPERS: Custom-stenciled walls with mother-of-pearl inlay bring a quiet elegance to a Southampton dining room.